The Bedford Bibliography for Teachers of Adult Learners

Barbara Gleason
City College of New York

Kimme Nuckles
Indiana Wesleyan University
University of Maryland, University College
Southern New Hampshire University
Warner University

Bedford/St. Martin's   Boston ♦ New York

For Bedford/St. Martin's
Publisher for College Success and Developmental Studies: Edwin Hill
Developmental Editor: Jonathan Douglas
Publishing Services Manager: Andrea Cava
Production Supervisor: Victoria Anzalone
Senior Marketing Manager: Christina Shea
Project Management: Books By Design, Inc.
Cover Design: William Boardman
Composition: Achorn International, Inc.
Printing and Binding: RR Donnelley and Sons

Manufactured in the United States of America.

9 8 7 6 5 4
f e d c b a

For information, write: Bedford/St. Martin's, 75 Arlington Street, Boston, MA 02116
  (617-399-4000)

ISBN 978-1-4576-1958-8

For adult learners in CUNY adult education and college courses, and for their teachers, tutors, and advisers.

—B. G.

For all adult learners in my classes, both on-ground and online.

—K. N.

Preface

The Bedford Bibliography for Teachers of Adult Learners is an outgrowth of many conversations and collaborative conference presentations at the annual Conference on College Composition and Communication (CCCC). Having first met at a CCCC panel presentation in 2000, we participated in cofounding a CCCC adult learning Special Interest Group (SIG), which first convened at CCCC 2002 in Chicago and has continued to meet every year subsequently. That SIG, Teaching Adult Writers in Diverse Contexts, has proven to be a valuable forum for developing professional relationships and has helped lay the foundation for this bibliography. Four Teaching Adult SIG members have served as consultants for this book: Linda Brender, Sonia Feder-Lewis, Michele Navarre Cleary, and Karen Uehling. Our fifth consultant, Thomas Peele, is a regular CCCC presenter who has expertise in digital literacies and has helped us survey scholarship on adult learners in online contexts.

This book would not have been possible without the ongoing support of our five consultants. Linda Brender is a Professor at Macomb Community College and the author of *Entrepreneurial Communication: A Health Care Ethnography* (VDM Verlag, 2009). Michelle Navarre Cleary, Associate Professor, Associate Dean of Curriculum, Instruction and Assessment, and Writing Coordinator at DePaul University School for New Learning, is author of "Anxiety and the Newly Returned Student" (*Teaching English in the Two-Year College*, May 2012) and other essays on adult learners and writing. Sonia Feder-Lewis, Core Professor in an adult learner–oriented doctoral program at St. Mary's University of Minnesota, has more than twenty years of experience teaching adult undergraduates and graduate students in diverse settings. Karen Uehling, Associate Professor in the English Department at Boise State University, is author of *Starting Out or Starting Over: A Guide for Writing* (HarperCollins, 1992), *Vision and Revision: A Reader for Writers* (HarperCollins 1994), and essays focusing on basic writing and creative nonfiction. Thomas Peele, Associate Professor of English at the City College of New York, is editor of *Queer Popular Culture: Literature, Media, Film, and Television*, 2nd ed. (Palgrave Macmillan, 2011) and essays focusing on basic writing, digital literacy, composition instruction, and queer theory. We are grateful to our consultants for their expertise, encouragement, research, and writing contributions.

We were initially inspired to conduct bibliographic research by the first two books in this series: *The Bedford Bibliography for Teachers of Writing* (now in a 7th edition and edited by Nedra Reynolds, Jay T. Dolmage, Patricia Bizzell, and Bruce Herzberg), and *The Bedford Bibliography for Teachers of Basic Writing* (edited first by Linda Adler-Kassner and Gregory Glau and then, in a 3rd edition, by Gregory Glau and Chitralekha Duttagupta). Having used these valuable resources for our own teaching and research, we envisioned a similar survey of scholarship on adult writing students enrolled in undergraduate college programs.

However, after delving into our research, we discovered a dearth of publications on undergraduate adult writers and, at the same time, a wealth of scholarship focusing on adult learners of language and literacy in diverse contexts outside academia. By widening the scope of our bibliographic survey, we were able to find sufficient published essays and books for the 300-abstract bibliography that we had originally proposed.

In keeping with our original focus, we have limited most of our survey to scholarship on adult learning and teaching within the United States. We maintained this focus not because we are interested exclusively in US education but because we could not adequately represent the extensive published research on adult learners in other countries while also surveying the scholarship on adult learning and teaching within the United States. Most publications included in this bibliography contain insights with implications for adult learning and teaching beyond US borders.

Acknowledgments

Among the contributors to this bibliography are twelve graduate students/recent graduates of the City College of New York's English Department. Eleven contributors are current graduate students or recent graduates of the CCNY MA in Language and Literacy, a graduate program that prepares individuals to teach adults seeking various types of formal education. One of these contributing authors, Brian Brice, is a recent graduate of the CCNY MA in Literature. All twelve of these authors wrote their abstracts while enrolled in Adult Learning and Development, a graduate course taught by Barbara in Fall 2012. We have included these graduate students as contributing authors to call attention to the growing professionalization of adult education and the increased presence of adult education master's programs. Each of these graduate students has written one abstract for this book. Our five consultants have collectively written sixty-five abstracts, and we (Barbara Gleason and Kimme Nuckles) have written all of the remaining abstracts for this bibliography.

Each abstract's author is identified by the author's initials:

Andrew Ahn, City College of New York (Graduate Student)	AA
Linda Brender, Macomb Community College	LDB
Brian Brice, City College of New York (Graduate Student)	BB
Sonia Feder-Lewis, Saint Mary's University of Minnesota	SFL
Caitlin Geoghan, City College of New York (Graduate Student)	CG
Barbara Gleason, City College of New York	BJG
Nargiza Matyakubova, City College of New York (Graduate Student)	NM
Nodira Matyakubova, City College of New York (Graduate Student)	NKM

Nayanda Moore, City College of New York (Graduate Student)   NMM

Michele Navarre Cleary, DePaul University   MNC

Kimme Nuckles, Indiana Wesleyan University; University of   KKN
    Maryland, University College; Southern New Hampshire
    University; and Warner University

Thomas Peele, City College of New York   TBP

Robert Ramos, City College of New York (Graduate Student)   RNR

Melisha Rose, City College of New York (Graduate Student)   MAR

Tessa Smith, City College of New York (Graduate Student)   TS

Natasha Thomas, City College of New York (Graduate Student)   NVT

Karen Uehling, Boise State University   KSU

Melissa Valerie, City College of New York (Graduate Student)   MCV

Maya Wojcik, City College of New York (Graduate Student)   MSW

We would like to thank three very supportive editors at Bedford/St. Martin's: Alexis Walker, Karrin Varucene, and Jonathan Douglas. We are especially grateful to Karrin and Jonathan for their insightful and conscientious editorial responses to the writing of more than 300 abstracts and two introductory essays.

We extend our warm appreciation to the family members and friends who encouraged us during the three years that we worked on this project. Kimme acknowledges the continuing support of her husband, Ron; her daughters, Jeanne, Angela, and Melissa; and her sons-in-law, Jason and Michael. For their professional support, Barbara thanks CCNY colleagues Carla Cappetti, Pam Laskin, Elizabeth Mazzola, Renata Miller, Harold Veeser, and Joshua Wilner. For moral support from family, Barbara thanks her mother, Virginia Gleason, and Anne Gleason-Roche, Joe Roche, Victoria Gleason, Randy Gleason, Sara Gleason, Mary Lilja, Joan Fergus, Patricia Quinn and her late husband, Edward Quinn. And for friends who encouraged her to stay the course, Barbara is grateful to Paul Dolan, Kathy Breidenbach, Joanna Clapps Herman, Bill Herman, Karl and Barbara Malkoff, Jason Malkoff, Qian Zhang Malkoff, Marie Squerciati, Lynn Reid, Wynne Ferdinand, Erika Zuker, James Gomez, Bennie Gomez, Erin Salamon, Anne Saidman, Sandy Ellison, and Bob O'Brien.

Contents

Preface   iv

INTRODUCTION   1

ADULT LEARNERS IN US
POSTSECONDARY EDUCATION   7

ADULT LEARNING AND DEVELOPMENT   20

Adult Learning   20
Adult Development   38
Survey Research, Overviews, and Large-Scale Studies   41
Case Studies and Ethnographies   57

WRITING AND READING CURRICULA   78

Writing and Reading in the Workplace   78
Writing and Reading in Adult Education Programs   81
*Writing and Reading in Undergraduate and Graduate
College Programs*   89
Writing and Reading in ELL Programs   103

INSTRUCTORS OF ADULTS AND
INSTRUCTIONAL APPROACHES   108

Instructors and Instructor Preparation   108
Theoretical Frameworks and Instructional Approaches   117
Curricula and Assessment   130

DIVERSE CONTEXTS FOR TEACHING AND
LEARNING READING AND WRITING   138

English Language Learner Classes   138
Online Environments   141
Prior Learning Assessment and Accelerated Degree Programs   151
Prison Education   155
Workplace Writing, Worker Education, and Labor Unions   158
Literacy in Family and Community   164
Adult Literacy Education Programs   169
College Environments and Programs   172

FOCUS ON ADULT LEARNERS   180

Adult Learners' Perspectives and Experiences   **180**
Multilingual Adults and English Language Learners   **182**
Learning Differences and Styles   **183**
Gender and Learning   **184**
Social Class, Culture, Race, and Learning   **189**
Soldiers and Veterans   **192**

Index of Authors Cited   **195**

Introduction

Kimme Nuckles

The idea for this bibliography began when we (Barbara Gleason and I) met in 2000 at the Conference on College Composition and Communication (CCCC). Because I was writing a dissertation on adult learners in composition classrooms, I decided to attend Barbara's talk on adult learners in the composition classroom. The title of her presentation was "Writing Workplace Ethnographies: Returning Adults Connect Work Experience and Academic Writing." We met each other at the end of the question-and-answer session and immediately began discussing adult education scholarship. We both understood the need for a greater awareness of adult learners and adult learning theory in college writing programs and at CCCC. We agreed that existing research on the topic of adult learners, particularly writers, was insufficient, and we knew that this group of students presented opportunities for research, especially as more adult learners continue to fill our classrooms. According to the National Center for Education Statistics (NCES), from 2000–2010, adult student enrollment in undergraduate programs increased by 42 percent, and the increases are predicted to continue at a rate of 20 percent by 2020 ("Fast Facts"). In contrast, only an 11 percent increase in the enrollments of traditional-age students is predicted between 2010 and 2020. With this predicted increase in adult learners in postsecondary institutions, we understood that more research on the effects these students were having on colleges, universities, and other educational programs intended for younger students was needed.

After meeting at Barbara's panel presentation and then again at another session at the same conference, we discussed co-presenting at future conferences. We developed the idea of creating a CCCC Special Interest Group (SIG) on adult learners. The following year, we collaborated with a few colleagues to present a half-day workshop on adult learners at CCCC, and we launched a SIG titled "Teaching Adult Writers in Diverse Contexts." The SIG has met annually at CCCC since 2002 with other faculty members such as Sonia Feder-Lewis, Karen Uehling, and Michelle Navarre Cleary, three of the consultants for this book, joining in the leadership of the group. It was through these interactions at CCCC that this book was born.

Who Are Adult Learners?

Adult learners have been identified in many ways, but the most frequently used method is to characterize adult students by age. Although age twenty-five is the most common dividing point, researchers differ on the exact age at which a student becomes an adult learner. Merle O'Rourke Thompson identifies returning students as older than twenty-two and as not having attended college courses within the previous five years. (See the articles under Writing and Reading in Undergraduate and Graduate College Programs.) Shelly Bennett, Tracy Evans, and Joan Riedle classify nontraditional students as age twenty-five and older. (See the section Survey Research, Overviews, and Large-Scale Studies.) Carol Kasworm categorizes adult learners as age thirty and older in undergraduate classes. (See the section Adult Learning.) The National Center for Education Statistics (NCES) defines older students as thirty-five years and older ("Fast Facts"). While the age at which students are considered adult learners varies, all of these age ranges are noticeably older than the ages of traditional college students, who range in age from eighteen to twenty-two.

Other researchers have questioned the importance of age as a factor for defining adult learners. Because many younger students have adult responsibilities such as full-time work or parenting, the term *nontraditional students* is sometimes used instead of *adult learners*. When these terms are used interchangeably, researchers usually identify the age they are using in defining adult learners. When the term *nontraditional students* is used alone, researchers seldom refer to age at all. For example, Michelle Hall Kells and Valerie Balester identify nontraditional students in these ways: lacking college-preparatory courses in high school, being marginalized because of power discrepancies between teachers and students, having low economic status, being a member of an ethnic group, and being part of language and discourse communities. In their research on ABE and ESL programs, Jeff Zacharakis, Marie Steichen, Gabriela de Sabates, and Dianne Glass do not focus on the students' ages. (See the section Theoretical Frameworks and Instructional Approaches.) In studies of English language learners, age is typically not a factor, as seen in studies by Jacqueline Lynch. (See Writing and Reading in Adult Education Programs.) Finally, learner age is often not mentioned by scholars investigating particular educational contexts, e.g., prison literacy (Jacqueline N. Glasglow; Thomas Laughlin), or an adult learner category, e.g., military veterans (Denis O. Kiely and Lisa Swift; Noreen M. Glover-Graf, Eva Miller, and Samuel Freeman) and graduate students (see contributions by Lornia Kerns [Adult Learning section] and Mary Miritello [Case Study and Ethnographies]). Therefore, in this bibliography, adult learners are being defined in a number of ways by the various authors.

Who Should Read This Book?

The purpose of this book is to present a survey of the literature on adult learners for readers who may be doing research on this topic. This book is intended for use by those who teach adult learners in various settings, those who teach courses on adult learners, graduate students who are researching adult learners, and any others who have a stake in the adult learner field, such as administrators or anyone associated with college-level education. As stated previously, the number of adult learners in postsecondary institutions is growing, so college instructors and professors will find this book useful. Thus, the book has multiple uses for those engaging in discussions about adult learners. For teachers of adult learners, reviewing the various sections and subtitles may help point to information needed for a particular situation or student. For researchers, exploring publications in various professions, academic disciplines, and related journals can help ensure that research is well informed and inclusive.

It is important to view adult learners from multiple perspectives to give a better picture of these individual students and the most pressing issues surrounding them. For instance, articles on veterans are beginning to appear within journals (see Veterans' Learning Experiences), as are essays on multigenerations within classrooms. Working with elderly adult learners is a new topic in the field, and we expect this trend to continue as Baby Boomers age and continue to learn. We also see that some topics within the overall subject of adult learners need more research: adult learners in religious settings, Native American adult learners, LGBT adult learners, adult learners with disabilities, and adult learners in the online classroom are among topics that readers may discover. These topics are possibilities for future doctoral students' research and for those who work with adult learners in various settings. As stated previously, this book is intended as a survey of research on adult learners but is not all-inclusive. The works included here have helped to shape how instructors and administrators who work with adult learners view these students and may assist them through instructional strategies, new programs, and different teaching situations. In differing ways, each of these 300-plus works points to significant issues facing adult learners.

How Is This Book Organized?

The five categories in the book were developed as we began our research on adult learners for this project. Focusing on the literacy skills adults need in academia and/or the workplace, we searched for sources that presented studies on writing, reading, and digital literacies, while also trying to acknowledge the need for research on adult learners in a broader context. We asked our consultants for titles and names of authors that focus on adult learners in a variety of settings. As we began to compile our lists, we realized that the sources fell within certain areas and that these areas could be further classified under broader headings. Using the publications on adult learners that we found, we created the following categories for our annotated bibliography: Adult Learning and Development; Writing and Reading Curricula; Instructors of Adults and Instructional Approaches; Diverse Contexts for Teaching and Learning Reading and Writing; and Focus on Adult Learners.

The first section, **Adult Learning and Development**, has four subsections: Adult Learning; Adult Development; Survey Research, Overviews, and Large-Scale Studies; and Case Studies and Ethnographies. These works offer some theories and larger studies on adult learners. For instance, Patricia Cross's seminal work, *Beyond the Open Door: New Students to Higher Education*, offers a basis for adult learning on which others have built their studies. This section also offers works from Paulo Freire ("The Adult Literary Process as Cultural Action for Freedom"), Carol Kasworm ("Adult Meaning Making in the Undergraduate Classroom"), and Jack Mezirow ("Learning to Think Like an Adult: Core Concepts of Transformation Theory"). Within the subsection of Adult Development are works on lifespan theory by authors such as Thomas L. Pourchot and M. Cecil Smith ("Some Implications of Life Span Developmental Psychology for Adult Education and Learning") and Barbara R. Bjorklund (*The Journey of Adulthood*, 7th ed.). In the section Survey Research, Overviews, and Large-Scale Studies are works such as "Comparing Academic Motivation and Accomplishments among Traditional, Nontraditional, and Distance Education College Students" by Shelly Bennett, Tracy Evans, and Joan Riedle and "Redefining Nontraditional Students: Exploring the Self-Perceptions of Community College Students" by Karen A. Kim, Linda J. Sax, Jenny J. Lee, and Linda Serra Hagedorn. Case Studies and Ethnographies includes works such as Mary Field Belenky, Blythe McVicker Clinchy, Nancy Rule Goldberger, and Jill Mattuck Tarule's *Women's Ways of Knowing: The Development of Self, Voice, and Mind* and Carol Berkenkotter, Thomas N. Huckin, and John Ackerman's "Conventions, Conversations, and the Writer: Case Study of a Student in a Rhetoric PhD Program."

The second section, **Writing and Reading Curricula**, focuses on courses designed for adult students learning to read and write. In a subsection titled Writing and Reading in the Workplace, you can find titles such as *Second Shift: Teaching Writing to Working Adults* by Kelly Belanger and Linda Strom. In the subsection Writing and Reading in Adult Education Programs, we have included an essay titled "Transforming Adult Students into Authors: The Writer to Writer Challenge" by Caroline Beverstock, Shanti Bhaskaran, Jacquie Brinkley, Donna Jones, and Valerie Reinke. Writing and Reading in Undergraduate and Graduate College Programs features works such as Barbara Gleason's "Returning Adults to the Mainstream: Toward a Curriculum for Diverse Student Writers" and Helen Johnson's "The PhD Student as an Adult Learner: Using Reflective Practice to Find and Speak in Her Own Voice." Writing and Reading in ELL Programs offers essays such as "Timed Writing and Adult English-Language Learners: An Investigation of First Language Use in Invention Strategies" by N. Eleni Pappamihiel, Takayuki Nishimata, and Florin Mihai.

The third section, **Instructors of Adults and Instructional Approaches**, presents instructional strategies and teachers' views of adult learners. This section includes works such as Stephen Brookfield's "Through the Lens of Learning: How the Visceral Experience of Learning Reframes Teaching" (in the subsection Instructors and Instructor Preparation). In the second subsection, Theoretical Frameworks and Instructional Approaches, Pierre Dominicé's *Learning from Our Lives: Using Educational Biographies with Adults* offers suggestions to help adult learners use learning narratives, whereas Raymond A. Mazurek's "Running Shoes, Auto Workers, & Labor: Business Writing Pedagogy in the Working-Class College" focuses on strategies for teaching writing within the workplace. Under Curricula and Assessment may be found sources such as Rhonda Beaman's "The Unquiet . . . Even Loud, Andragogy! Alternative Assessments for Adult Learners" and Kathleen

Cercone's "Characteristics of Adult Learners with Implications for Online Learning Design."

In the fourth section, **Diverse Contexts for Teaching and Learning Reading and Writing**, the sources examine how adult learning takes place in several venues, some of which would be good areas for future research. The first subsection, English Language Learner Classes, includes sources such as Van E. Hillard's "A Place in the City: Hull-House and the Architecture of Civility" and *Preparing for Success: A Guide for Teaching Adult English Language Learners* by Brigitte Marshall. Online Environments includes works by Lauren Marshall Bowen ("Resisting Age Bias in Digital Literacy Research") and Angela Crow ("What's Age Got to Do with It? Teaching Older Students in Computer-Aided Classrooms"). The subsection Prior Learning Assessment and Accelerated Degree Programs includes Raymond J. Wlodkowski's "Accelerated Learning in Colleges and Universities." In the subsection Prison Education, you can find Jane Maher's "'You Probably Don't Even Know That I Exist': Notes from a Prison College Program" and Thomas Laughlin's "Teaching in the Yard: Student Inmates and the Policy of Silence." The subsection Workplace Writing, Worker Education, and Labor Unions has sources by writers such as Judy Kalman and Kay M. Losey ("Pedagogical Innovation in a Workplace Literacy Program: Theory and Practice") and Mike Rose (*The Mind at Work: Valuing the Intelligence of the American Worker*). The subsection Literacy in Family and Community includes works such as *Cora Wilson Stewart and Kentucky's Moonlight Schools: Fighting for Literacy in America* by Yvonne Honeycutt Baldwin and "Understanding African American Learners' Motivations to Learn in Church-Based Adult Education" by E. Paulette Isaac, Guy Talmadge, and Tom Valentine. Adult Literacy Education Programs includes Krista Hiser's "A Paragraph Ain't Nothin' But a Sandwich: The Effects of the GED on Four Urban Writers and Their Writing." The subsection College Environments and Programs includes sources by Rosemary Ann Blanchard, Felicia Casados, and Harry Sheski ("All Things to All People: Challenges and Innovations in a Rural Community College") and by James P. Pappas and Jerry Jerman ("Accreditation Issues Related to Adult Degree Programs").

The fifth section, **Focus on Adult Learners**, shifts the focus to the adult learner. Adult Learners' Perspectives and Experiences includes Patricia Connors's "Some Attitudes of Returning or Older Students of Composition" and Francis E. Kazemek's "They Have Yarns: Writing with the Active Elderly." Multilingual Adults and English Language Learners offers works such as Julie Mathews-Aydinli's "Overlooked and Understudied? A Survey of Current Trends in Research on Adult English Language Learners" and "Timed Writing and Adult English-Language Learners: An Investigation of First Language Use in Invention Strategies" by N. Eleni Pappamihiel, Takayuki Nishimata, and Florin Mihai. The subsection on Learning Differences and Styles includes articles such as "Teaching a Learning Disabled Adult to Spell: Is It Ever Too Late?" by Marianne Mazzei Hanlon and R. Jeffrey Cantrell. The subsection Gender and Learning features works such as *In a Different Voice: Psychological Theory and Women's Development* by Carol Gilligan and "Inspiration from Home: Understanding Family as Key to Adult Women's Self-Investment" by

Annemarie Vaccaro and Cheryl D. Lovell. Juanita Johnson-Bailey's "Race Matters: The Unspoken Variable in the Teaching-Learning Transaction" may be found in the subsection of Social Class, Culture, Race, and Learning. The final subsection, Veterans' Learning Experiences, includes works such as Denis O. Kiely and Lisa Swift's "Casualties of War: Combat Trauma and the Return of the Combat Veteran" and Thomas G. Sticht's "Swords and Pens: What the Military Can Show Us about Teaching Basic Skills to Young Adults."

Within all five of these sections, we find that the research surrounding adult learners crosses many diverse professional groups. For instance, in Adult Learning and Development, we find articles within the fields of composition, adult education, postsecondary education, and psychology. The category of Diverse Contexts for Teaching and Learning Reading and Writing includes studies in the workplace, with veterans, in urban and rural settings, and online. When we review the literature, we realize the need to move out of our professional fields and into reading works of other professional fields so that we can understand the adult learner better and aid this population in gaining access to the education they need to fully participate in a democratic society. We also understand that adult learners are defined in multiple ways and that adults continue to learn throughout their lives, as noted by W. Ross Winterowd (*Senior Citizens Writing: A Workshop and Anthology, with an Introduction and Guide for Workshop Leaders*). It is our hope that this bibliography serves as a useful resource for all of those who work with this growing population of adult learners.

Works Cited

Balester, Valerie M., and Michelle H. Kells, eds. *Attending to the Margins: Writing, Researching, and Teaching on the Front Lines*. Portsmouth, NH: Boynton/Cook Heinemann, 1999. Print.

"Fast Facts: Enrollment." Institute of Education Sciences. National Center for Education Statistics. 2012. Web. 23 Feb. 2014.

Adult Learners in US Postsecondary Education: A Brief Overview

Barbara Gleason

Instructors of adult college students generally know about the rewards and challenges associated with teaching adults. Many instructors also understand that adult education inside (and outside) the United States has a rich and complex history and that several professional organizations support adult educators and adult-oriented programs and colleges—e.g., the American Association for Adult and Continuing Education, the Council for Adult and Experiential Learning, the American Council on Education, and the Association for Continuing Higher Education. Less widely recognized are the many curricular and institutional changes traceable to a heightened demand for more education of all kinds and especially for college degrees among adults: these changes include (but are not limited to) the community college movement, adult-oriented degree completion programs, increased attention to high school equivalency certificates, the rise of for-profit colleges, and online education. One important consequence of adults' increasing demand for education is an expansive scholarship on adult learning and teaching.

Influential Adult Education Scholars

Although adult learners have gained national prominence in recent decades as subjects of research and scholarship, as catalysts for curricular innovation, and as sources of revenue for postsecondary institutions, adult education is by no means a recent phenomenon. In addition to formal and nonformal learning opportunities afforded by settlement houses, nontraditional courses, and a few activist adult educators in the nineteenth and early twentieth centuries (Addams; Baldwin; Hollis), educational opportunities for adults were established by government programs, the YMCA, and the military during the first half of the twentieth century (Bound and Turner; Knowles, *The Making of an Adult Educator*, 6–12; Sticht). In these decades, adult education was both a newly developing teaching focus and an emerging subject of scholarship.

A good example of an early-twentieth-century adult education scholar is Eduard C. Lindeman, a professor at The New York School of Social Work who, in 1926, argued that learning should continue throughout adulthood: "From many quarters comes the call to a new kind of education with its initial assumption that *education is life*—not a mere preparation for an unknown kind of future living" (4). In a prescient commentary on the future of adult education, Lindeman argued that effective adult education would alter not only individual adult lives but the "social order" (105). In the 1930s, a decade after publishing *The Meaning of Adult Education*, Lindeman accepted a worker training position in the federal government's Works Progress Administration (WPA).

While working for the WPA, Lindeman became a mentor to a young man named Malcolm Knowles, a Harvard graduate recently hired to work for the National Youth Administration, a US government agency established to help young adults become more employable (Knowles 6). In 1946, Knowles began graduate studies in adult education at the University of Chicago, where he was taught and mentored by influential adult educator and scholar Cyril Houle (Knowles 27–28). Two decades later, after having taught in several colleges, published widely, and developed courses for adult educators, Malcolm Knowles was nationally recognized as a leader in the growing professional field of adult education.

Knowles is particularly well-known for introducing to American educators a set of adult learning principles, collectively referred to as andragogy (Holton, Swanson, and Naquin; Knowles, "Andragogy, Not Pedagogy"; Knowles, *The Making of an Adult Educator*; Knowles, Holton, and Swanson, *The Adult Learner*, 7th ed.; Merriam; Smith). These principles, based on the ideas of German instructor Alexander Kapp, have offered an especially longlasting and influential framework for developing adult-oriented instructional approaches and curricula:

> Despite years of critique, debate, and challenge, the core principles of andragogy have endured . . . and few adult learning scholars would disagree with the observation that Knowles' ideas sparked a revolution in adult education and training. . . . Brookfield (1986), positing a similar view, asserts that andragogy is the "single most popular idea in the education and training of adults." (Holton, Swanson, and Naquin 119)

As Holton et al. suggest, Knowles's influence on adult educators is unparalleled. Among the many adult learning scholars who have relied on Knowles's ideas to develop curricula and instruction is Stephen S. Brookfield. Arguably the most prolific and publicly honored American adult education scholar, Brookfield has won the Cyril O. Houle Award for Outstanding Literature in Adult Education six times and has discussed Knowles's contributions to adult education in *Understanding and Facilitating Adult Learning*.

As a framework of core principles, the andragogical model has recently been expanded and rearticulated (Holton, Swanson, and Naquin; Knowles, Holton, and Swanson). The six core principles are:

1. Adults learn best when they know why they need to know something.
2. Adults learn more effectively when they are self-directed rather than dependent on a teacher.
3. Adults have more experiences and different kinds of experiences than children, and these experiences can serve as important resources for learning.
4. Adults learn best when they are ready to learn.

5. Rather than being subject-centered, adults are task-centered learners and problem solvers.
6. Internal motivations, rather than external rewards, are particularly important for adults. (Summarized from Knowles, Holton, and Swanson, 63–67)

The andragogical model has been extensively critiqued for its focus on the individual, lack of attention to social contexts, and failure to examine existing social inequities. However, even as new theories of adult learning (e.g., transformational learning, situated learning, narrative learning) have been introduced and debated, Knowles's andragogical principles continue to be an important touchstone for both new and experienced adult educators.

How Adult Learners Influenced Twentieth-Century Undergraduate Education

While a handful of college instructors and scholars were paying attention to adult learners during the first half of the twentieth century, adult undergraduates began attending college in significant numbers just after World War II with the support of the Serviceman's Readjustment Act of 1944, or the GI Bill (Jolly). These new college students registered in the traditional degree programs designed for young adults and also in junior colleges, which were a growing presence in the United States. For some returning World War II veterans, higher education opportunities were out of reach: After the US government lowered the draft age from 21 to 18 in 1942, young men were increasingly being accepted into the military without having earned a high school diploma. To assist these individuals, the US armed forces adapted the Iowa Tests of General Educational Development to establish a General Education Development (GED) certificate in 1942 (Hanford, Smith, and Stern). Originally restricted to military personnel and veterans, the GED certificate was made available to the New York state general population in 1947 and to residents of all fifty states twenty-five years later (Hanford, Smith, and Stern). While the GED was originally intended for military veterans and adults who had not completed high school, it is now commonly offered for people age 16 and older.

The influx of college students under the GI Bill had a second major influence on the education landscape: These World War II veterans helped spur the growth of two-year degree institutions, which came to be known as community colleges (especially with reference to public institutions) during the 1960s and 1970s ("junior college"). Ever since the 1970s, adult undergraduates (particularly individuals who come from working-class families, are self-supporting, or are immigrants to the United States) have increasingly enrolled in publicly financed community colleges, where admissions standards are generally less restrictive and tuition and fees are more affordable than for senior colleges. Community colleges offer short-term certificate programs, which can improve employment opportunities for students, and associate degrees, which can both increase employment options and allow for credit transfers to senior colleges.

More Twentieth-Century Influences: Opening Access to Higher Education

Two decades after the GI Bill was enacted, widespread social unrest and related sociopolitical movements (e.g., the civil rights movement, the women's movement, and the peace movement) inspired many educators to create academic programs that would support students being admitted as a consequence of newly lowered college admissions policies. Community colleges proliferated while senior colleges began offering special counseling services specifically for adult undergraduates, remedial courses for students of all ages, and specially designed adult-oriented courses and degree programs. Two examples of adult-oriented divisions in traditional colleges are the Program for Adult College Education (PACE) at California State University–Dominguez Hills and the Center for Worker Education (CWE) at the City College of New York.

In addition to community colleges and adult-oriented courses and programs housed within traditional colleges, entirely new institutions have been established to attract adult undergraduates: two well-known examples of postsecondary institutions designed for working adults are the University of Phoenix (founded in 1976) and Empire State College, State University of New York (founded in 1971). The University of Phoenix has been a leader in accelerated learning and online education, helping usher in a wave of for-profit colleges that are designed for working adults (Wolfe). Empire State College has emphasized its use of individualized instruction from professors who are called "mentors" (Herman and Mandell) and offers a well-designed prior learning assessment (PLA) program for adults who wish to earn college credit on the basis of learning derived from life experience ("Prior Learning Assessment System").

Together with a handful of other colleges in the 1970s and 1980s, Empire State pioneered the use of PLA to award college credits. Today, PLA is widely available at traditional colleges and universities and at nontraditional colleges, another outcome that illustrates the influence of adult undergraduates on higher education. Perhaps the most consequential innovation in adult-oriented college curricula, PLA programs award college credit for learning experienced outside the college classroom and then documented while a student is in college. Learning achieved in both informal contexts (e.g., unstructured, unplanned, experiential learning that can take place anywhere) and nonformal contexts (described by Merriam et al. as "organized learning opportunities outside the formal education system" [30]) can provide college students with opportunities to claim college credit (sometimes called "life experience credit") via prior learning assessment. One widely used PLA approach requires students to compile portfolios of their own written and artistic productions and, very often, of additional documents—e.g., letters from employers, workshop certificates, military service documents, community service awards, and workplace reports (Colvin; Michelson and Mandell). Examples of actual students' PLA portfolios have been compiled by Denise M. Hart and Jerry H. Hickerson in *Prior Learning Portfolios: A Representative Collection*. Two professional organizations provide PLA guidance for institutions and support for individual educators: the National Institute on the Assessment of Prior Learning and the Council for Adult and Experiential Learning.

PLA credits can be obtained via testing or individualized portfolio assessment. A recent survey conducted by the Council for Adult and Experiential Learning (CAEL) on PLA practices in the United States reveals that in 2006, 85 percent of higher education institutions participating in the survey reported using College Level Examination Program (CLEP) exams, 84 percent reported use of Advanced Placement (AP) practices, 27 percent reported use of Excelsior exams, 48 percent reported use of DSST (DANTES Subject Standardized Tests), 57 percent reported use of challenge exams, 70 percent reported use of guidelines by the American Council of Education, and 66 percent of study participants reported using portfolio evaluations to assess experiential learning/prior learning (Hart and Hickerson 7). Current availability of PLA opportunities is far greater than in 1974, when only a little more than forty institutions offered PLA programs (Hart and Hickerson 5).

Early Generations of Adult Undergraduates: 1960s and 1970s

In *Adults as Learners*, K. Patricia Cross identifies three main influences explaining the increases in adults' participation in formal learning activities during the 1960s and 1970s: changing population demographics with more older adults available to pursue formal learning, social changes that encouraged more women and ethnic minorities to pursue learning as adults, and technological innovations that promoted greater participation in distance education (Cross 2–3).

As for adults returning to college, Cross has profiled US adult undergraduates of the 1970s as upwardly mobile individuals with working-class backgrounds and better jobs than working-class people of the same age who are not attending college and have no college degrees. Typically first-generation college students, these 1970s adult undergraduates were often more focused on their own goals than were younger adults and more likely than younger college students to attend classes part-time and to enroll in community colleges or special degree-granting programs for nontraditional students. A similar, more recent analysis of adult undergraduates' motivations is provided by James Peter Loftus, whose descriptive study of returning adult undergraduates reveals that they cite one or more of five reasons for (re)entering college: career advancement, personal satisfaction, family considerations, encouragement from an employer, and/or tuition reimbursement (60).

The social science research conducted by Cross on "new students" (Cross's term for adult learners) in the 1960s and 1970s has been compared to the scholarship of Mina Shaughnessy and her focus on basic writers at the City College of New York in the 1970s (McAlexander). Although they expressed their ideas in different discourses and relied on different research methods, Cross and Shaughnessy were both advocates for opening access to higher education for new generations of college students who were often the first generation in their families to attend college.

Adult Participants in Twenty-First-Century American Education Systems

From 1970 to 2010, the proportion of adult college students age 25 and older has increased dramatically. In 1970, 27 percent of all enrollments (undergraduate and graduate students) were age 25 or older while in 2010, 44 percent of enrollments (undergraduate and graduate) were age 25 or older (National Center for Education Statistics 2011). Furthermore, in 2010, women, students of color, English language learners, and multilingual students were more prevalent on college campuses in all age groups than ever before, in part because of changing social expectations and in part because of widened educational and employment opportunities for women, ethnic minorities, and recent immigrants during the past fifty years.

While adult undergraduates are usually defined by age (most commonly by age 25 or older), these students typically share one or more characteristics of nontraditional students. According to the National Center for Educational Statistics, a student is classified as "nontraditional" if he or she:

- delays enrollment (does not enter postsecondary education in the same calendar year that he or she finished high school);
- attends part-time for at least part of the academic year;
- works full-time (35 hours or more per week) while enrolled;
- is considered financially independent for purposes of determining eligibility for financial aid;
- has dependents other than a spouse (usually children, but sometimes others);
- is a single parent (either not married or married but separated and has dependents); or
- does not have a high school diploma (completed high school with a GED or other high school completion certificate or did not finish high school). (National Center for Educational Statistics, Nontraditional Undergraduates, 3)

Since many college students under age 25 also exhibit one or more of the traits above, there is debate about who "adult undergraduates" are and how they are best described. For instance, according to the National Center for Educational Statistics, college students younger than 25 are frequently financially independent and working full-time, two key indicators of adult status.

Another indicator of nontraditional student status is the attainment of a GED certificate rather than a traditional high school diploma. GED preparatory courses represent a growing segment of the US adult education system, with "nearly half [of all] GED certificate holders eventually enroll[ing] in postsecondary education" (Garvey 1). In their analysis of high school degrees awarded in the United States and the growing use of GEDs as substitutes for high school diplomas, Heckman and LaFontaine explain that when high school completion rate reports conflate GED attainment with high school diplomas earned, US high school completion rates are inflated to levels that reach 88 percent (see, for example, National Center for Higher Education Management Systems). However, analyses based on US Census data and on data compiled by individual states (Common Core Data) reveal that high school diplomas are earned by anywhere from 68 percent to 77 percent of high school students today, depending on how the calculation is being made (Heckman and LaFontaine 251), and, in addition, another 15 percent of all new US high school credentials are attained via GED certification (Heckman and LaFontaine 247). The majority of GED test-takers (65 percent) are young adults under the age of 24 (Heckman and LaFontaine 247) and a "disproportionate number of GED certificates are earned by minorities"—a fact that conceals the lower high school completion rates among minorities (Heckman and LaFontaine 248).

For adult educators, GED preparatory classes represent a professional opportunity to teach, develop curricula, conduct research, and enter into the public debate about high school graduation standards and alternate pathways to earning high school completion credentials. Although not all GED students are over age 25, most GED students are nontraditional students who benefit from adult-oriented curricula and instructional strategies. Moreover, opportunities for adult educators in GED preparatory programs are likely to become more prominent in the near future: GED testing is currently undergoing a transition that will make preparatory instruction even more important than it already is. Obtaining the GED certificate will soon be made more difficult by a requirement that every test-taker complete the test online (making use of a computer mandatory) and by a higher fee for test-taking due to the fact that the GED program is being privatized (Hanford et al.; Rich; Winter). These changes in the GED program will also affect the educational options of adult learners who drop out of high school and impact the number of students eligible to enter college.

Portrayals of Adult Learners in General Higher Education Journals

Although "adult education" is sometimes conflated with GED instruction, remediation, and "adult basic education," many returning adult undergraduates are in fact highly prepared academically, focused, and goal-oriented. These adult undergraduates often apply their goal-oriented habits of mind to their practices as college students and can sometimes be very successful academically. Unfortunately, well-prepared, highly motivated adult undergraduates and their potential for positively influencing higher education receive relatively little attention in published journals. A recent analysis of seven higher education journals reveals a lack of focus on adult undergraduates in general higher education journals such as *Research in Higher Education* and *Journal of Higher Education* (Donaldson and Townsend). Deploring this void, the study's authors call for "research that does not treat adults as invisible or problematic because they are different from traditional students" (Donaldson and Townsend 45–46). They argue further that the dearth of research on adult students diminishes available information on "increasingly diverse students represented on many commuter campuses, community colleges, and other institutions" (Donaldson and Townsend 45).

While general higher education journals have been paying scant attention to adult undergraduates, for-profit colleges have focused heavily on this group as potential customers, especially recently. For-profit (or proprietary) vocational schools and colleges have been available for decades but have only recently gained a major share of the undergraduate student population nationwide. For-profit colleges have employed effective marketing strategies for attracting working adults to college, and their targeted marketing strategies have paid off: these colleges now enroll about 10 percent of US undergraduates.

The Rise of For-Profit Private Colleges

One of adult undergraduates' most significant impacts on postsecondary education is the growth of for-profit colleges. While community colleges attract working adults in high numbers, public community colleges operating on restricted budgets are often unable to provide the services or the courses that these students need ("Discounted Dreams"; Moltz); moreover, community colleges generally require reading, writing, and math remedial coursework that lengthens students' time spent in college, consumes limited amounts of financial aid, and discourages some students from remaining in school. These limitations of community colleges have fueled a growing need for a new type of college, and for-profit colleges have increasingly filled that need.

For-profit colleges often require fewer remedial classes, offer accelerated degree programs, provide online courses, and emphasize coursework leading directly to employment in areas such as nursing, culinary arts, and teaching. For all of these reasons, for-profit colleges are attracting working adults in large numbers. However, for-profit colleges have also proven controversial. While charging a relatively high tuition (compared to public colleges), for-profit colleges tend to attract students who qualify for government-sponsored financial aid but who also accumulate more debt than they can repay: "Although for-profit-colleges, which typically serve low income students, enroll only about 10 percent of the nation's undergraduates . . . , their students made up 150,000, or almost half, of the [student loan] defaults [in 2010]" (Lewin). Some for-profit colleges have been known to use excessively persistent recruitment strategies, so much so that "[a] new Federal Communications Commission rule now prevents private, for-profit universities from making unsolicited marketing robocalls" (Krupnick). In recent years, these colleges have become a focus of careful scrutiny by government officials, state and federal legislators, and journalists ("College, Inc."; Lewin).

Despite controversies surrounding for-profit colleges' recruitment tactics, tuition, and student loan defaults, it is clear that these colleges are attracting students. According to the National Center for Educational Statistics, in 2010 about 10 percent of all 18 million undergraduate students in US postsecondary institutions (approximately 1.8 million students) were enrolled in private for-profit colleges (National Center for Educational Statistics, Nontraditional Undergraduates, 4). In addition to the 10 percent share of undergraduate enrollments in Fall 2010, for-profit colleges increased the number of college degrees that they granted (at all levels) "by a larger percentage . . . than public institutions and private non-profit institutions" for academic years from 1999–2000 to 2009–2010 (National Center for Educational Statistics, Nontraditional Undergraduates, 5). And even though for-profit colleges have recently experienced some setbacks in the form of reduced enrollments, increased regulation, and financial woes, these colleges remain a forceful presence in postsecondary education and might well have a bright future (Krupnick). One reason for these colleges' popularity is their frequent offering of accelerated learning programs.

Accelerated Learning in Adult-Oriented College Programs

Because adult undergraduates frequently must balance home, work, and school responsibilities, finance their own education, and sometimes attend college part-time, adults are attracted to programs that promise to speed up academic progress. This is the central feature of accelerated learning educational programs, sometimes referred to as intensive education.

> The core element in accelerated learning programs is the accelerated course. Ground-based (as opposed to online) accelerated courses are presented in less time than the conventional number of instructional contact hours (for example, twenty hours vs. forty-five hours) and for a shorter duration (for example, five weeks rather than sixteen weeks). (Wlodkowski, "Accelerated Learning" 6)

Additional features of these programs include learner-centered classrooms, adult-oriented curricula designed by specialists (not individual teachers), and a particularly strong reliance on part-time faculty. While these programs have proven attractive to working adult students (Kasworm), they have also been criticized for not offering sufficient time for learning and for being too market-driven (Traub).

Concluding Observations

As the curricular and institutional changes outlined in this essay suggest, increases in adult undergraduate enrollments have radically transformed post-secondary education and changed the "social order," an outcome predicted by Eduard Lindeman in 1926. How does adult education change the social order? Increased adult education opportunities enhance the possibility of upward social mobility, not just for young adults but for middle-aged and working adults as well. In search of better lives for themselves and their families, adult undergraduates have fueled the growth of community colleges, inspired the development of adult-oriented degree programs and colleges, filled class-rooms in for-profit colleges, and established a growing need for professionally prepared adult educators. In fact, master's degree programs in adult education are currently a growth industry, with many of these new master's programs being offered entirely online.

One crucially important reason for adults returning to classrooms is a need for more and better employment options, which can yield basic benefits in housing, health, and safety. While new employment patterns can certainly affect people in all income brackets, it is adults with the lowest income levels who have the most to gain from education opportunities. In *Back to School: Why Everyone Deserves a Second Chance at Education*, Mike Rose calls attention to a Pell Institute report finding of an "astonishing 47 percent gap in the attainment of bachelor's degrees between young people at the top half versus bottom half of our country's income distribution" (21). Simply stated, young adults from middle-class and wealthy families generally attain higher levels of education than young adults from working-class and low-income families, with all related benefits. Moreover, because educational attainments correlate positively with employment options and annual earnings, individuals who were raised in families with lower incomes generally have more to gain from educational opportunities afforded to adults than individuals who were raised in families with higher incomes. And that means that individuals who have grown up in lower-income and working-class families are most likely to benefit from alternative high school programs, GED programs, and adult-oriented college degree programs.

While economic, institutional, and personal barriers still prevent many US adults from attending college, and these barriers themselves merit our attention and a higher-volume public policy discussion, it is also true that in recent decades an impressive array of higher education options have opened up for working adults who aspire to a college education. A variety of educational programs are now widely available for adults who meet college admission eligibility requirements, have the means to finance a college education, and are sufficiently motivated to attend college classes. Increased support for adult degree programs, innovative new curricula, and adult education graduate programs are entirely justified by twenty-first-century US workforce needs and by the alarmingly wide disparity in personal income and access to goods and services here in the US. Clearly, there is a corresponding need for more professionally prepared adult educators and for much greater visibility of existing and future scholarship on adult learning and adult education.

Works Cited

"ACS Educational Attainment by Degree Level and Age Group (American Community Survey): Percent of Adults Age 25 to 64 with a High School Diploma, 2011." *National Center for Higher Education Management Systems*. Web. 1 Nov. 2013.

Addams, Jane. *Twenty Years at Hull-House*. Ed. Victoria Bissell Brown. Boston: Bedford, 1999. Print.

Adult Learning in Focus. Council for Adult and Experiential Learning and National Center for Higher Education Management Systems. 2008. Web. 11 Nov. 2013.

Baldwin, Yvonne Honeycutt. *Cora Wilson Stewart and Kentucky's Moonlight Schools: Fighting for Literacy in America.* Lexington: UP of Kentucky, 2006. Print.

Bound, John, and Sarah Turner. "Going to War and Going to College: Did World War II and the G.I. Bill Increase Educational Attainment for Returning Veterans?" *Journal of Labor Economics* 20.4 (2002): 784–815. Print.

Brookfield, Stephen. "The Contribution of Eduard Lindeman to the Development of Theory and Philosophy in Adult Education." *Adult Education Quarterly* 34.4 (1984): 185–96. Print.

Brookfield, Stephen. *Understanding and Facilitating Adult Learning.* San Francisco: Jossey-Bass, 1986. Print.

"College, Inc." *Frontline.* Public Broadcasting Service. 2010.

Colvin, Janet. *Earn College Credit for What You Know.* 4th ed. Chicago: Kendall Hunt/CAEL, 2010. Print.

Coombs, P. H. "Formal and Nonformal Education: Future Strategies." *Lifelong Education for Adults: An International Handbook.* Ed. C. J. Titmus. New York: Pergamon, 1989. 57–60. Print.

Cross, K. Patricia. *Adults as Learners.* San Francisco: Jossey-Bass, 1981. Print.

"Discounted Dreams: High Hopes and Harsh Realities at America's Community Colleges." Public Broadcasting Service. 2007. Radio.

Donaldson, Joe F., and Barbara K. Townsend. "Higher Education Journals' Discourse about Adult Undergraduate Students." *Journal of Higher Education* 78:1 (2007): 27–50. Print.

Garvey, John, with Terry Grobe. *From GED to College Degree: Creating Pathways to Postsecondary Success for High School Dropouts.* Jobs for the Future. May 2011. Web. 2 Nov. 2013.

Hanford, Emily, Stephen Smith, and Laurie Stern. "Second-Chance Diploma: Examining the GED." *American RadioWorks.* Sept. 2013. Web. 3 Nov. 2013.

Hart, Denise M., and Jerry H. Hickerson. *Prior Learning Portfolios: A Representative Collection.* Dubuque, IA: Kendall Hunt, 2009. Print.

Heckman, James J., John Eric Humphries, and Tim Kautz. *The Myth of Achievement Tests: The GED and the Role of Character in American Life.* Chicago: U of Chicago P, 2014. Print.

Heckman, James J., and Paul A. LaFontaine. "The American High School Graduation Rate: Trends and Levels." IZA Discussion Paper No. 3216. Dec. 2007. Web. 1 Oct. 2013.

Herman, Lee, and Alan Mandell. *From Teaching to Mentoring: Principle and Practice, Dialogue and Life in Adult Education.* New York: RoutledgePalmer, 2004. Print.

Hiser, Krista. "A Paragraph Ain't Nothin' But a Sandwich: The Effects of the GED on Four Urban Writers and Their Writing." *City Comp: Identities, Spaces, Practices.* Ed. Bruce McComiskey and Cynthia Ryan. Albany: SUNY Press, 2003. 57–70. Print.

Hollis, Karen. *Liberating Voices: Writing at the Bryn Mawr Summer School for Women Workers.* Carbondale: U of Southern Illinois P, 2004. Print.

Holton III, Elwood F., Richard A. Swanson, and Sharon S. Naquin. "Andragogy in Practice: Clarifying the Andragogical Model of Adult Learning." *Performance Improvement Quarterly* 14.1 (2001): 118–43. Print.

Jolly, Jennifer L. "Historical Perspectives: The Servicemen's Readjustment Act of 1944." *Gifted Child Today* 36.4 (2013): 266–68. Print.

"junior college." *Encyclopædia Britannica Online.* Encyclopædia Britannica. 2013. Web. 20 Oct. 2013.

Kasworm, Carol E. "From the Adult Student's Perspective: Accelerated Degree Programs." *Accelerated Learning for Adults: The Promise and Practice of Intensive Educational Formats.* Ed. Raymond J. Wlodkowski and Carol E. Kasworm. Hoboken, NJ: Wiley, 2003. 17–28. Print. New Directions for Adult and Continuing Education 97.

Knowles, Malcolm S. *The Making of an Adult Educator: An Autobiographical Journey.* San Francisco: Jossey-Bass, 1989. Print.

Knowles, Malcolm S., Elwood F. Holton III, and Richard A. Swanson. *The Adult Learner: The Definitive Classic in Adult Education and Human Resource Development.* Burlington, MA: Elsevier, 2005. Print.

Krupnick, Matt. "Will Beaten Down For-Profit Colleges Bounce Back?" *The Hechinger Report.* CNN Money. 11 Nov. 2013. Web. 11 Nov. 2013.

Lewin, Tamar. "Student Loan Default Rates Rise Sharply in Past Year." *International New York Times Online.* 12 Sept. 2011. n. pag. Web. 11 Nov. 2013.

Lindeman, Eduard C. *The Meaning of Adult Education.* Norman, OK: Harvest House, 1961. Print.

Loftus, James Peter. "Adults Returning to College: A Descriptive Study." Diss. U of Iowa, 1998. Print.

McAlexander, Patricia J. "Mina Shaughnessy and K. Patricia Cross: The Forgotten Debate over Postsecondary Remediation." *Rhetoric Review* 19.1/2 (2000): 28–41. Print.

Merriam, Sharan B. "Andragogy and Self-Directed Learning: Pillars of Adult Learning Theory." *The New Update on Adult Learning Theory.* Ed. Sharan B. Merriam. Hoboken, NJ: Wiley, 2001. 3–13. Print. New Directions for Adult and Continuing Education 89.

Merriam, Sharan B., Rosemary S. Caffarella, and Lisa M. Baumgartner. *Learning in Adulthood: A Comprehensive Guide.* 3rd ed. San Francisco: Jossey-Bass, 2007. Print.

Michelson, Elana, and Alan Mandell. *Portfolio Development and the Assessment of Prior Learning: Perspectives, Models and Practices.* Sterling, VA: Stylus, 2004. Print.

Moltz, David. "The Quest to Get into Class." *Inside Higher Education.* 15 Sept. 2010. n. pag. Web. 10 Apr. 2014.

National Center for Education Statistics. Digest of Education. Table 200. 2011 Tables and Figures. Web. 1 Nov. 2013.

National Center for Educational Statistics. "Nontraditional Undergraduates. Findings from the Condition of Education, 2002." US Department of Education & Office of Educational Research and Improvement. NCES 2002–2012. Web. 23 Apr. 2014.

"Prior Learning Assessment System (PLA Planner)." *Empire State College, State University of New York.* Web. 29 Oct. 2013.

Quinn, Lois M. *An Institutional History of the GED*. Unpublished manuscript. 1990, 2002. Web. 30 Oct. 2013.

Rich, Motoko. "Raising the G.E.D. Bar Stirs Concern for Students." *International New York Times Online*. 11 Oct. 2013. n. pag. Web. 17 Oct. 2013.

Rose, Mike. *Back to School: Why Everyone Deserves a Second Chance at Education*. New York: The New Press, 2012. Print.

Smith, Mark K. "Andragogy." *The Encyclopedia of Informal Education*. Web. 30 Oct. 2013.

Sommer, Robert F. *Teaching Writing to Adults: Strategies and Concepts for Improving Learner Performance*. San Francisco: Jossey-Bass, 1989. Print.

Sticht, Thomas G. "Swords and Pens: What the Military Can Show Us about Teaching Basic Skills to Young Adults." *American Educator* (Fall 2000): n. pag. Web. 1 June 2011.

Traub, James. "Drive-Thru U.: Higher Education for People Who Mean Business." *New Yorker*. 20–27 Oct. 1997: 114–23. Print.

Winter, Caroline. "GED Faces New Rivals for High School Dropouts." *Bloomberg Businessweek*. Companies & Industries. 10 Oct. 2013. n. pag. Web. 19 Oct. 2013.

Wlodkowski, Raymond J. "Accelerated Learning in Colleges and Universities." *Accelerated Learning for Adults: The Promise and Practice of Intensive Educational Formats*. Ed. Raymond J. Wlodkowski and Carol E. Kasworm. Hoboken, NJ: Wiley, 2003. Print. 5–15. New Directions for Adult and Continuing Education 97.

Wolfe, Alan. "How a For-Profit University Can Be Invaluable to the Traditional Liberal Arts." *The Chronicle of Higher Education* (4 Dec. 1998): B4–B5. Print.

Adult Learning and Development

Adult Learning

1   Baumgartner, Lisa. "An Update on Transformational Learning." *The New Update on Adult Learning Theory*. Ed. Sharan B. Merriam. Hoboken, NJ: Wiley, 2001. 15–24. Print. New Directions for Adult and Continuing Education 89.

Defined as learning that changes perception of self or external realities, transformational learning is a bedrock concept for adult education. Four approaches to transformational learning are described: the cognitive rational model, the social justice model, the developmental model, and a spiritually oriented model. The author pays special attention to Jack Mezirow's cognitive rational theory and examines recent expansions of this model. She then explores pedagogical implications of transformational learning and ethical concerns. — BJG

2   Compton, Jonathan I., Elizabeth Cox, and Frankie Santos Laanan. "Adult Learners in Transition." *Students in Transition: Trends and Issues*. Ed. Frankie Santos Laanan. Hoboken, NJ: Wiley, 2006. 73–80. Print. New Directions for Student Services 114.

Compton, Cox, and Laanan note that the adult learner population is rapidly growing in postsecondary institutions, and they argue that a difference exists between nontraditional and adult students, even though many academics use the terms interchangeably. Compton, Cox, and Laanan then present the characteristics that distinguish adult students from nontraditional students. These characteristics include pursuing a vocational certificate or degree, using education to create new opportunities in the workplace, thinking of themselves as workers first and students second, enrolling in distance education, and often being English language learners. The authors then review the top six schools for adult learners as recognized by the Council for Adult and Experiential Learning (CAEL). The common features of these institutions include a validation of experiential learning, customized learning plans for the students, support for distance learning, and student support services for adult learners specifically, independent from services for other students. Compton, Cox, and Laanan conclude by discussing the implications of their findings for student affairs personnel and institutions. — KKN

3   Cross, K. Patricia. *Beyond the Open Door: New Students to Higher Education*. San Francisco: Jossey-Bass, 1971. Print.

In *Beyond the Open Door*, Cross characterizes "New Students" in higher education as those scoring in the lowest third academically. A 200-page book, *Beyond the Open Door* contains ten chapters, three appendices, and some thirty-five tables, and resulted from Cross's analysis of four major educational surveys conducted between 1960 and 1969. These studies generally centered on high school seniors and often were longitudinal, extending backward as far as seventh grade or forward to a year after high school graduation or community college entrance. The data includes (1) academic measures like standardized tests or high school grades and (2) interests, attitudes, preferences, socioeconomic status, and the like. Cross learned that most New Students are Caucasians from blue-collar backgrounds; they are first-generation college students who earned Cs in high school. They plan to attend community colleges or vocational schools, not for the joy of learning but to obtain a better life than their parents have. New Students should not be equated with low socioeconomic status or ethnic minorities, although there is overlap. In fact, one cannot assume that the effectiveness of traditional education breaks down along class lines, with the affluent well served and the poor badly served. Instead, Cross argues that traditional education has served people who can learn using the narrow approach of "traditional academic discipline-bound curricula" (16). In response, Cross calls for educational reform. Rather than remediation for traditional academic excellence, remediation should reorient students' attitudes toward learning. Colleges should offer a range of subjects, which Cross classifies into working with people, with things, and with ideas; of these, the New Students appear strong in fields dealing with human problems and technology (165). She advises adult learning methods, especially self-selected learning projects, such as group or shop work and industrial or community experience, be evaluated by performance, interviews, or competency exams. Ultimately, Cross hopes to establish education that moves students "Beyond the Open Door." Ethnic minorities and women are also new students to higher education but differ from the general profile. Women possess aptitude for traditional academic work but need support services to thrive in college. While minority enrollment has increased, the proportion of minorities remains small, and Cross calls for strategies to assist minorities in dealing with a majority culture. —KSU

4   Dill, Patricia L., and Tracy B. Henley. "Stressors of College: A Comparison of Traditional and Nontraditional Students." *Journal of Psychology* 132.1 (1998): 25–32. Print.

Noting the lack of studies on stress in nontraditional students, Dill and Henley present their study of traditional college students, ages 18–23 years, and nontraditional college students, ages 24 and older. The authors used the Adolescent Perceived Events Scale for college students with the participants. The results show that nontraditional students desired to return to school after breaks, but traditional students attended class more often. Nontraditional students felt better about completing homework, but traditional students worried more about performance in school. Also, nontraditional students were impacted by bad classes or bad teachers more than traditional students. Traditional students desired spending time with friends more than nontraditional students did, and traditional students considered breaks and vacations as fun and relaxing more than nontraditional students did. The effects of family and friends were different for both groups, also. Dill and Henley note that their findings "indicate that there are significant differences between traditional and nontraditional students in their perceptions of stressful events" (31). One caution they mention is the need for a more valid instrument for measuring stress in nontraditional students as the test that the students took is geared toward traditional students. —KKN

5   Dougherty, B. Christopher. "Measuring Effectiveness in Transfer Practices for Adult Learners." *Journal of Continuing Higher Education* 57(1) (2009): 54–58. Print.

Dougherty reviews statistics on the success of transfer students in earning their degrees. He focuses on adult learners, particularly those 35 years and older. Noting that adult learners comprise 40 percent of college students, Dougherty reports that only one-third will graduate with a bachelor's degree. He notes that most research focuses on students transferring from community colleges to four-year institutions, but there is little data on adult learners who transfer. He argues that institutions should be concerned with adult learners who move from institution to institution, which has a negative effect on degree completion. Dougherty notes that students who enroll in postsecondary institutions after age 31 "are 20% less likely to complete any degree than their traditional age counterparts" (55). Articulation between two-year and four-year institutions helps adult learners by providing individual paths for them. Dougherty calls for both two-year and four-year institutions "to articulate programs enrolling returning adult learners and to promote the transfer so as to clearly identify the pathways to degrees following the completion of the associates" (57). —KKN

6   Flint, Thomas & Associates. *Best Practices in Adult Learning: A CAEL/ APQC Benchmarking Study.* Canada: Council for Adult and Experiential Learning, 1999. Print.

With support from the Council for Adult and Experiential Learning (CAEL), staff from the American Productivity and Quality Center (APQC) undertook a benchmarking study of best practices at adult learner-friendly institutions of higher education during the year of 1998. As defined in the first chapter (written by Marisa Martin Brown, Joseph A. Camillus, C. Jackson Grayson Jr., and Ron Webb), benchmarking involves studying a group of similar organizations in order to identify their best practices with the end goal of adapting these best practices within one's own institution. This procedure has been less commonly applied to educational institutions than to business organizations, so this study is groundbreaking in that it focuses on higher education. The study first involved inviting sixty-three institutions to participate in completing a survey questionnaire, a process that yielded a response rate of 54 percent (thirty-four institutions). From this group of thirty-four private and public institutions, six were selected for the study on the basis of their responses in sixteen screening categories—e.g., student admission criteria, professional development for faculty, and a variety of instructional approaches. The approach to this study was divided into five phases: (1) planning; (2) screening a pool of nominated institutions; (3) a review meeting by staff who selected the six higher educational institutions for this study; (4) site visits for data collection; (5) preparing and distributing a report of study findings. The key finding is that adult learner–friendly higher education institutions promote an environment in which adult learner–centered practices are implemented, sensitivity is shown to students' needs, institutional structures and roles are flexible, and effective communication strategies are routinely practiced. Ten appendices offer the reader specific information about this study and the opportunity to review study protocols, evaluation instruments, and discussion questions. —BJG

7   Freire, Paulo. "The Adult Literacy Process as Cultural Action for Freedom." *Harvard Educational* Review 40:2 (May 1970): 205–25. Rpt. in *A Sourcebook for Basic Writing Teachers.* Ed. Theresa Enos. New York: Random, 1987. 158–75. Print.

Freire describes critical consciousness by considering adult literacy primers for learning to read. Arguing that literacy is not a neutral technology but that all encounters with language are politically charged, Freire contends that primers present a simplistic view of the world and objectify students as empty vessels to be filled. This kind of pedagogy assumes a passive learner, both a passive language learner and a passive learner of the social structure and one's place within it. Passivity and objectification lead to dehumanization and oppression and promote silence. That is, until one can name and see a structure, one cannot see or challenge social phenomena or question power relationships. Instead, Freire argues that literacy educators recognize the capacity of all to create text, including the poor and illiterate, and the universal right to voice. Effective teachers do not simply transmit information; they engage in a dialogic process. Then, "the literacy process, as cultural action for freedom, is an act of knowing in which the learner assumes the role of knowing subject in dialogue with the educator" (162–63). This sort of pedagogy is based on study of the world and the learner's situation within it, focusing both on form and content. Freire advises teachers to choose concepts for study that learners need to understand so they can act on critical issues, and within those concepts, teachers choose words for study that generate many forms. Such literacy work allows learners to engage in "critical analysis of the social framework" (168).—KSU

8   Hansman, Catherine A. "Context Based Adult Learning." *The New Update on Adult Learning Theory*. Ed. Sharan B. Merriam. Hoboken, NJ: Wiley, 2001. 43–51. Print. New Directions for Adult and Continuing Education 89.

Context-based adult learning theories offer a valuable alternative to behaviorist psychology models, which posit learning as stable, context-independent, and portable. Twentieth-century European psychologist L. S. Vygotsky articulated a sociocultural model of learning that has proven widely influential; he explained learning as occurring in culturally defined contexts in which people interact with one another and use technical tools (computers, calculators, pencil and paper) or psychological tools (language, numbers, learning strategies). Drawing on Vygotsky's theory, situated cognition theory argues that real-world situations offer the best learning environments. It expands experiential learning and self-directed learning to include context as essential to explanations of learning. Two useful concepts are cognitive apprenticeship and communities of practice. Cognitive apprenticeships involve learners in observing modeled behaviors, talking with mentors, practicing previously modeled activities, and benefitting from scaffolding provided by mentors and coaches. Communities of practice are groups of people who voluntarily participate in shared interests and activities. The emphasis on everyday activities and environments makes context-based learning theory more egalitarian than formal learning models. — BJG

9   Hill, Robert J. "Troubling Adult Learning in the Present Time." *Third Update on Adult Learning Theory*. Ed. Sharan B. Merriam. Hoboken, NJ: Wiley, 2008. 83–92. Print. New Directions for Adult and Continuing Education 119.

Hill tempers modern theories and scholarship about adult education with Michel Foucault's concept of how the present moment interacts with accepted methodology to produce a successful approach to education. The present moment, described as postmodern by many scholars, integrates traces of various historical moments. Prior moments — especially intellectual precursors born during the Enlightenment and eighteenth-century humanism — produced a manner of knowing defined as "foundational," based on the concept of a "stable, coherent, autonomous, rational, unitary self" (84). Foundational knowing posits that authentic knowledge must be distilled from observation over time and is "evidence-based" (84). Recently, a new way of knowing has been juxtaposed with this existing hypothesis on what can be considered valid learning. The Convergence Movement disavows the concept of a unitary self and deconstructs the definitions of identity — including a concept of self based on race, gender, or sexuality. Learning, in the Convergence Movement, is found in a fusion of modernist and postmodernist perspectives, creating a third space called an "epistemological ecotone" (88) — a zone of transition between adjacent movements, old and new, that shares elements of both but is defined by neither and produces new possibilities. In this third space, a new paradigm called the Convergence Movement proposes a form of meaning-making in which students are encouraged to answer "what if" questions— e.g., "What if empathy for marginalized and oppressed people is nothing more than forced intimacy that, in the end, appropriates the Other and erases difference?" (88). These "what if" questions suggest a relativistic type of meaning-making, but the learning espoused by the Convergence Movement is not relativistic: its "foundational values" are "purpose, creation, and interpretation within a radical critique" (89). Questions surrounding social justice are blended with adult learning within this peri-postmodern framework for learning and knowing.—CG

10   Hinkson, Christina, and Marilyn Butler. "A Proactive Approach for Community Colleges to Respond to the Adult Learner." *Catalyst* 39.1 (Spring 2010): 22–27. Print.

When unemployment rates are high, people enter higher education, particularly community colleges, so Hinkson and Butler argue that community colleges need to be aware of the need for programs that prepare students to work in various other industries. They note that community colleges make up the largest system of postsecondary education; therefore, they need to cater to the needs of displaced workers and workers looking to move forward in their careers. Thus, community colleges greatly affect their communities. Hinkson and Butler note that adult learners are different from traditional 18-year-old students, so community colleges need to adjust their programs to meet the needs of adult learners. The institutions need to address adult learners' fear of failure and their life experiences. Additionally, the authors argue that community colleges need to be "active in workforce development" (26). They also state that community colleges should consider how they deliver their courses and look at industries that are booming so that students' skills match the job market.—KKN

11   Kasworm, Carol. "Adult Learners in a Research University: Negotiating Undergraduate Student Identity." *Adult Education Quarterly* 60.2 (2010): 143–60. Print.

Kasworm presents statistics on adult learners in postsecondary institutions, particularly public four-year research universities, to support her argument that four-year research universities need to recreate their missions and environments to support a diverse population in regard to students' ages. She then reviews past studies on adult learners, noting that few studies have considered adult students as learners at research universities. For her study, Kasworm used interpretive qualitative research to analyze the interviews of students who were at least 30 years old and in various stages of their education at two universities. She found the students had positional and relational identities. Positional identities were "influenced through both their actions and their interactions in relation to the cultural context" (148). Relational identities were based on their anxiety and confidence, as students were concerned about being accepted in the classroom by the faculty. Their relational identities were multilayered, as the students wanted to be accepted academically and socially. The students found they had limited supportive relationships with both older and younger students and with some faculty. Kasworm summarizes her study by stating, "the student role is highly complex. . . . Adult student role identity and agency are based within coconstructed positional and relational identities" (157). —KKN

12   Kasworm, Carol. "Adult Meaning Making in the Undergraduate Classroom." *Adult Education Quarterly* 53.2 (Feb. 2003): 81–98. Print.

Using the constructivist view of knowledge-making, Kasworm studied how adult learners, whom she identified as at least 30 years old, created and dealt with their learning as college undergraduates. Her research question considered how the learning they engaged in during class related to their involvements in their broader lives. The results of the study showed that adult undergraduate students believed the classroom was the main place for learning and making meaning, and they acted on that learning by connecting it to their lives outside of class. The adult students also classified their learning. The instructor of each course and the focus of the course determined how the students negotiated meaning. Kasworm then discusses each of these results based on the students' level in college and their various voices (cynical, inclusion, straddling, and outside voice). Finally, she calls for more research on adult students' beliefs about learning. —KKN

13   Kasworm, Carol. "What Are They Thinking? Adult Undergraduate Learners Who Resist Learning." *Journal of Research in Innovative Teaching* 1.1 (2008): 25–34. Print.

Kasworm argues that while instructors need to create learning environments that help adults to mature and increase their understanding of the world, some adult learners resist the learning that is considered important in the classroom. She identifies a unique group of resistant adult learners who do well academically (GPAs) but do not engage in the classroom: "In the classroom, they resisted learning new content beyond their current world of understanding" (25). Most of the resistant adult learners in this study were returning to the classroom for job advancement and were in their 40s and 50s. Within this group were three subgroups: the outwardly compliant but not engaged students; the vocally questioning who voiced concerns about the incongruence of the ideas in the classroom with the work world; and the openly resistant learners who challenged the faculty and shared their work experiences that countered the faculty information. Most of the students thought their instructors did not value their real-world experience and did not want to hear the students' experiences and opinions. The students also evaluated what was taught in the classroom as to its value, whether important only for a test or for long-term use in the workplace. The students needed to see value in the college degree. Kasworm argues that instructors need to "determine how to create meaning-making connections through the design of the course, the presentation and engagement in context, the development of classroom discussion and in-class experiences, and the nature of assessment of learning through presentations, papers, and tests" (31). She states that instructors need to get into their resistant adult learners' mental models and use these as a way of engaging the students in the course content and widening their points of view. Kasworm ends the article with six suggestions for instructors to use to connect with resistant adult learners: design courses based on understanding the learners; gather information on the learners at the outset of the course to help them understand how to value and broaden their knowledge; develop course materials and activities to make inferences and apply course information to the world of work; have a supportive classroom so that adults feel valued and free to speak openly about their experiences and knowledge; develop exercises to help adult learners experience a different view on a topic; and "respect the learner, even when the individual disagrees with the content or your beliefs" (33). —KKN

14   Kazis, Richard, et al. *Adults in Higher Education: Barriers to Success and Strategies to Improve Results.* Employment and Training Administration Occasional Paper 2007-03. US Dept. of Labor. Mar. 2007. Web. 20 Dec. 2010.

This study is divided into five sections: Adult Learners in Education, Accessibility, Affordability, Accountability, and Recommendations. The authors' goal is to "synthesize the research literature on the challenges facing adult learners in higher education today and emerging strategies for increasing the number of adults over 24 who earn college credentials and degrees" (1). The study notes that although adult learners "over age 24 currently comprise about 44 percent of U.S. postsecondary students, . . . [t]he practices and policies of the higher education system continue to favor traditional, financially dependent, 18- to 21-year-old high school graduates who enroll full time" (2). The labor market continues to demand that adults have degrees and training beyond the secondary level, and this demand will intensify as the job "categories with the fastest expected growth in the next decade require postsecondary education" (2). Since most adults are financially independent, the "flexibility and convenience of online education makes it particularly attractive to adult learners" (3). To make education more accessible, traditional institutions of higher education should consider, as for-profit institutions have done, how to increase accessibility for students who are likely to have many work and family responsibilities. Online course delivery systems can increase accessibility for nontraditional students. Instructional methods that allow students to use their work- and home-life experiences are also likely to promote student success. Institutions can create greater flexibility of credit transfer between institutions. Alternative forms of financial aid should be made available for students who do not qualify for traditional financial aid based on full-time status. Credit also should be awarded when students demonstrate competence rather than relying solely on completion of credit hours. In addition to improving accessibility and affordability, institutions of higher education need to be more accountable for student success. Conventional learning outcomes are geared toward traditional students. Nontraditional students need concrete information about "employment outcomes, earnings potential, or return on education investment when choosing a postsecondary institution" (40). Educators, however, "express concern that overly simplistic metrics and reporting systems will fail to drive improvement" (40). The study reports proposed federal legislation that would allow students access to comparative information about institutions and also would compel institutions to include part-time and transfer students in their graduation rates. This inclusion would provide useful information to nontraditional students. The study recommends the incorporation of "lessons from employer methods of measuring skills and learning into design of accountability systems" and the development of "state data systems that can report economic as well as educational outcomes" (41). The report recommends the development of "federal-state partnerships," changes in financial aid programs, a national tracking system to report on student experience over time, and the establishment of "research and development programs to encourage employer engagement in the postsecondary education of working adults" (50).—TBP

15   Keeton, Morris T., Barry G. Sheckley, and Joan Krejci Griggs. *Effectiveness and Efficiency in Higher Education for Adults: A Guide for Fostering Learning*. Dubuque, IA: Kendall Hunt, 2002. Print.

This book offers a research-based framework for increased learning effectiveness and efficiency in higher education. The authors argue that a set of key learning principles and related strategies, together with creative uses of technologies, can help colleges enhance accountability and reduce costs. This twin focus on demonstrating successful learning and increasing efficiency has come more sharply into focus as college student populations have trended toward older learners and working adults. Eight learning principles are presented along with strategies for their implementation and illustrative anecdotes. Principles one and two are "early and ongoing clarification of goals" and "deliberate practice" (6). Principle three advocates support for individual learners, while principle four emphasizes the value of experiential learning. Reflecting on learning achieved and pursuing solutions to actual problems form the bases for principles five and six. Principles seven and eight call attention to monitoring individual learners' experiences and creating college-wide cultures of learning. Concrete suggestions for teachers are provided in eight of the ten chapters. What makes this book distinctive, according to the authors, are (1) an emphasis on skills development rather than a sole focus on theory and fact-based knowledge, and (2) attention to recent observations about learning and problem-solving.—BJG

16   Kerns, Lorna. "Adult Graduate Students in Higher Education: Refocusing the Research Agenda." *Adult Learning* 17.1-4 (2006): 40–42. Print.

Kerns argues that most research on adult learners in college focuses on undergraduate students and ignores graduate school adult learners. She then states that while undergraduate and graduate adult learners have some things in common, they have some differences, including already having a bachelor degree, "familiarity with the culture and mastery of the demands of the higher education environment," a link to their career and issues, and little time to complete the graduate work (41). Kerns makes suggestions for studies on graduate adult learners as more adults will enter graduate school to keep up with the global economy and increase their skill levels. — KKN

17   Kilgore, Deborah W. "Critical and Postmodern Perspectives on Adult Learning." *The New Update on Adult Learning Theory*. Ed. Sharan B. Merriam. Hoboken, NJ: Wiley, 2001. 53–61. Print. New Directions for Adult and Continuing Education 89.

The author challenges the generic view of adult learners, pointing out that individuals differ by gender, race, class, and life experience, and proposes that critical and postmodern theories can better serve adult educators than empiricist and positive epistemologies, which present knowledge as stable and unaffected by the knower or by social and linguistic processes. Critical theory and a postmodern perspective share common ground in that both epistemologies posit knowledge as socially constructed. The two perspectives diverge in the area of validity and certainty: critical theories view rationality as key to arriving at more solid conclusions and self-interest as playing a key role in knowing. In contrast, postmodernists view knowledge as "tentative, fragmented, multifaceted, and not necessarily rational" (54). Taken together, both of these perspectives can play useful roles in adult education, both as frameworks for policy decisions by adult educators and as orientations toward learning and knowing that can be useful for curriculum development, instructional practices, and conversations among teachers and learners. — BJG

18   Knowles, Malcolm S., Elwood F. Holton, and Richard A. Swanson. *The Adult Learner: The Definitive Classic in Adult Education and Human Resource Development*, 7th ed. Burlington, MA: Elsevier, 2011. Print.

The seventh edition of this classic book presents Knowles's core view of andragogy, an expanded section on the future of andragogy, added readings on andragogy in practice internationally, and a new presentation on adult-oriented instruction supported by computers. By introducing theory, learning, growth, and development, the authors explain learning theory conceptually and identify key components of learning theories. These theories can be classified as either behaviorist/connection theories or cognitivist/gestalt theories and further categorized as machine-based models or holistic models. The authors survey historical learning theory (e.g., Edward Thorndike's nineteenth-century research, behaviorism, and contributions of psychologists Sigmund Freud, Carl Jung, Erik Erikson, Abraham Maslow, and Carl Rogers) and identify the origin of *andragogy*, dating back to German teacher Alexander Kapp's use of *andragogik* in 1833. In 1950, Knowles introduced the term *andragogy* to US educators with a groundbreaking discussion of ways in which adult learning differs from child learning. Contrasts between child learning (pedagogy) and adult learning (andragogy) are focused on six areas: (1) preparing learners, (2) climate, (3) planning, (4) diagnosis of needs, (5) setting of objectives, (6) setting learner plans, (7) learning activities, and (8) evaluation. Theories of teaching are also described (chapter 5), followed by a discussion of the andragogical process model (chapter 6). Applications of andragogy to the discipline of human resource development are discussed (chapter 8), while new perspectives on andragogy are explained (chapter 9) with reference to learning models developed by Daniel Pratt and D. A. Kolb as well as an analysis of motivation by R. J. Wlodkowski. Theory and research expanding beyond the scope of andragogy include research on learning differences, cognitive controls (e.g., field dependence/independence theories of perception), learning how to learn, and individual learners' needs and learning styles, among others. The future life of andragogy will partially be determined by how flexible the concept is in new contexts and in the face of developments, e.g., in educational uses of technology. Changing conceptions of teachers (to learning facilitators) and teaching (e.g., use of learning contracts) challenge adult learning theories to adapt to evolving educational contexts. —BJG

19   Marsick, Victoria J., and Karen E. Watkins. "Informal and Incidental Learning." *The New Update on Adult Learning Theory.* Ed. Sharan B. Merriam. Hoboken, NJ: Wiley, 2001. 25–34. Print. New Directions for Adult and Continuing Education 89.

Embedded in activity and influenced by context, informal learning is more pervasive than formal learning, although it often goes unrecognized by adult learners, teachers, employers, and organizations. Incidental learning (e.g., learning by mistake or by trial and error) —an important type of informal learning—is an unanticipated byproduct of other activities and a constant presence in adult life. Adults can learn informally by reflecting on experience, talking to others, exploring topics independently, participating in a group, or absorbing an organization's policies, procedures, and values. That is, informal learning can occur at the level of the individual, team, or organization. Research reveals that informal learning is often triggered by an event or a sudden understanding, it tends to be haphazard, and it is often connected to other people's learning. A proposed model for enhancing informal learning involves a sequence of events starting with a trigger, continuing with interpretation of experience, and ending with lessons learned inside a frame. Because lessons learned via informal learning are vulnerable to group power dynamics, cultural and social norms, and individual beliefs, informal learning can lead to false assumptions and error. Adult educators are advised to encourage informal learning while finding ways to make learned lessons more open to question and critique. Substantial progress has been made on researching informal learning; more research is still needed in areas such as tacit knowledge of erroneous information, the influence of emotion, and interfaces between informal learning of individuals, teams, and organizations. —BJG

20   McAlexander, Patricia J. "Mina Shaughnessy and K. Patricia Cross: The Forgotten Debate over Postsecondary Remediation." *Rhetoric Review* 19.1/2 (2000): 28–41. Print.

McAlexander compares the "iconic" Mina Shaughnessy with a lesser known but influential contemporary, K. Patricia Cross. Both Shaughnessy and Cross worked at public universities in the 1960s and 1970s and supported open admissions. Both were affected by the civil rights movement, but influenced by it in different ways, particularly how they looked at what both called the "new students." Shaughnessy's work consists primarily of *Errors and Expectations* and a few essays, while Cross wrote many articles and several books. Shaughnessy studied drama, literature, and religion; her work is narrative and metaphorical, demonstrating rhetorical skill drawn from personal experience and observation. Cross was a math major with a PhD in psychology who relied on quantitative methods. Shaughnessy offers readers elegant narrative, while Cross's mode is numbers and figures drawn from her analysis of existing national data banks of information on the new students. These differing inquiries led Shaughnessy and Cross to conflicting profiles of the new students, reasons for their underachievement, and recommendations for curriculum. Shaughnessy, whose inner-city New York students were mainly ethnic minorities, condemns the racist and classist assumptions of earlier education and believes in the potential of her students to obtain a traditional education. Cross argues that most developmental students are not minorities and identifies low test scores and ability as well as weak motivation and effort as characteristic of new students. Shaughnessy focuses on improving remedial methods and, in fact, suggests that teachers remediate themselves. Cross recommends not remediation for academic excellence but vocational, business, and paraprofessional alternatives in two-year colleges. McAlexander concludes that while Shaughnessy was right that "the academic background of minorities *is* often to blame," Cross emerges as "more accurate in describing the students and predicting the direction of basic education" (37). —KSU

21   Merriam, Sharan B. "Andragogy and Self-Directed Learning: Pillars of Adult Learning Theory." *The New Update on Adult Learning Theory*. Ed. Sharan B. Merriam. Hoboken, NJ: Wiley, 2001. 3–13. Print. New Directions for Adult and Continuing Education 89.

This essay offers a review of scholarship on two adult learning concepts: andragogy and self-directed learning. Both concepts served key roles in jumpstarting the professional field of adult education in the United

States: Malcolm Knowles first introduced andragogy to a US readership in the 1960s, and Allen Tough and Cyril Houle offered comprehensive investigations of self-directed learning (SDL) in the 1960s and early 1970s. Extensive scholarship on both andragogy and self-directed learning during the three decades spanning 1970 through 2000 expanded these concepts and suggested many instructional applications but concluded with severe criticisms of both concepts. The most scathing critique was that they focus too strongly on individual learners while ignoring social contexts for learning and cultural influences on learners. Sociocultural contexts for learning and the influence of political and economic forces became far more prominent in adult learning theory than acontextual conceptions of adult learners common to early formations of andragogy and SDL, calling into question the relevance of these two foundational concepts for contemporary scholars and teachers. Sharan Merriam argues that despite these criticisms, both andragogy and SDL continue to influence adult education scholarship today and have the potential to enrich continued explorations of the nature of adult learning. She suggests specific questions that can be useful for exploring these concepts and connecting them to contemporary concerns with social contexts and cultural influences on learning. — BJG

22   Merriam, Sharan B., Rosemary S. Caffarella, and Lisa M. Baumgartner. *Learning in Adulthood: A Comprehensive Guide*, 3rd ed. San Francisco: Jossey-Bass, 2007. Print.

The authors provide a comprehensive survey of publications on adult learning and development. Part One focuses on North American contexts for adult learning, forces that have shaped adult education, and characteristics of adult participants in formal education programs. Part Two, "Adult Learning Theories and Models," presents major contemporary adult learning theories, starting with andragogy, a model articulated by Malcolm Knowles to contrast learning in adulthood with learning in childhood, and continuing with theories articulated by Howard McClusky, Knud Illerus, and Peter Jarvis. Also described are three types of learning strongly associated with adults: self-directed learning, transformational learning, and experiential learning. Part Three introduces modern perspectives on learning, including, for example, narrative knowing, postmodernism, feminism, and embodied learning. Part Four opens with a review of more established learning theories, beginning with concepts presented by Aristotle and Plato, and continuing with behaviorist psychology, Gestalt psychology, the humanist orientation, and cognitive psychology. Adult development research is summarized in the fourteenth and fifteenth chapters, with attention to changes in memory and cognition, and a final chapter connects ideas about adult learners, learning, and educational programs. — BJG

23   Mezirow, Jack. "Learning to Think Like an Adult: Core Concepts of Transformation Theory." *Learning as Transformation: Critical Perspectives on a Theory in Progress*. Mezirow, Jack, and Associates. San Francisco: Jossey-Bass, 2000. 3–33. Print.

Mezirow articulates Transformation Theory as a form of meaning-making that is fundamentally important in adulthood. It involves "becoming critically aware of one's own tacit assumptions and expectations and those of others and assessing their relevance for making an interpretation" (4). This experience can lead to transformative learning, a process whereby a person may expand on an existing meaning perspective (or frame of reference), adopt a new perspective, change a habit of mind (e.g., a liberal or conservative orientation), or change a point of view (which Mezirow describes as a fully expressed habit of mind). Transformations of habits of mind may be sudden and dramatic or progressive and incremental. Transforming a point of view often results from considering another person's perspective and viewing it as one's own. Transformative learning can follow from a meaningful event (such as a disorienting dilemma, self-analysis, or experiencing a new role) and will focus on either external realities or one's own assumptions and beliefs. Becoming critically reflective about one's own beliefs is an underlying precondition for transformative learning. Although critical self-reflection can occur prior to adulthood, it is more likely to occur in adults. Therefore, critical self-reflection and transformative learning are more closely associated with adults than with children. —BJG

24 Mezirow, Jack, and Associates. *Fostering Critical Reflection in Adulthood: A Guide to Transformative and Emancipatory Learning*. San Francisco: Jossey-Bass, 1990. Print.

A breakthrough work in its time, this collection of essays edited by Mezirow continues to serve as a baseline text for understanding the transformative power of critical reflection for adult learners. Written by leaders in the field of adult learning, the essays provide insights into both the theoretical underpinnings of critical reflection as an andragogical tool and practical methodologies for introducing these strategies into the classroom and workplace. In his introductory chapter, Mezirow explains the ideas and purposes of the work: "Emancipatory education is an organized effort to help the learner challenge presuppositions, explore alternative perspectives, transform old ways of understanding, and act on new perspectives" (18). He describes the nature of critical reflection, which allows students to "make meaning" of their experiences, with meaning being a facet of understanding, learning, and knowledge. While engaged in this process, students are encouraged to "reassess the presuppositions on which [their] beliefs are based" (18). Following this introduction are essays that build on this theme of transformative learning through critical reflection, including an essay in which Peter Dominicé explains the idea of education biographies as a way for students to contextualize their learning and to gain perspective on their understanding of knowledge, and one in which Stephen Brookfield leads a reader through understanding the media's deep influence on students' perceptions and the ways in which they make meaning. The collected essays contain a rich vein of insights into the nature of transformative learning alongside strategies for invigorating student learning. — SFL

25   Ozanne, Julie L., Natalie Ross Adkins, and Jennifer A. Sandlin. "Shopping [for] Power: How Adult Literacy Learners Negotiate the Marketplace." *Adult Education Quarterly* 55.4 (Aug. 2005): 251–68. Print.

Noting that adult education focuses not only on teaching reading, writing, and math, but also on life skills such as consumer education, Ozanne, Adkins, and Sandlin argue that these programs do not consider what adult literacy students actually do in the marketplace. The authors review literature on functional literacy, which focuses on the transference of skills across various settings. Using interviews and observations, the authors studied participants' consumer practices. Two dimensions resulted from the study: "(a) acceptance or rejection of the stigma of low literacy and (b) subjection or power in the marketplace" (254). Based on these two dimensions, the authors divided the study participants into two groups: alienated consumers and conflicted identity managers. One finding of the study is that literacy is not a skill set that can transfer from one setting to another. Additionally, within the marketplace setting, specific contexts require specific skills in a wider range. This range of skills is used competently to meet the needs of the situation. Also, those adult literacy learners who reject the label of low literacy are more successful in the marketplace. Ozanne, Adkins, and Sandlin call for a critical approach that encourages consumers to see themselves with agency and know how to participate in and change marketplace interactions. — KKN

26   Richardson, John T. E., and Estelle King. "Adult Students in Higher Education: Burden or Boon?" *Journal of Higher Education* 69.1 (1998): 65–88. Print.

Citing studies prior to 1998, Richardson and King discuss the realities of adult students who return to higher education in comparison to how they are perceived. First, the authors discuss the various definitions of *adult learner* based on age, and then they summarize the various characteristics that have been given to adult learners in postsecondary education. They note that researchers cannot group all adult learners together based on select characteristics. Richardson and King then refute some of the common misconceptions about adult learners: Isolated courses on study skills are ineffective with adult learners as they often praise the courses; the students lack time management skills as they have learned to manage time with their domestic and career responsibilities; and they lack cognitive abilities, which does not consider that adult learners perceive tasks based on how they relate to everyday life. Finally, the authors call for stereotypes of adult learners to be rejected, especially by organizations. — KKN

27   Rossiter, Marsha, and M. Carolyn Clark. *Narrative and the Practice of Adult Education*. Malabar, FL: Krieger, 2007. Print.

Building on the recent "narrative turn" in the humanities and social sciences, Marsha Rossiter and M. Carolyn Clark explore relationships between narrative and adult learning and between narrative and adult education. Chapters 1 and 2 introduce narrative theory and its applications to knowing and interpretation, with reference to the work of Jerome Bruner and D. E. Polkinghorne, who both argue that a narrative epistemology involves the knower in discovery and creation of knowledge. Chapter 3 presents applications of narrative to life span theories of adult development. In chapter 4, the authors discuss relationships between narrative and adult learning, a theme that is related to writing practices in chapter 5. Journal writing and autobiographical writing are of particular importance for applying narrative epistemologies to adult learning practices. Facilitating narrative learning in the classroom is addressed in chapter 5, while narrative's applications to program development are explored in chapter 6 and narrative's relationship to developing self-understanding is addressed in chapter 7. The book's overarching argument is that narrative epistemology can redefine the field of adult education and provide a solid foundation for theories of adult learning. — BJG

28   Taylor, Edward W. "Transformative Learning Theory." *Third Update on Adult Learning Theory.* Ed. Sharan B. Merriam. Hoboken, NJ: Wiley, 2008. 5–15. Print. New Directions for Adult and Continuing Education 119.

Taylor reviews Jack Mezirow's adult learning theory, transformative learning, which is based on the learner's frame of reference. He then reviews various alternative conceptions about transformative learning, which include "psychoanalytic, psychodevelopmental, and social emancipatory" (7). He adds the views of "neurobiological, cultural-spiritual, race-centric, and planetary" (8). All of these alternative concepts approach transformative learning from a new perspective, theorizing how each one affects how adults learn. Taylor then presents "emerging alternative perspectives on transformative learning theory" (10) that emphasize reflection, holistic approaches, and barriers to transformative learning. Finally, Taylor argues that transformative learning theory has "replaced andragogy as the dominant educational philosophy of adult education" (12). — KKN

29   Taylor, Kathleen, and Annalee Lamoreaux. "Teaching with the Brain in Mind." *Third Update on Adult Learning Theory.* Ed. Sharan B. Merriam. Hoboken, NJ: Wiley, 2008. 49–59. Print. New Directions for Adult and Continuing Education 119.

Taylor and Lamoreaux begin by discussing how the brain operates, putting the anatomy terminology into simpler terms, and then explain how learning takes place by connecting new information to past patterns and experiences. In other words, new information is filtered through the knowledge gained from previous experiences. Relating this information to how adults learn, the authors argue that teachers of adults can aid their students with learning course material by using strategies that align with brain functions. Instructors need to help students relate new information to current and past experiences in order for students to learn properly. Taylor and Lamoreaux provide examples of activities instructors could use to help students relate previous experiences to the new information in their courses. They lead the reader through the processes of experience, reflection, abstraction, and testing before discussing the role of adult educators in the process. Adult learners need to have "their maturity, knowledge, and experience" recognized (57), and scaffolding assists them with constructing new levels of learning. —KKN

30   Tisdell, Elizabeth J. "Spirituality and Adult Learning." *Third Update on Adult Learning Theory*. Ed. Sharan B. Merriam. Hoboken, NJ: Wiley, 2008. 27–36. Print. New Directions for Adult and Continuing Education 119.

After defining *spirituality* and distinguishing it from *religion*, Tisdell explains why the topic is important for adult learning. She argues that spirituality has had a great influence in adult education and discusses how spirituality has influenced research in the field. Recently, spirituality has become more prominent in adult education because of the amount of discussion on the topic within the field. In her study, Tisdell found that "*significant* spiritual experiences of deep learning seem to happen only occasionally," but these "lead to continued development" (31). These experiences help people reframe earlier experiences and make new discoveries that are transformative. Each significant spiritual experience helps to develop one's identity, which "often happens in concert with further cognitive and moral development" (33). Tisdell concludes by stating that instructors do not need to focus on spirituality in their classrooms; rather, they can help students focus on "shimmering moments" (34) and their development. —KKN

31   Zacharakis, Jeff, Marie Steichen, Gabriela Diaz de Sabates, and Dianne Glass. "Understanding the Experiences of Adult Learners: Content Analysis of Focus Group Data." *Adult Basic Education and Literacy Journal* 5.2 (2011): 84–95. Print.

These authors focus on understanding why adults entered ABE and ESL classes, what aspects of the programs helped them be the most successful, and how the programs could be improved. The authors then discuss the literature on adult learners and the aspects of programs that retain adult learners and help them be successful. To complete the research, the authors used focus groups and the Strategic Analysis of Representations Approach (SARA) "to better understand the ways in which adults reinvest in the self through change" (85). After discussing the pluses and minuses of focus groups and the SARA, Zacharakis, Steichen, de Sabates, and Glass present their research process and findings. The 104 students in their study were from various adult learning centers in Kansas, and the students were in English speaking ABE groups and Spanish speaking ESL groups. The students in the ABE groups were 18 to 30 years old, and the ones in the ESL groups were 19 to 65 years old. Using content analysis, they coded the transcripts from the groups. The content was grouped into six areas, and examples of what students said are included. They found that student-teacher relationships are essential for adult students to experience success. The students had to overcome barriers such as old friends or habits that were developed when they were younger in order to succeed in the classes. They also used successes as empowerment to continue in their educational endeavors. The authors then discuss the limitations of the study but note that the focus groups allowed the students to share their experiences, which allowed them to inspect their own lives and to redesign their journeys to forge ahead in their education. — KKN

32   Zaffit, Cynthia K. "Bridging the Great Divide: Approaches That Help Adults Navigate from Adult Education to College." *Adult Learning* 19.1–2 (2008): 6–11. Print.

Zaffit discusses adult students who complete adult education programs and whether or not they have goals to attend college. She says it is difficult to learn the real goals of these nontraditional students. One study cited showed that students who completed one year in community college earned more than those who did not. These students face multiple obstacles in school, but if they succeed in completing one year and continuing in college, their grades are not significantly different from students who earned a high school diploma in the traditional manner. Zaffit then discusses three models — advising, career pathways, and college prep — to help adult education students transition to college. Finally, she calls for "a systematic approach" (9) for helping these students transition to college and for colleges "to see adult learners as potential college students" (9). — KKN

33   Zemke, Ron, and Susan Zemke. "Thirty Things We Know for Sure about Adult Learning." *Training* (1988): 57–61. Print. Rpt. of *Training/ HRD* 18.6 (1981): 45–46, 48–49, 52.

Training magazine labels this brief article a "classic" because readers requested it more than any other between 1981 and 1988. The Zemkes review a huge body of research on adult learning and classify it into three categories: what we know about learner motivation, curriculum design, and classroom practice. Under each category, the authors identify key researchers and research directions and then extract characteristics of adult learners and guidelines for instructors. The Zemkes argue that adults seek learning experiences to cope with life changes, so learning should be practical, not an end in itself. Further, critical life changes are teachable moments. Adults prefer, according to the authors, focused curriculum with time to integrate and practice new concepts. A key curriculum researcher, R. B. Catell, developed the notions of "fluid," fact-based intelligence as opposed to "crystallized" intelligence based on knowledge and experience. The teaching implications of Catell's work, identified by influential adult learning theorist K. Patricia Cross, include meaningful presentations of information with aids to help organize material, a pace that allows for mastery, focusing on one idea at a time with minimal competing demands, and frequent summary. A second set of research affecting curriculum is life stage theory and work on values. This material suggests that curriculum designers iden-tify content that may support or challenge students' values and allow for learners in different life stages with differing values. Another form of curriculum research focuses on modes of instruction—adults favor self-directed learning projects, delivered in varied forms: lectures, short seminars, consultation with an expert, on-site visits, and the like. Adults prefer to carry out these projects in collaborative work groups, not in isolation. Research on classroom practice suggests that the classroom be physically and psychologically comfortable. Instructors should clarify expectations before delving into content; honor adults' life experience; allow for dialogue; use active learning techniques; pro-tect minority opinion; and plan for practice, applications of learning, accountability, and follow-up. In short, the "instructor is less advocate than orchestrator" (60). —KSU

Adult Development

34   Bjorklund, Barbara R. *The Journey of Adulthood*, 7th ed. Upper Saddle River, NJ: Pearson/Prentice, 2011. Print.

Informed by lifespan developmental psychology, this book covers mul-tiple developmental phases and many different aspects of adult life, for example, work, social relationships, health, and retirement. While the author summarizes the work of many psychologists (e.g., Freud, Jung, and Maslow), she argues that Erik Erikson's theory of psycho-social development has been particularly influential (253). Drawing on research from such fields as "biological and medical sciences, the social sciences, gender studies, economics, education and vocational psychology, clinical psychology, epidemiology, and anthropology" (xv), the author addresses topics such as physical changes, cognition, social roles, retirement, and death and bereavement. Because adult learners anticipate changes in memory and learning ability as they age, the section on "cognitive abilities" (chapter 4) has special relevance for adult learners and their teachers. The author explains different types of memory and summarizes research reports, stating that adults experience various levels of memory loss within different types of memory, e.g., short-term and long-term memory. In the area of long-term memory, for example, there are two types of mental operation: semantic memory (ability to recall words, names, and facts) and episodic memory (the ability to recall recent events). While semantic memory remains gen-erally stable as people age into their seventies, episodic memory does decline with age. Research shows that unless speed is a component of the assessment, older adults can learn new skills ("procedural memory") nearly as well as younger adults. As for cognitive declines associated with aging, individual differences can be accounted for by factors such as health, schooling, exercise, and an active mental and social life. Of special interest for teachers of adult learners are topics discussed in chapter 9, "The Quest for Meaning." Older adults can also experience development in the area of moral reasoning and spiritual growth. Kohlberg's stage theory of moral development is summarized (283), as is Carol Gilligan's critique of that theory. In the final two chapters, the author argues that adults continue to learn all through their lives and that later stages of development must account for quality of life issues and adults' perceptions of death and dying. — BJG

35   Lytle, Susan L. "Living Literacy: Rethinking Development in Adulthood." *Linguistics and Education* 3.2 (1991): 109–38. Rpt. in *Literacy: A Critical Sourcebook*. Ed. Ellen Cushman, Eugene R. Kintgen, Barry M. Kroll, and Mike Rose. Boston: Bedford, 2001. 376–401. Print.

Lytle argues that too little is known about adult literacy development, especially for adults with low literacy competencies. In order to learn more about adult literacy development, scholars should examine competing views of literacy and investigate common assumptions about low-literacy adults' abilities and lifestyles. For example, the assumption that low-literacy adults are weak and embarrassed (and therefore seek private, one-on-one tutoring) does not align with the realities of individuals who attend adult literacy classes. Many such individuals have highly varied self-concepts, interests, and literacy experiences. Rather than relying on generalizations, adult literacy educators and researchers should develop a richer conceptual framework for understanding adult literacy, taking into account cultural scripts for learning and for using written language. Ultimately, effective adult literacy theory building will require researchers to include adult literacy learners' perspectives and active participation in inquiry projects. In so doing, researchers can develop a theory of adult literacy development that can prove useful to educators and policymakers. — BJG

36   Pourchot, Thomas L., and M. Cecil Smith. "Some Implications of Life Span Developmental Psychology for Adult Education and Learning." *PAACE Journal of Lifelong Learning* 13 (2004): 69–82. Print.

Pourchot and Smith discuss theories of life span development and how these apply to adult learning and to the adult education classroom. The authors divide life span development into three areas: psychometric research, which explains that humans develop over a lifetime in many different ways and through many changes; everyday cognition, which explains that adult learning occurs in contexts; and postformal thought in adulthood, which involves problem finding and represents "mature adult thought" (73). After discussing these theories, Pourchot and Smith discuss the importance of integrating these theories in the adult learning environment and use headings of curriculum development, instruction, and evaluation, as well as the administration of the programs in the remainder of the article. The authors conclude, "Adult educators, however, need to make the connections between life span development, adult education and learning explicit in their teaching" (79). —KKN

37   Smith, M. Cecil. "Does Service Learning Promote Adult Development? Theoretical Perspectives and Directions for Research." *Linking Adults with Community: Promoting Civic Engagement through Community-Based Learning*. Ed. Susan C. Reed and Catherine Marienau. Hoboken, NJ: Wiley, 2005. 5–15. Print. New Directions for Adult and Continuing Education 118.

Smith reviews the benefits of service learning to college students, but the findings of studies on service learning usually focus on traditional undergraduate students. Following the review of adult development, Smith discusses how service learning affects three of the domains of adult development by using the dimensions of service learning. He reasons that service learning affects the moral development of adults as they learn to care for others in need and develop close relationships, may contribute to the maturity of the psychosocial aspect of adults, and increases the cognitive growth of adult learners in some areas. Smith then calls for research on how service learning meets the growth in the various domains of adult development. Finally, he calls for caution in requiring service learning for adult learners until studies show definitively that service learning aids in the growth of adult learners. —KKN

38   Spitzer, Tam M. "Predictors of College Success: A Comparison of Traditional and Nontraditional Age Students." *NASPA Journal* 38.1 (Fall 2000): 82–98. Print.

Spitzer states that nontraditional age students, whom she identifies as age 25 and older, are growing in number in colleges and universities. Noting that both traditional and nontraditional students share a common goal of performing academically and progressing in their career development, the author argues that predictors of academic performance and career development with nontraditional students need to be studied as much as they have been studied for traditional students. Academic performance, self-efficacy, and intrinsic motivation affect academic performance and have been studied in traditional students, but few studies have looked at these factors with nontraditional students. Spitzer's study looked at self-efficacy, self-regulation, and social interactions as predictors of collegiate goals with both traditional and nontraditional students. Using student questionnaires, Spitzer found that "nontraditional students and females have higher GPAs and greater career decidedness than traditional students and males" (92). Self-regulation and intrinsic motivation also were greater in nontraditional students than traditional students. As expected, greater academic self-efficacy, self-regulation, and social support predicted higher GPAs regardless of students' ages. Lower GPAs were related to higher social acceptance and self-worth. No correlation between GPA and career decidedness was found with either age group, so Spitzer concludes that academic performance and career development evolve concurrently and are not interdependent. Nontraditional students were found to have greater motivation and self-regulation, leading to higher GPAs. Spitzer suggests instructors use activities that group together traditional and nontraditional students to share self-regulation strategies. She also suggests career counseling for traditional students, as these students tend to be less decided about their final goals and have fewer experiences than nontraditional students. — KKN

Survey Research, Overviews, and Large-Scale Studies

39   *Adult Learning in Focus: National and State-by-State Data.* Council for Adult and Experiential Learning and National Center for Higher Education Management Systems. 2008. Web. 18 Feb. 2008.

With funding support from The Lumina Foundation for Education and in partnership with the National Center for Higher Education Management Systems (NCHEMS), the Council for Adult and Experiential Learning (CAEL) presents a comprehensive national and state-by-state survey of US adults' educational attainments and workforce participation. In addition to providing research findings, the report describes areas where more information is needed about adults' educational attainments and explains some of the difficulties in obtaining data. The report also provides links to useful resources: one particularly valuable resource for researching adults' educational attainments is the NCHEMS's Information Center for State Higher Education Policymaking and Analysis (www.higheredinfo.org.). This Web site provides up-to-date information on topics such as college access, retention and graduate rates, and college degree attainments. The authors of this report argue that more educational attainments are needed by US adults, both to benefit individuals and to fill the jobs that require increasingly advanced levels of education. In particular, barriers to education experienced by nontraditional adult students should be lifted. For example, financial aid for students seeking post-secondary education is commonly available only to full-time students, yet many nontraditional college students attend classes part-time. An annotated bibliography of research on adult learning is appended to the report. — BJG

40   Aldrich, Pearl G. "Adult Writers: Some Factors That Interfere with Effective Writing." *Technical Writing Teacher* 9.3 (1982): 128–32. Print.

To find out more about her students' writing practices, Aldrich distributed a survey to 165 working adults "who spend a significant portion of their time on the job writing and who are responsible for originating substantive written documents" (128). Some of the respondents worked for the military while others worked in the private sector. Aldrich tabulated the results, refined the survey, and distributed it to 89 more people who were working professionals in government and private sector jobs but were also students in the author's Effective Writing courses. Many of the respondents were engineers; over half of them had college degrees. Question 9 prompted students to order a list of eight prewriting activities. Few of the respondents ordered the list correctly: the necessary steps of determining a purpose and identifying an audience for the document were often not the first items on the list. Aldrich concludes that the writers' failure to complete these steps is one major reason for their poor writing. Another survey question asked students to rewrite a sentence if it needed to be rewritten. The sentence was poorly written and "contained a violation of parallel structure," but only 64 of the 165 respondents corrected the error and improved the style (131). Aldrich concludes that the respondents lacked knowledge about the value of preparation, and this lack of knowledge "causes them to be anxious, defensive, and reluctant to approach their writing tasks until the last minute" (132). For these reasons, the writing they produce is weak. — TBP

41   Baer, Justin, Mark Kutner, John Sabitini, and Sheila White. *Basic Reading Skills and the Literacy of America's Least Literate Adults: Results from the 2003 National Assessment of Adult Literacy (NAAL) Supplemental Studies* (NCES 2009-481). Washington, DC: US Dept. of Education, Institute of Education Sciences, National Center for Education Statistics, 2009. Web. 18 Feb. 2013.

Baer et al. report on the basic reading skills of participants in the 2003 National Assessment of Adult Literacy (NAAL) — a study of adults' functional literacy. The definition of functional literacy used for this research is "[u]sing printed and written information to function in society, to achieve one's goals, and to develop one's knowledge and potential" (3). Baer et al. focus on the performance of low-literate adults. All of the NAAL study participants were first asked to answer seven simple literacy questions. Most study participants were able to respond to these questions and were then assigned tasks in the main literacy assessment, results for which were presented by classifying participants according to numerical scores in three areas: prose literacy, document literacy, and quantitative literacy. A very small proportion of the study participants were unable to respond to the initial seven literacy questions and were then assigned to the supplementary assessment. Administered in either Spanish or English, the Adult Literacy Supplemental Assessment (ALSA) used common, everyday objects to assess "letter-reading, word-reading, word-identification, and basic comprehension skills" (iv). In addition, all 19,000 study participants responded to questions in a Fluency Addition to NAAL (FAN), which tested print skills, or the ability to read "letters, words, and continuous text — accurately and efficiently" (iv). The ALSA answers two key questions: "What basic functional literacy tasks can adults at the lowest level of literacy perform?" (v); and how do various groups of study participants compare on these functional literacy tasks? Key findings involve characteristics of the adults who participated in the supplemental assessment and the percentage of adults who correctly answered ALSA questions. For example, most ALSA study participants were Hispanic and most had not attained a high school diploma or a GED. In addition, poverty correlated strongly with being assigned to the supplementary assessment group. — BJG

42   Ballard, Sharon M., and Michael Lane Morris. "Factors Influencing Midlife and Older Adults' Attendance in Family Life Education Programs." *Family Relations* 54.3 (July 2005): 461–72. Print.

Older adults have shifting roles, including caregivers, family roles, retirement planning, and preserving independence while aging, but it is unknown if these older adults attend family life education programs to meet these needs. After reviewing the literature on older adults and the factors that affect their attendance in family life education programs, Ballard and Morris present their study that surveyed adults age 50 and older. The data considered deterrents to attendance in family life education programs, and these were categorized as programmatic deterrents, personal deterrents, time deterrents, and attendance deterrents. The study had a few limitations, which the authors discuss. The primary finding was that program promotions should focus on specific aspects of the programs. Nighttime driving and cost were two major deterrents to attendance, but each program needs to assess its particular audience. Ages within the group of older adults also need to be considered, as younger adults have different needs and interests than older adults. Ballard and Morris discuss the implications of the study before making recommendations. —KKN

43   Bay, Libby. "Twists, Turns, and Returns: Returning Adult Students." *Teaching English in the Two-Year College* 26.3 (1999): 305–12. Print.

This essay reports on a study of ninety-five returning adults at Rockland Community College, State University of New York (SUNY). The study was conducted in the context of rising enrollments of older students nationwide and in the SUNY community colleges. The research seeks answers to three questions: (1) Why do older adults attend college classes? (2) What challenges and satisfactions are experienced by older students? (3) How can colleges serve the needs of adult students? A survey questionnaire was mailed to two hundred students, of which eighty-five responded, and interviews were conducted with ten additional students. These students were primarily white and female. All students were older than 24 years of age, with most being over 50. As for the reasons why these students returned to college, 50 percent stated that they were pursuing a degree, 25 percent indicated that they were returning for "general interests," 25 percent cited social reasons for returning, and 7 percent claimed they were returning out of "boredom" (307). Complementing this survey was a prior survey (conducted in 1992 at the same college), which asked older students why they had not entered college at a younger age. Financial concerns had prevented most of these students from attending college earlier, together with lack of guidance, encouragement, and self-confidence. When asked about their difficulties, students most frequently mentioned time (e.g., time management and finding time for school). As for satisfactions, nearly all participants mentioned new knowledge and skills and most indicated a "new sense of self" (309). Forming new friendships and receiving praise from family were also identified as important. In response to questions about needed services for older students, study participants reported a need for flexibility and sensitivity from faculty, child care provisions on campus, and special class sections for older adults only. In a final commentary, the author points out a need for a special office to address the needs of older adults on campus. —BJG

44   Bennett, Shelly, Tracy Evans, and Joan Riedle. "Comparing Academic Motivation and Accomplishments among Traditional, Nontraditional, and Distance Education College Students." *Psi Chi Journal of Undergraduate Research* 12.4 (2007): 154–61. Print.

Bennett, Evans, and Riedle used questionnaires to study the differences among traditional college students, whom they identified as attending college immediately following high school graduation (less than 25 years of age); nontraditional college students, who were identified as 25 years or older and did not attend college right after high school; and distance education students, who were identified as taking only online courses to obtain their degrees and included both traditional and nontraditional students. After reviewing the works of Eppler et al. and Dill and Henley, which researched the differences between traditional and nontraditional students regarding college students, Bennett, Evans, and Riedle sought to find the differences between traditional, nontraditional, and distance education college students in learning or goal performance, stressors, self-concept, and academic performance. The results of the study were that nontraditional and distance education students were more learning-oriented whereas traditional students were more performance-oriented; nontraditional and distance education students had higher GPAs than traditional students, and nontraditional students spent more time on studying. Distance education students took the fewest credits of the three groups but worked the most hours of the three groups. Stressors were not a significant factor in this study's findings. The authors conclude that nontraditional and distance learners "would benefit from a different learning environment than traditional students" (160) and these students "embrace challenges more than traditional students and are less anxious about failure" (160). Because most classrooms include both traditional and nontraditional students, instructors must work hard to create a supportive environment for both, which is not an easy task. —KKN

45   Brown, Betsy A. "Four Puzzles in Adult Literacy: Reflections on the National Adult Literacy Survey." *Journal of Adolescent & Adult Literacy* 42.4 (Dec. 98/Jan. 99): 314–24. Print.

The National Adult Literacy Survey of 1992 shows that adult literacy needs to be addressed more, but it also shows that the findings do not match expectations, according to Brown. She argues, "Basic literacy instruction for adults remains a largely piecemeal enterprise, provided by a variety of state and federal initiatives, workplace programs, and volunteer literacy associations" (314). After discussing the parameters of the survey, Brown addresses how the literacy rates in the United States compare to those in other countries: Sweden, Switzerland,

Poland, The Netherlands, Canada, and Germany. She finds that while the United States is richer and more advanced than other countries, its adults read information and apply it inadequately. While this is true, the United States has more adults who read in a refined manner than the other countries. Brown explains that this is the result of the disparity between rich and poor school districts in the United States. She also examines the relationship between literacy skills and income and finds that increased literacy skills do not necessarily mean higher income—enough for people to support themselves—as other factors such as employment opportunities, race, home situations, disabilities, and addictions need to be considered. Finally, Brown addresses the issue of women and literacy, stating that few literacy programs are based on gender, but some now are addressing family literacy with parents, primarily women, and children.—KKN

46   Calvin, Jennifer, and Beth Winfrey Freeburg. "Exploring Adult Learners' Perceptions of Technology Competence and Retention in Web-
based Courses." *Quarterly Review of Distance Education* 11.2 (2010):
63–72. Web. 16 Apr. 2014.

Calvin and Freeburg reviewed literature that showed adult learners feared computer technology and don't have basic computer skills. Therefore, the authors' study looked at adult students' self-reporting on their skills and how they felt about Web-based learning. The study included 1,000 students with two or more years of work experience who were enrolled in a bachelor program at a university, but the program was delivered in various places such as community education centers and military bases. The students were required to take several courses on the Web, not in face-to-face classrooms. The average age of the students was 36 years. The study found that most students considered themselves as having intermediate skills and that access to computers was not a problem for them. The findings also indicate that more work on Web-based courses is needed instead of continuing the focus on technology issues students have. The students wanted clearer assignment instructions and more guidance for assignments in online courses, which Calvin and Freeburg recommend.—KKN

47   Chao, Ruth, and Glenn E. Good. "Nontraditional Students' Perspectives on College Education: A Qualitative Study." *Journal of College
Counseling* 7.1 (Spring 2004): 5–12. Print.

Beginning with a description of recent research on nontraditional students ages 25 and older, the authors note that the research has not focused on these students' counseling needs. They argue, "Just as coun-
selors work to provide services that are appropriate for diverse client populations, such as people from different cultural backgrounds, they also need to recognize nontraditional students' issues that set them apart from traditional-age students" (5). Thus, the authors conducted a qualitative study to research why nontraditional students return to college and the effects the experience has on those students, their

families, and their work. After explaining their methodology, Chao and Good present the results of the study. They learned that nontraditional students have a hopefulness that affects their motivation and other aspects of their lives. They also state that nontraditional students make use of their life experiences and motivation to overcome barriers they experience in their college careers. These students also had a clear connection between their college work and careers, which is not found in traditional students. Chao and Good note that counselors need to address the life transitions nontraditional students experience and that cause the students to return to college. —KKN

48   Chen, Li-Kuang, Young Sek Kim, Paul Moon, and Sharan B. Merriam. "A Review and Critique of the Portrayal of Older Adult Learners in Adult Education Journals, 1980–2006." *Adult Education Quarterly* 59.1 (Nov. 2008): 3–21. Print.

Noting that the population of people age 65 and older is growing in the United States, the authors argue that research in adult education programs that serve these older adults will need to become a focus in the literature on adult education. Therefore, the authors reviewed how adult learners age 65 and older have been portrayed in journals and the assumptions about these students that have developed. In the 1970s, the University of Michigan "established the first graduate program in educational gerontology" (4). Following the establishment of this program, others began to study how older adults learn, and the journal *Educational Gerontology* was created. Since 1948, handbooks on adult education have included chapters on older adult learners. The authors selected mainstream journals on adult education for their study. They used qualitative content analysis to analyze the ninety-three journals, and all of the authors of this study reviewed every article. In their analysis, the authors found three categories of topics for the 1980s: "educational experiences and participation of older adults, instructional designs and strategies, and descriptions of educational programs for older adults" (7). The articles of the 1990s focused more on "contexts and projects for older adults' learning." (8). In their review of articles from the twenty-first century, the authors found that writers focused on similar topics as in the previous decades, but with the added concentration on educational participation of older adult learners. The authors then discuss the main themes they found in the literature and what these articles omit, namely, the diversity of the older adult population. —KKN

49   Clark, M. Carolyn, and Marsha Rossiter. "Narrative Learning in Adulthood." *Third Update on Adult Learning Theory*. Ed. Sharan B. Merriam. Hoboken, NJ: Wiley, 2008. 61–70. Print. New Directions for Adult and Continuing Education 119.

Clark and Rossiter review narrative learning, which is part of constructivist learning theory, and its applications for adult education, beginning with a review of the narrative learning literature. They argue, "Narrative is . . . how we craft our sense of self, our identity" (62), so as students tell the stories of their life experiences, they are sharing their sense of themselves and making connections with the course material. Clark and Rossiter argue that people understand their stories in relation to their lifespan development. Narrative learning is tied to lived experience, so adult education instructors need to connect students' experiences to their learning. The authors believe that narrative learning comes from stories and "conceptualizing the learning process" (65). They provide methods to help students share narratives of their learning, including learning journals, concept-focused autobiographical writing, and instructional case studies. Clark and Rossiter argue that using narrative learning in the adult education classroom will lead to an enriched learning experience for students. —KKN

50   Donohue, Tambra L., and Eugene H. Wong. "Achievement Motivation and College Satisfaction in Traditional and Nontraditional Students." *Education* 118.2 (Winter 1997): 237–43. Print.

After reviewing literature on various studies of nontraditional college students, who are identified as 25 years old and older, Donohue and Wong discuss the studies' inconsistent results. The authors also call for more research on the satisfaction of older college students, especially since this population is growing on college campuses. Then Donohue and Wong present their study and findings. They used two questionnaires, the College Student Satisfaction Questionnaire and the Work and Family Orientation Questionnaire, to survey 126 students ranging in age from 19 to 57 years. The results are that significant correlations exist between college satisfaction and achievement motivation, and traditional and nontraditional students differ in the correlations. They found "partial support . . . that nontraditional students demonstrate higher achievement motivation" (241). Then the authors call for more research on college satisfaction for these two groups of students, including the development of a survey that compares the relationship between achievement motivation and satisfaction for nontraditional students. —KKN

51   Dzindolet, Mary T., and Lawrence Weinstein. "Attitudes of Traditional and Nontraditional Students toward Their Classmates of Various Ages." *Psychological Reports* 75 (1994): 1587–92. Print.

Dzindolet and Weinstein review research on traditional and nontraditional students and argue that universities need to respond to the various needs of nontraditional students. Then they introduce their research that "investigated the attitudes traditional and nontraditional students held toward their classmates of various ages" (1588). The students in their study ranged in age from 17 to 68 years, and the students were surveyed about their attitudes toward traditional and nontraditional students. The authors found that traditional students favored students their own age in their classes while nontraditional students preferred diverse ages. Dzindolet and Weinstein found they had difficulty assimilating their results into other research because different studies define traditional and nontraditional students differently. They argue that universities cannot disregard the effects older students have on traditional students and suggest future research for these institutions. — KKN

52   Frey, Ruth. *Helping Adult Learners Succeed: Tools for Two-Year Colleges*. CAEL. Sept. 2007. Web. 3 Jan. 2011.

Frey describes the development and use of a community college version of the Adult Learning Focused Institution (ALFI) Assessment Toolkit. Because our economy is increasingly knowledge-based, many adults are seeking postsecondary education. Yet their nontraditional status, characterized by "part-time enrollment, full-time employment, financial independence, and/or parental responsibilities — create needs and priorities that differ from those of traditional students and make it difficult for adults to enter into and succeed in the traditional postsecondary environment" (3). To respond to these needs, the staff at the Council for Adult and Experiential Learning (CAEL) created a survey instrument designed to promote understanding of what nontraditional students need to succeed. The survey instrument was based on the Adult Learning Focused Initiative Assessment Toolkit, "which offers colleges a mechanism to formally assess programs for adult learners" (3). The assessment toolkit was revised specifically to meet the needs of community colleges and piloted in 2005–2006 by twenty-five community colleges. The toolkit comprises two assessments that measure nontraditional students' "perceptions of their experience as compared to faculty and administration's perceptions of institutional programming" (5). The survey results can help guide administrators in program design. One of the key results of the survey is an emphasis on transitions, which refer to "a college's ability to explain what is needed to complete an academic program, classes that are closely related to life and work goals, and guidance on classes that transfer to other programs both within and outside of the college" (6). The twenty-five institutions participating in the pilot study used the results to change their programs. These changes included a wider range of course time offerings, enhanced support for nontraditional students in the form of Web sites and orientation sessions, establishing noncredit programs, creating advising programs, and enhanced advising training for faculty. Colleges also pursued articulation agreements with local four-year colleges and to "inform strategic planning and program review, or as part of the accreditation review" (7). Students strongly indicated the need for good advising, flexibility in course delivery options, and clearly stated course goals. They were very appreciative of course delivery software that allowed them to track their progress online. — TBP

53   Gere, Anne Ruggles. "Kitchen Tables and Rented Rooms: The Extracurriculum of Composition." *College Composition and Communication* 45.1 (1994): 75–92. Web. 2 Dec. 2010.

This revised 1993 CCCC Chair's Address is a call to attend to the vitality of writing development that happens outside of schools, workplaces, and other formal learning environments, often among those excluded from or marginalized in academia. Although Gere supports the professionalization of composition and rhetoric, she critiques overly narrow efforts to professionalize as having neglected the history and ignored the current reality of this extracurriculum. By *extracurriculum*, she means an environment in which individuals, alone or more often together, voluntarily work on improving their writing outside of formal education. Gere gives current and historical examples of extracurriculum that range from a contemporary writing group in San Francisco's impoverished Tenderloin District to the nineteenth-century New York Garrison Society, a self-help organization for middle-class African Americans. She argues that groups like these are virtually unknown by composition scholars because, in our efforts to professionalize, we have told our history as one based within the academy. The extracurriculum has only been considered in these historical accounts when it has been a stepping-stone to disciplinarity, such as student literary clubs. While this disciplinarity history is largely a story featuring white males, Gere shows that the extracurriculum is marked by gender, race, and class diversity. She argues that the extracurriculum accomplishes the goals we hope for but do not always achieve in composition classes with students often dismissed as not able to write. Gere finds writers who work on their writing because they want to in a curriculum "constructed by desire" (80), who are affirmed by their writing, who perform their writing and, in doing so, are motivated to continue to develop as writers, and who write to effect personal and sometimes community transformation. She invites us not to appropriate but to learn from and open dialogue in nonacademic environments where some of our students are already writing, where writers of many backgrounds feel welcome, where writers take control of their learning, and where writing enhances connection to community. — MNC

54 Giancola, Jennifer Kohler, David C. Munz, and Shawn Trares. "First-Versus Continuing-Generation Adult Students on College Perceptions: Are Differences Actually Because of Demographic Variance?" *Adult Education Quarterly* 58.3 (2008): 214–28. Print.

This study was developed because the authors found that literature on nontraditional students focused on first-generation or adult students, but it did not focus on adult learners who were first-generation versus those who were continuing-generation students. The study was conducted at a college for professional studies where the students were over age 22, with most over age 25. The Noel-Levitz Adult Student Priorities Survey (ASPS) was administered to over three hundred students. The findings of the study demonstrate that students were satisfied with the various aspects of the institution. However, the authors indicate that different models of the test are needed for traditional and adult first-generation students. The authors then propose further research that is needed to understand the differences between the two groups of adult learners. — KKN

55   Gillam, Alice M. "Returning Students' Ways of Writing: Implications for First-Year College Composition." *Journal of Teaching Writing* 10.1 (1991): 1–20. Print.

Gillam presents research with two groups of adult writers enrolled in first-year writing in the early 1980s, totaling sixty-four students. Her research methods include beginning- and end-of-term questionnaires, pre- and post-course responses to the Daly and Miller Writing Apprehension Test (WAT), interviews, and four in-depth case studies. Gillam illustrates this material with two of her case studies, including sample essays. The most salient feature emerging from this research is gender differences. Gillam finds that returning men rarely engage in personal writing and bring experience with workplace writing to the classroom, such as memos, proposals, documentation, and histories; these genres are structured, purposeful, written for a definite audience, and assume the writer's authority. Women engage in personal writing, specifically journals and letters, which are organic in form, expressive, conversational, and written for an audience of the self or a known other. Women's work-related writing encompasses employment and volunteering, largely business letters, memos, nursing documents, and minutes taken for organizations. These tasks are formal, sometimes formulaic, purposeful, and written for a specific audience, but they do not foster women's authority as writers. Both genders, like most traditional students, have some difficulty with authorial voice, particularly integrating personal experience with secondary sources. Gillam argues that returning women are exceptionally intimidated by the authority of print sources, amplified by insecurity about age and gender. Gillam proposes the use of "an experience portfolio including a prose vitae describing significant life experiences, a writing history and writer's profile, and writing samples" (12) and describes how this portfolio can be used in the classroom and analyzed by instructors for strategies to design assignments and reduce anxiety.—KSU

56   Hayes, Elizabeth R. "A New Look at Women's Learning." *The New Update on Adult Learning Theory.* Ed. Sharan B. Merriam. Hoboken, NJ: Wiley, 2001. 35–42. Print. New Directions for Adult and Continuing Education 89.

After providing an historical view on women as learners, Hayes argues that the research on women as learners remains questionable even today. She states that other factors—such as race and ethnicity—need to be prioritized over gender in studies. She then presents recent views on women as learners, beginning with how relationships affect women's learning. Connected knowing, which is discussed in *Women's Ways of Knowing* by Belenky, Clinchy, Goldberger, and Tarule, is how women "embrac[e] new ideas and [seek] to understand different points of view" (37). Hayes argues that this idea has been misinterpreted and applied incorrectly, resulting in stereotypes of women in the classroom. The second view on women as learners states that women are subjective, rely on intuition, and are emotional, a common historical view. Hayes calls for a review of beliefs about gender and learning, noting that most studies are based on psychology and biology. More recent studies have considered the social and cultural aspects of learning, which affect how women learn. Hayes argues, "We can be alert to potential gender patterns while trying to avoid gender stereotypes" (40). Instructors may ask students to consider how gender has affected them as learners. Thus, instructors need to create learning environments that support both men and women.—KKN

57   Houser, Marian L. "Are We Violating Their Expectations? Instructor Communication Expectations of Traditional and Nontraditional Students." *Communication Quarterly* 53.2 (2005): 213–28. Print.

Houser reviews the literature on instructor communication with students, but it mainly has focused on traditional students, whom she defines as 18–23 years old. However, more studies on how nontraditional students (24 years and older) respond to instructor communication are needed, as this group of students is growing rapidly on college campuses. The communication literature has focused on "instructor communication behaviors associated with positive student responses" (216). Houser then discusses expectancy violations theory and presents her research questions based on this theory. Her study used a survey instrument with an equal number of traditional and nontraditional students, and the results she shares indicate that traditional and nontraditional students prefer different communication behaviors from their instructors. Houser found that a main difference is that "traditional students want instructors who are friendly and attentive to their needs" (224) whereas nontraditional students want instructors simply to provide the information, show them how to apply it, and then move on. However, she found both groups of students want instructors to provide clear directions and expectations and provide feedback in a timely manner. "Nontraditional students desire instructors who are organized, offer structure in the syllabus as well as class routine, and stay on task" (225).—KKN

58   Johnson-Bailey, Juanita. "Race Matters: The Unspoken Variable in the Teaching-Learning Transaction." *Contemporary Viewpoints on Teaching Adults Effectively*. Ed. Jovita M. Ross-Gordon. Hoboken, NJ: Wiley, 2002. 39–49. Print. New Directions for Adult and Continuing Education 93.

Johnson-Bailey, noting that adult education reflects our society, argues that barriers such as race, gender, and others impair accomplishing the goals of adult education. She also argues that the hierarchy in society follows students and teachers into the adult education classroom; therefore, teachers need to acknowledge this fact. She states educators need to understand how "life conditions of underprivileged learners play out in their [instructors'] everyday classroom circumstances" (41–42). She outlines the three basic ways in which race is addressed in adult education literature. First is the color-blind perspective, which does not acknowledge race in the curriculum or the classroom and "is the most widely used approach among adult educators" (42). The multicultural or cultural diversity perspective acknowledges that culture has its own values, mores, and experiences, and each group is valued for its accomplishments so that equity is more readily recognized in the classroom. The third perspective, entitled the social justice perspective, "takes a moral position that critiques society as unjust toward minorities and other disenfranchised groups and calls for the field to remember its mission to work toward democratization" (43). Johnson-Bailey then discusses some of the studies on power in the classroom and how these affect the adult education classroom. She argues that adult education's current embrace of critical reflection is a positive move; instructors need to consider how race affects their classrooms and how to manage this. Johnson-Bailey then discusses her experiences as an adult educator and a black woman. From her experiences, she makes recommendations for teachers to address race in the classroom. —KKN

59   Kim, Karen A., Linda J. Sax, Jenny J. Lee, and Linda Serra Hagedorn. "Redefining Nontraditional Students: Exploring the Self-Perceptions of Community College Students." *Community College Journal of Research and Practice* 34.5 (2010): 402–22. Print.

The authors review literature that defines traditional students and argue that the use of *nontraditional* to describe students in community colleges marginalizes the students. Using role theory, the authors analyzed data from the Transfer and Retention of Urban Community College Students (TRUCCS) survey completed at institutions in Los Angeles. The analysis looked at how students view themselves and at the ages of the students. From the analysis, the authors found that employment was an important factor for student identification, regardless of age. The most noteworthy difference between the group of students under 25 and the group over 25 was doing housework or caring for children, and the social aspect of college was the second significant difference between the two groups of students. However, the authors note that students in both age groups work and/or have children and household responsibilities, so age alone does not define nontraditional students. Other factors also need to be considered, particularly when examining community college students. —KKN

60   Kirsch, Irwin S., Ann Jungeblut, Lynn Jenkins, and Andrew Kolstad. *Adult Literacy in America: A First Look at the Findings of the National Adult Literacy Survey* (NCES 93-275). Washington, DC: National Center for Education Statistics, Institute of Education Sciences, US Department of Education, 1993. Web. 18 Feb. 2013.

The 1992 National Adult Literacy Survey grew out of a 1988 call from the United States Congress for the US Department of Education to study US adults age 16 and older. During eight months in 1992, 13,600 adult household residents and 1,100 prison inmates participated in the study by completing various literacy tasks and responding to questions about their educational and work backgrounds and their reading practices. The definition of literacy used for this study is "[u]sing printed and written information to function in society, to achieve one's goals, and to develop one's knowledge and potential" (4). The report analyzes adults' literacy levels in three areas: prose literacy, document literacy, and quantitative literacy. Kirsch et al. conclude that the most significant finding of this study is that 21 to 23 percent of study participants performed at the lowest level of prose, document, and quantitative literacy. Translated into real numbers and applied to the population as a whole, this finding suggests that 40 to 44 million of 191 million adults living in the United States have low literacy skills. This study focused on English literacy, not literacy in all languages, so immigrants comprised 25 percent of the low-performing adults. Educational attainment also correlates strongly with low literacy levels: 62 percent of the individuals who scored at the lowest levels had not completed high school. Older adults (age 65 and older) were found to perform literacy tasks at lower levels, and physical, mental, or medical issues were also found to be significant factors. Adults scoring in the second lowest level (Level 2) for all three literacy areas (prose, document, and quantitative) comprised 25 to 28 percent of study participants. Although study participants found to perform at Level 1 or Level 2 are described as "Below Basic" or "Basic" by authors of this report, the low-performing study participants do not generally recognize themselves as possessing weak reading and writing skills. The majority of these participants report that they read and write English "well" or "very well" (xvii). —BJG

61   Kutner, Mark, Elizabeth Greenberg, Ying Jin, Bridget Boyle, Yung-chen Hsu, Eric Dunleavy, and Sheila White. *Literacy in Everyday Life: Results from the 2003 National Assessment of Adult Literacy* (NCES 2006–477). Washington, DC: National Center for Education Statistics, Institute of Education Sciences, US Department of Education, 2006. Web. 18 Feb. 2013.

Kutner et al. report on the National Assessment of Adult Literacy (NAAL), the first comprehensive study of adult literacy conducted since the National Adult Literacy Survey (NALS) conducted in 1992. NAAL uses many of the same procedures and instruments as the 1992 NALS, so comparisons between the two studies are made in NAAL. Nineteen thousand adults age 16 and older were interviewed for this research. They lived in households or were prison inmates. All except for a very few low-literacy study participants were evaluated by questions in the main literacy assessment. This main literacy assessment was comprised of literacy tasks in three areas: prose literacy, document literacy, and quantitative literacy. Study participants were assigned numerical scores for their performance in these three areas and assigned to one of four levels: *Below Basic, Basic, Intermediate,* and *Proficient.* Only people who could converse in English or Spanish were able to participate in this research: literacy in languages other than English was not analyzed. One key finding was that between 1992 and 2003, scores on prose literacy declined for people with high school diplomas and, similarly, scores on prose and document literacy were lower in 2003 for study participants with some college education. —BJG

62   Lynch, Jean M., and Cathy Bishop-Clark. "A Comparison of the Non-traditional Students' Experience on Traditional Versus Nontraditional College Campuses." *Innovative Higher Education* 22.3 (1998): 217–29. Print.

Because many studies on nontraditional students in college are based on campuses that cater to this type of student, Lynch and Bishop-Clark studied how nontraditional students compare to traditional students at, and affect the environment of, a traditional university. They propose that traditional university faculty may be biased against nontradi-tional students because of the lack of experience faculty have with this group of students. This study labeled nontraditional students as over 25 years of age; the researchers interviewed students in this category. Nontraditional students were selected from the main campus and two branch campuses of a major university. The branch campuses had more nontraditional students than the main campus, so the researchers were able to compare responses based on the population of the campuses. Lynch and Bishop-Clark found that the nontraditional students indi-cated they liked the mixed age classrooms; however, they recognized differences between themselves as older students and traditional stu-dents. They felt that younger students did not take their schoolwork seriously and that each group learns differently. Nontraditional students on the main campus, which catered to traditional students, felt that instructors designed their syllabi and classrooms for the traditional stu-dent. Additionally, the nontraditional students on the main campus felt their instructors did not allow for the additional responsibilities these students had. Lynch and Bishop-Clark encourage more research on this topic so that additional variables may be considered. —KKN

63   Manheimer, Ronald J., and Diane Moskow-McKenzie. "Transforming Older Adult Education: An Emerging Paradigm from a Nationwide Study." *Educational Gerontology* 21.6 (Sept. 1995): 613–32. Print.

Arguing that the number of older adult educational programs is in-creasing, Manheimer and Moskow-McKenzie note that the number of people age 55 and older has tripled in these programs. However, tuition-free courses for older adults in college programs are not well attended or advertised. Instead, programs are being offered at community-based institutions. The authors then review five organizational models that are common: college- and university-based learning-in-retirement institutes, Older Adult Services and Information Systems institutes, community colleges, senior centers, and Shepherd's Centers in religious centers. They note that these programs are "financially viable, evolv-ing organizations" (615) that empower older adults as leaders. One trend is that the seniors become more involved in community pro-grams as a result of these models. The authors' national study reviewed 430 programs that serve senior adults through surveys sent to the organizations. Generally, the programs began in or around 1982, and most were local programs that had host organizations. Most of the programs did not complete a needs assessment before beginning the programs, but some used findings from surveys completed by government agencies or higher education institutions. Planning groups included senior adults, and most of the programs initially were supported by donated services, funding, and volunteers. Many of the programs have bylaws, with seniors helping with decision making. However, most of the programs did not aggressively recruit people to be part of the programs. Initially, these programs offered life-enrichment courses, but later they added vocational courses and other courses. The authors note that these senior adult programs continue to evolve and grow. — KKN

64   Mathews-Aydinli, Julie. "Overlooked and Understudied? A Survey of Current Trends in Research on Adult English Language Learners." *Adult Education Quarterly* 58.3 (2008): 198–213. Print.

Mathews-Aydinli describes adults learning English in nonacademic situations in North America and states that 45 percent of students in adult education programs are English language learners (ELLs) or in English literacy classes. These students are from greatly diverse backgrounds with unique and vastly different needs. They are different from international students in higher education courses. Mathews-Aydinli argues that the needs of adult education ELLs are not being met as many of these learners drop out or have limited achievement. She then reviews recent literature on adult ELLs in nonacademic settings. She reviewed databases that limited the articles of primary research to North America, the United Kingdom, or Australia and from 2000 and later. She then categorized the articles and dissertations into three categories: "ethnographic studies, teacher-related studies, and second-language acquisition studies" (201). Ethnographic studies was the largest group of research, and the studies focus on power, identity, and socialization. From these studies, Mathews-Aydinli found three common threads, which include addressing practical issues for ELLs in nonacademic settings, recognizing the diversity of this group of adult learners, and raising questions about the expectations for this group. Teacher-related studies either focused on teachers in ESL programs or teacher practices and individual teachers' experiences. Mathews-Aydinli then reviews some of the articles within this category. She notes, "one common thread . . . runs throughout them all—namely, a particular sensitivity toward the students' cultural backgrounds" (207). The final category, second-language acquisition studies, includes works on themes in second-language acquisition, not necessarily with a focus on adult ESL students, although very few studies fit this last category. Mathews-Aydinli concludes by calling for more research on adult language learners not in postsecondary settings. — KKN

65   Melichar, Barbara E. "Instructors' Attitudes toward Nontraditional Students Positive, Study Shows." *Adult Learning* 6.1 (Sept./Oct. 1994): 27–28. Print.

Instructors in postsecondary vocational technical institutes completed a questionnaire for this study by Melichar. She designed the study after hearing that instructors had negative attitudes regarding nontraditional students, whom she defined as 26 years and older. Melichar's study found that instructors had a positive attitude toward nontraditional students. The results of the study show that instructors rated nontraditional students higher in twenty-three of forty areas. In only four areas did the instructors indicate more positive attitudes toward traditional students. Melichar suggests several studies that might be conducted to further understand instructors' attitudes toward nontraditional students. —KKN

66   Merriam, Sharan B., and Young Sek Kim. "Non-Western Perspectives on Learning and Knowing." *Third Update on Adult Learning Theory*. Ed. Sharan B. Merriam. Hoboken, NJ: Wiley, 2008. 71–81. Print. New Directions for Adult and Continuing Education 119.

Merriam and Kim distinguish between Western and non-Western regions and the characteristics of each region. In their discussion of the differences between the two regions, they review the differences in how learning is perceived and the manner in which philosophic and religious systems contribute to ideas on learning. Because Western and non-Western systems think differently about learning, the way in which students construct knowledge is different. For instance, in non-Western systems, learning is more communal, meaning the entire community is responsible for learning, which builds the community. Additionally, learning takes place over a lifetime and is informal, as well as holistic. Merriam and Kim provide various examples of cultures (for example, Hindu, Native American, and Muslim, among others) to demonstrate these characteristics of learning in non-Western regions. They then discuss the importance for adult educators to understand the differences between Western and non-Western systems and the thinking about education and learning within each one. —KKN

67   Thompson, Merle O'Rourke. "The Returning Student: Writing Anxiety and General Anxiety." *Teaching English in the Two-Year College* 10.1 (Fall 1983): 35–39. Print.

By administering the Anxiety Scale Questionnaire and the Thompson Attitude Survey to over 150 traditional and adult students, Thompson measured their levels of anxiety in general and with writing. Overall, the entire group of students had low general anxiety before and after the composition course in which they were enrolled. The results of the general anxiety test given before the composition class showed that traditional students had more anxiety than the adult students, however, which is contrary to the general belief about adult learners. The writing anxiety test showed that returning females had more writing anxiety than any of the other students, while returning males had the lowest writing anxiety. At the end of the course, Thompson found adult male students still had less writing anxiety than any of the other students, and their anxiety was considerably less than adult women's. Thompson theorizes that the instruction in the composition class reduced these adult learners' writing anxiety. She then suggests that instructors who have students who demonstrate anxiety should be aware that the student also may have writing anxiety, and they should assure their returning students that their writing anxiety will not last.—KKN

Case Studies and Ethnographies

See: Libby Bay, "Twists, Turns, and Returns: Returning Adult Students." [43]

68   Belenky, Mary Field, Blythe McVicker Clinchy, Nancy Rule Goldberger, and Jill Mattuck Tarule. *Women's Ways of Knowing: The Development of Self, Voice, and Mind.* New York: Basic Books, 1986/1997. Print.

This book was written to "show how women's self-concepts and ways of knowing are intertwined" (3). The four authors are psychologists who were curious about why women "doubt their intellectual competence" (4), yet they still learn through their relationships, life catastrophes, and community work. Their study was based on Carol Gilligan's work on women's development and William Perry's work on development based on male subjects. The authors observed that women often feel alienated from the academic world. In this study, Belenky, Clinchy, Goldberger, and Tarule interviewed 135 women in various settings, including formal education institutions and family agencies that provide assistance with parenting. When they analyzed the interviews, they used five categories for the information: silence, received knowledge, subjective knowledge, procedural knowledge, and constructed knowledge. Part one is divided into chapters based on these five categories. Part two is divided into chapters based on the contexts in which the women learn. The chapter on silence is based on the interviews of women in the social agencies, and these women tended to be young and deprived socially, economically, and educationally. These women perceived words "as weapons" (24). Chapter 2 on received knowledge focuses on how women "learn by listening" (37), although these women are not confident about their own ability to speak. In educational settings, these women did not feel capable when they had to do original work because they were recipients of knowledge, not givers of knowledge as the teachers were. These women do feel good about their ability to retain information as they listen, unlike the women in the silent group. Subjective knowledge results from women listening to their inner voices, which results in gaining strength that transitions women in their relationships and growth. Most of the women in this group were from less advantaged or more permissive homes. In the chapter on procedural knowledge, the group of women was more homogeneous and "practiced in the art of being students" (87), as they attended prestigious colleges. Their ways of knowing were challenged when authorities attempted to force the women to believe the authorities' opinion, but the women did not stifle their inner voices to keep their beliefs. The authors state these women were working at "acquiring and applying procedures for obtaining and communicating knowledge" (95), which causes them to gain a sense of control. When women enter constructed knowledge, they are reclaiming themselves and trying to integrate personal knowledge with what they have learned from others. During the transition to constructed knowledge, women begin to ask themselves questions about themselves, creating a new "way of thinking about knowledge, truth, and self" (136). These women also distinguish between real talk and didactic talk. In the last part of the book, the authors discuss the family lives of each type of woman, their educational experiences, and their views and reactions to teachers. — KKN

69   Belzer, Alisa. "'It's Not Like Normal School': The Role of Prior Learning Contexts in Adult Learning." *Adult Education Quarterly* 55.1 (2004): 41–59. Print.

Belzer examines the experience of five African American women taking part in a GED class at a community-based learning center. Intrigued by resistance shown by some of her students to the nontraditional, participatory learning experience offered at the center, Belzer sought to understand "the ways in which prior experiences in formal learning contexts influence learners' perceptions of the current context" (42). She argues that previous researchers, including Mezirow and Knowles, have viewed experience primarily in a positive light — i.e., as a well from which to draw and build rather than a potential hindrance to learning. Belzer's interviews revealed, however, that the women were deeply ambivalent about their current learning, both enjoying their classroom activities and doubting the value of GED exam preparation. Their experiences at the program conflicted with their expectations of school, which had been consistent, if negative, due to a prior focus on homework, tests, and rules. Belzer places the responses from her students into a framework that draws on adult learning theory and recognizes that experience can be either empowering or an impediment to learning, depending on the student's ability to contextualize that experience. — SFL

70   Belzer, Alisa. "What Are They Doing in There? Case Studies of Volunteer Tutors and Adult Literacy Learners: Volunteer Tutors and Adult Literacy Learners Face a Number of Challenges as They Work Together." *Journal of Adolescent & Adult Literacy* 49.7 (Apr. 2006): 560–72. Print.

Belzer describes and discusses her case study on the interaction between literacy volunteer tutors and their adult tutees from different programs. After citing information about US literacy programs, Belzer discusses how volunteers are trained and the programs they use with their tutees. Her research required the tutors to record their sessions, and the article provides transcripts with commentary on the recordings. From the analysis of the tapes, Belzer concludes that volunteers deal with many challenges when tutoring because their training is limited. One example is the selection of texts that tutors use when the tutees want other readings. In spite of the challenges, both the volunteer tutors and the tutees felt that their work together was successful. Belzer ends with possible solutions to the challenges that the tutors faced. — KKN

71 Berkenkotter, Carol, Thomas N. Huckin, and John Ackerman. "Conventions, Conversations, and the Writer: Case Study of a Student in a Rhetoric PhD Program." *Research in the Teaching of English* 22.1 (1988): 9–44. Print.

A case study of one doctoral student's advanced academic literacy reveals that, for this student, learning content (declarative knowledge) preceded learning to write (procedural knowledge) in the register and style of one academic research community. Additionally, the doctoral student's participation in various communities of practice influenced his writing development and acquisition of particular discourse forms and rhetorical strategies. "Nate," the subject of this study, was enrolled in his first year graduate courses at Carnegie Mellon University when his writing development was investigated. Berkenkotter, Huckin, and Ackerman framed their study by asking how advanced academic literacy is acquired, how novice writers become members of discourse communities, and what factors inhibit or encourage learning necessary linguistic behaviors. The primary object of analysis was Nate's texts — writing he produced prior to graduate school and during his first year of doctoral studies. Sociolinguistics, the sociology of science, and a model of literacy acquisition that contextualizes learning in home cultures and everyday situations frame the analysis. The researchers discovered three problems with Nate's writing: he used "I" too frequently, the writing was not always sufficiently cohesive and coherent, and Nate's diction did not sufficiently conform to expectations of the targeted academic discourse community (language was sometimes too informal or too formal). Nate was initially observed to be a highly competent informal prose writer whose compositions revealed lower proficiency levels when he was required to comment on abstract concepts while using unfamiliar discourse conventions and a style not yet fully mastered. As Nate progressed through his first year of graduate studies, his writing began to more closely resemble social science expository prose, a change that the authors attribute to Nate's desire to become a member of his doctoral program community and the larger professional community of composition and rhetoric research writers. — BJG

72 Berkenkotter, Carol, and Thomas N. Huckin, with John Ackerman. "Conventions, Conversations, and the Writer: An Apprenticeship Tale of a Doctoral Student." *Genre and Knowledge in Disciplinary Communication: Cognition/Culture/Power.* Ed. Carol Berkenkotter and Thomas N. Huckin. Mahwah, NJ: Erlbaum, 1995. 117–44. Print.

Berkenkotter and Huckin present their findings from case study research focusing on one graduate student acquiring genre knowledge while enrolled in a doctoral program at Carnegie Mellon University (CMU) in 1984 and 1985. The purpose of this study was to examine the influence of educational context on a graduate student's writing for different professors in different courses. A key premise is the view that academic discourse conventions and conversations constitute *advanced literacy* (as pointed out by David Bartholomae) which students must acquire to succeed academically. The student whose writing is central to this research is "Nate," a skilled novice writer enrolled in the CMU Rhetoric PhD program. Following in the tradition of Donald Murray, Nate expressed the view (in self-reports addressed to Berkenkotter and Huckins) that his voice is uniquely his own; he was therefore surprised when a professor suggested that his informal, self-expressive prose style and his thinking processes would need to change to reflect the conventions of research scientists. Nate is described by the authors as highly skilled in an informal, oral style of writing but struggling to acquire a more formal, academic register. This struggle manifested itself in academic writing performances marred by weaknesses in paragraph structure, focus, cohesion, and vocabulary. Receiving negative criticism from a professor about his prose style made Nate acutely aware of his shortcomings and led Nate to write a memo to one of his professors about his struggles with academic discourse. Writing this memo allowed Nate to use narrative and a more informal style — resulting in greater fluency and increased opportunity for Nate to work out his ideas. The strategy worked so well as a heuristic that Nate would employ it repeatedly in order to build a bridge from his existing oral style to the more literate style required by his academic program. As Nate continued writing for his graduate professors, he gradually acquired skill in the use of the registers associated with graduate-level academic writing. In analyzing Nate's writing progress, Berkenkotter and Huckins call attention to Nate's proactive stance as a learner of academic prose literacy. — BJG

73   Blanton, Linda Lonon. "Student, Interrupted: A Tale of Two Would-Be Writers." *Journal of Second Language Writing* 14.2 (2005): 105–21. Print.

In a case study of two young adults who immigrated to the United States as children, Blanton analyzes the literacy development of college students who learned literacy in their home languages (in Ethiopia and Vietnam) until age 11 and then began learning to read and write in English after immigrating to the United States. Second-language acquisition research indicates that individuals with a solid literacy foundation in a first language acquire literacy in a new language more rapidly and effectively. However, due to insufficient research, it is not known whether effective literacy development can be achieved by starting literacy acquisition in one language and then continuing literacy learning in a second language. Both of the individuals profiled in this case study developed strong oral fluency but only rudimentary literacy skills in English after having immigrated to the United States, earning a high school diploma, and starting college. Neither individual had developed full literacy in a first language, since home language schooling ended for each at age 11. In college, both students received mixed messages by earning satisfactory grades in various credit-bearing courses but being unable to pass a gateway exam for enrollment in college composition. Blanton argues that while several different models exist for college composition curricula, all these curricula assume that students start with a strong literacy foundation. The academic writing skills taught in college composition courses may benefit traditional students (with strong literacy skills) but do not benefit nontraditional students with weak literacy skills. Therefore, college composition curricula based on academic skills that are to be learned should be supplemented or replaced by curricula that focus on students' particular learning experiences and needs. — BJG

74   Bowen, Lauren Marshall. "Resisting Age Bias in Digital Literacy Research." *College Composition and Communication* 62.4 (2011): 586–607. Print.

Bowen shares her experience of studying an 81-year-old woman and her digital literacy practices. Bowen argues that literacy research has neglected the study of the elderly, particularly in relation to their digital literacy. She also argues that groups such as AARP continue to marginalize elders in the discussion of Web 2.0, limiting elders to Web 1.0 or even leaving them out of the digital literacy discussion. Through her study, Bowen learns that many elderly have transferred past literacy practices and/or blended them with digital literacy practices, continuing their learning of digital use through work experiences and help from family and friends. Bowen calls for more research on elderly literacy, particularly digital literacy, so that "we might see literacy less in terms of measuring up to the most recent technological innovations and more in terms of how individuals regularly innovate in order to make meaning in their everyday lives" (603). — KKN

75   Brandt, Deborah. "Accumulating Literacy: Writing and Learning to Write in the Twentieth Century." *College English* 57.6 (Oct. 1995): 649–68. Print. Rpt. in *Literacy and Learning: Reflections on Writing, Reading, and Society*. Ed. Deborah Brandt. San Francisco: Jossey-Bass, 2009. 67–90.

Deborah Brandt presents findings from interviews with sixty-five Americans of different backgrounds and ages. Because literacy is always evolving in response to emerging technologies and changing economic and social structures, Brandt argues, the literacy learning and reading/writing practices of individuals should be studied in relation to specific social contexts and considered from a historical perspective, especially in eras marked by rapid social transformation. Three members of one white family and one African American man are profiled in order to portray literacy learning at home, in church, and at school and changing literacy expectations over time. A contrast between Genna May (born in 1898) and her grandson Michael May (born in 1981) demonstrates sharply rising achievement standards for readers and writers across three generations. A description of Jordan Grant (born in 1948) illustrates the interplay of church, home, school, and the civil rights movement as social contexts for literacy learning in the life of one well-educated man whose identification with the African American culture and with his own community significantly influenced his literate practices. Ultimately, Brandt argues, literate practices do not simply change from one form to another. Rather, older literacies continue to exist as newer literacies emerge, and together they accumulate as "literate artifacts and signifying practices that haunt the sites of literacy learning" (87). Moreover, Brandt contends, while existing scholarship has documented contrasts between home literacies and school literacies, we have not yet explored the overlap of different literacies learned in various social contexts during the life of one individual. — BJG

76   Brandt, Deborah. *Literacy in American Lives*. New York: Cambridge UP, 2001. Print.

In a study of literacy learning in the lives of eighty twentieth-century Americans, Brandt employs interviews and life-story research to analyze relationships between individuals' literacy pursuits and broad-sweeping economic changes. When fully articulated, these relationships form a conceptual frame Brandt terms *sponsors of literacy*. Literacy sponsors can be "any agents, local or distant, concrete or abstract, who enable, support, teach, and model, as well as recruit, regulate, suppress, or withhold literacy — and gain advantage by it in some way" (19). In her interviews with study participants, Brandt asked about individuals and agencies that had influenced their literacy learning — especially with regard to writing. In emphasizing writing, Brandt seeks to redress former literacy researchers' tendency to focus mainly on reading. Beyond the analysis of individual lives is a larger focus on generations of individuals with similar literacy pursuits and experiences related to a shared socio-economic cultural context. In each of six chapters, Brandt examines one aspect of literacy sponsorship in twentieth-century American lives. Among the themes presented in these chapters are (1) learning to read and write in rural farm communities before and after corporate agribusiness took control of family farms, (2) a family of four generations who learned to write in different periods of the twentieth century, (3) self-help educational initiatives in African American communities, and (4) variation in literacy learning among individuals with disparate economic backgrounds. Drawing together her findings from the case studies and her analysis, Brandt argues that literacy learning has evolved from a process controlled by mainly conservative forces (such as the church and the state) to a decentralized, destabilized process facilitated by innovative social media and new technologies. Finally, Brandt argues that inequities in literacy learning opportunities must be addressed as a civil rights issue. Rather than discussing literacy from the perspective of our economy's needs, Brandt contends, we should focus on the interests of individuals and the responsibility of our economy to meet the needs of teachers and students. — BJG

77 Buckmiller, Tom. "Contradictions and Conflicts: Understanding the Lived Experiences of Native American Adult Learners in a Predominantly White American University." *Widening Participation and Lifelong Learning* 12.3 (Dec. 2010): 6–18. Print.

Buckmiller begins by providing a historical perspective of Native Americans and how schooling was used to remove their culture, which explains why many Native Americans remain conflicted about education today. Noting that Native American adult students are underrepresented in US postsecondary institutions, Buckmiller also argues that the study of Native American adult students has not received enough attention in the field. Using Grande's "'Red' pedagogy" (9), Buckmiller interviewed three Native Americans age 25 and older in his qualitative study. These students spoke of the culture shock they experienced as the lone Native Americans in their classes. They felt prejudice from both fellow students and teachers, and their perspectives often were dismissed when they offered them in the classroom. Buckmiller calls for instructors to remove hidden barriers that are unique to Native American students. For instance, recognizing that the mourning period for Native Americans is longer than it is in other cultures and that Native American culture works cooperatively, not competitively, is important. Accordingly, Native American adult students need strong support systems, both at the university and at home. Buckmiller ends with a call for an effort that will result in higher education that respects Native American adult students, their worldview, and who they are. —KKN

78 Castaldi, Theresa M. "Adult Learning: Transferring Skills from the Workplace to the Classroom." *Lifelong Learning: An Omnibus of Practice and Research* 12.6 (1989): 17–19. Print.

Castaldi presents her study of students in a US Labor History class to demonstrate how these adult students used their writing experiences in the workplace to develop their essays for the class. She found that of the twenty students in the course, 80 percent read and wrote for their jobs to some degree. She interviewed the students at school, home, and the workplace. She discovered that the students based their course writing on what they knew from work, and they often incorporated their personal experiences into their writing. Then Castaldi presents three case studies of students in the class to show how they wrote based on their work writing. She found that one student's work writing was not a good model for writing in the classroom, so she suggests that instructors discuss with students the writing they do so that they can discover which writing skills transfer to the college setting and which do not. Also, instructors should clearly articulate the requirements for the students for the assignments and encourage students to write often. —KKN

79 Castles, Jane. "Persistence and the Adult Learner: Factors Affecting Persistence in Open University Students." *Active Learning in Higher Education* 5.2 (2004): 166–79. Print.

Citing research in adult learning literature in the late twentieth century, Castles notes two threads that emerged: persistence and student drop-outs. While drop-out rates were researched quantitatively, persistence of adult learners was researched qualitatively. She notes that adult learners have their own goals, which sometimes do not match the goals of the institution. Using the programs at Open University in the United Kingdom, Castles reviews some of the research the institution has done on adult learner persistence. The research revealed three categories of factors that affect adult learners' persistence: support systems and employment patterns present in the student's life; factors that arise during the course that cause stress; and intrinsic factors such as motivation, time management, and organization that affect learning. The adult learners were not a homogenous group, but the most common age group was 25 to 40 years. Castles then discusses the literature on each of these areas. She found that the factors were interdependent, but nothing was found about the relative importance of each one or how they affected one another. She then discusses her interviews with students in Open University, including the questions about and the difficulties with some of the research. The analysis of the data collected showed that support factors figured the most in the success of adult learners. She also found that students mentioned a love of learning as very important, which was a new factor in the research. Castles then calls for institutions to provide study advisors and other support staff for adult learners. —KKN

80   Clark, Gregory, and Stephen Doheny-Farina. "Public Discourse and Personal Expression: A Case Study in Theory-Building." *Written Communication* 7.4 (Oct. 1990): 456–81. Print.

This essay describes the writing of Anna, a returning adult woman undergraduate who wrote and read in two environments: an upper division literature class and a workplace. Anna's literature course writing involved expressions of personal perspective based on lived experience despite the literary analysis task assigned. As an employee at Responsibility Childbirth, Anna became enmeshed in a controversy over providing abortions and receiving government funding. Anna's workplace writing entailed composing and editing articles for a newsletter and writing a report. Anna's writing tasks at work became increasingly persuasive and political over time because of the controversy surrounding provision of abortions. As Anna wrote in two different environments, she was using two different rhetorics and learning to write for different purposes. Her college writing is characterized by these authors as "individualistic" and her workplace writing is described as a "collective rhetoric" that is "transactional" in the sense that James Berlin uses that term to assume that "knowledge . . . is necessarily embedded in a negotiated process and is thus provisional" (471). While the authors started this project with a focus on Anna's writing and writing experiences, they conclude with a focus on their own experiences of interpreting Anna's writing and understanding her experiences as a participant in two different types of rhetoric. They conclude that by analyzing the conflicting experiences of one writer, such as Anna, they can contribute to developing a theory of writing that can inform writing instruction practices. —BJG

81   Courage, Richard. "The Interaction of Public and Private Literacies." *College Composition and Communication* 44.4 (1993): 484–96. Print.

Courage presents two case studies of adult women in a college composition course in order to study their academic literacies as opposed to their public and private literacies. He bases his study on Shaughnessy's, Bizzell's, and Bartholomae's research on academic literacies. Courage argues that the composition field needs to understand "the ways in which our students are simultaneously immersed in different patterns of language use, the sociocultural logic of those patterns, and the complex relations among them" (490). He emphasizes that we also must understand the hierarchy we place on academic discourse over public discourse. Courage argues that when we do this, we will understand how public literacies develop self-worth that helps students enter into academic literacies. —KKN

82   Darkenwald, Gordon G., and Richard J. Novak. "Classroom Age Composition and Academic Achievement in College." *Adult Education Quarterly* 47.2 (1997): 108–16. Print.

Darkenwald and Novak studied the effects of age composition on classrooms at both a community college and a university. Their study was based on similar work by Elder (1967), who found that adults in the classroom had a positive effect on younger students. Darkenwald and Novak found that adults had a positive effect in the classroom more in community colleges than in the university. However, this was not true in math classes. The implications of the study are for policies and programs, but the authors recognize that institutional missions would influence these. The greatest finding is that adult learners "bring some very desirable attributes to college and university campuses that are not always recognized" (116). —KKN

83   Dillon-Black, Liz. "A Rose Abused: Literacy as Transformation." *Journal of Adolescent & Adult Literacy* 42.1 (1998): 20–24. Print.

Dillon-Black presents a case study of a literacy student named Rose to demonstrate her transformation as a reader. Dillon-Black states, "My question in writing this case study was to consider whether I, as a literacy provider, reflected in practice what existed in theory" (21). In her presentation about Rose, Dillon-Black shows the change that takes place in Rose's perception of herself and her interaction with her classmates. The author attributes the changes to some of the learning theories she used with Rose in the course, one being the critical reflection strategy. The transformation in Rose was not permanent, which Dillon-Black attributes to Rose not making social, political, and economic changes as a result of the course. —KKN

84   Doheney-Farina, Stephen. "A Case Study of One Adult Writing in Academic and Nonacademic Discourse Communities." Ed. Carolyn B.

Matalene. *Worlds of Writing: Teaching and Learning in Discourse Communities of Work*. New York: Random, 1989. 17–42. Print.

A case study of one adult writer working in two institutional contexts reaffirms the established principle that particular forms of writing are sanctioned in different discourse communities while stretching beyond this focus to analyze a writer's rhetorical decision making. The study focuses on Anna, a 38-year-old undergraduate who is writing for a senior literature seminar as an English major and interning at a public relations department of a women's health clinic for college credit. By observing and interviewing Anna, her professor, and her supervisor, the author explores Anna's writing practices from the perspective of expected norms and her own decisions to meet those norms. For his analysis of Anna's literature course writing, the author asks questions regarding how Anna learns the instructor's expectations for composing a critical essay and how Anna produces writing that does or does not conform to these expectations. To analyze Anna's writing for a women's clinic public relations office, the author asks questions related to how Anna learns to write as a member of that discourse community. Doheney-Farina reports a key finding that institutional and social roles influence decision making about use of specific discursive practices; moreover, a writer's institutional and social role can influence a decision to produce or not produce the normal discourse expected in a community. While the findings of this research are preliminary and limited in scope, the author's analysis suggests that college professors should explore their own assumptions about what counts as acceptable forms of writing in college courses, about boundaries for stretching beyond accepted norms in an academic discourse community, and about influences on writers' decisions related to their own discursive practices in particular communities. — BJG

85   Glover-Graf, Noreen M., Eva Miller, and Samuel Freeman. "Accommodating Veterans with Post-traumatic Stress Disorder Symptoms in the Academic Setting." *Rehabilitation Education* 24.1 & 2 (2010): 43–56. Print.

Because more veterans are surviving their traumas in the Iraq and Afghanistan wars, more veterans entering postsecondary institutions are bringing disabilities into the classroom, so academia must help these veterans, who may or may not disclose their situations, to transition to college classrooms, argue the authors. Many of these veterans will exhibit symptoms of post-traumatic stress disorder (PTSD), which will affect their experience in college classrooms and completion of their degrees. Actions and responses of professors and classmates may affect the veteran with PTSD. The authors studied veterans of the Iraq war as they participated in focus groups. The seven participants were males ages 26 to 39. Through the analysis of the veterans' responses, the authors make some recommendations for academic institutions with veterans of the Iraq and Afghanistan wars, including having counselors who can advise administrators of ways to accommodate these veterans with PTSD and helping the veterans to obtain credit for their military education. — KKN

86   Hanlon, Marianne Mazzei, and R. Jeffrey Cantrell. "Teaching a Learning Disabled Adult to Spell: Is It Ever Too Late?" *Journal of Adolescent & Adult Literacy* 43.1 (1999): 4–11. Print.

Hanlon and Cantrell present a case study of a 31-year-old man who had been diagnosed with dyslexia as a child and now was seeking assistance with his reading and spelling. The study includes an interview with the man's mother, who confirms her son's experiences in elementary and secondary schools. The authors used three strategies — word sorting, spell checks, and homophone rummy — with the student, and reading and spelling levels increased from a second- or third-grade level to a sixth-grade level over nine months. Hanlon and Cantrell call for further research on working with adults like this one who struggle with reading and spelling because of an early diagnosis that labels them. They also suggest that all teaching strategies focus on the same areas of learning rather than having a diverse focus. — KKN

87   Houser, Marian L. "Expectancy Violations of Instructor Communication as Predictors of Motivation and Learning: A Comparison of Traditional and Nontraditional Students." *Communication Quarterly* 54.3 (Aug. 2006): 331–49. Print.

Houser uses Burgoon's expectancy violations theory to "compare the instructor communication expectations and classroom experiences of traditional and nontraditional students" (332). She defines nontraditional students as those ages 25 and older. Houser reviews the literature on expectation theory and the findings within these articles. Following this review, Houser provides an in-depth description of her study. The results of Houser's study were that instructors violated the communication expectations of both traditional and nontraditional students; however, how the students viewed the communication differed in the two groups. Traditional students expected instructors to be clear in their communication and "nonverbally immediate with both communication behaviors influencing classroom motivation and learning" (343). Nontraditional students also expected instructor clarity in explanations, preparation for the required work, and instructor feedback. Because instructors violated the desired communication expectations of both traditional and nontraditional students, the students' motivation and learning were affected. — KKN

88   Jackman, Mary Kay. "Where the Personal Becomes Professional: Stories from Reentry Adult Women Learners about Family, Work, and School." *Composition Studies* 27.2 (1999): 53–67. Print. Rpt. in *Teaching Developmental Writing: Background Readings.* Boston: Bedford, 2001.

Jackman discovered the importance of the narrative through her ethnographic research in a first-year writing course. In this article, she discusses three women, two adult students and the teaching assistant instructor, and how they use narratives to intertwine their personal lives with their academic lives. Through the case studies, Jackman shows the importance of learning more about adult women students as they are a growing part of postsecondary institutions. One of the students intertwines her wife and mother identities with her student identity as she writes; much of her writing in the course was based on her life experiences. The other student worked while attending college, and she also used her life experiences in her writing as she connected her academic writing to her jobs and family. Finally, the instructor used her own personal stories to teach writing to the students, and the two women mentioned that they liked the instructor's teaching style. The course helped these two students to see themselves as writers, which they did not see upon entering the course. Jackman calls for instructors to use personal writing in the classroom in order to break up the boundaries between the community and the university. — KKN

89   Key, Daphne. *Literacy Shutdown: Stories of Six American Women*. Newark, DE: International Reading Assn., 1998. Print.

After interviewing six women of different races about their literacy histories and then analyzing interview transcripts, the author identifies particular moments when each woman chose to withdraw from educational experiences and opportunities because of emotional insecurities or negative reactions to others. By describing these interviewees' emotional responses to important educational moments, the author proposes a theory that rests primarily on emotions and women's psychological histories. Calling this theory "literacy shut-down," the author argues that teachers and researchers must pay much closer attention to emotional experiences surrounding literacy scholarship and in educational programs. — BJG

90   Li, Yongyan. "Apprentice Scholarly Writing in a Community of Practice: An Intraview of an NNES Graduate Student Writing a Research Article." *TESOL Quarterly* 41.1 (2007): 55–79. Print.

Li reviews research on academic writing, noting that most of the research has been on writing in the humanities and social sciences, and most of the research was completed in North American institutions. With this in mind, the author notes that most science graduate students must write for specialty journals in place of coursework. Then Li presents the case study of a graduate science student engaging "with his community of practice" (57) by looking at four areas of engagement: "(a) the local research community, (b) the laboratory data, (c) his own experience and practice of research article (RA) writing, and (d) the global specialist research community" (57). Li reviewed the chemistry student's process logs that are kept while writing the first draft of a research article for international publication, noting that these logs have been reviewed in previous studies but not for students in non-Anglophone settings. The author discovered that the student had struggled with the English portion of the entrance examinations for universities in China. His process logs were posted as blogs, and Li responded to the posts in English. Additionally, Li interviewed the student. The drafts of the article were uploaded to the student's blog also, and Li analyzed all parts of the blog. The student relied on the lessons he learned from writing previous articles in his master's program. Li says that the student developed a deeper understanding of the data in his research by using the writing process, although he struggled with sorting his data and claims. His interaction with his research community and the global specialist research community show the importance of the social aspect of writing. Li argues that English for Academic Purposes (EAP) educators can help students like the one in this study by assisting students more systematically and earlier in graduate programs. — KKN

91   Michaud, Michael J. "The 'Reverse Commute': Adult Students and the Transition from Professional to Academic Literacy." *Teaching English in the Two-Year College* 38.3 (Mar. 2011): 244–57. Print.

Michaud presents a case study of an adult student in a college for adult education. He argues that adult students enter postsecondary institutions with experience in a wide range of professional writing, and he seeks to understand what happens when adult learners transition "from writing-for-the-boss to writing-for-the-teacher" (245). Through Michaud's interviews and analysis of the student's writing, he argues that adult learners try to balance the requirements of the courses with their own concerns and their "workplace knowledge and experience" (247). One of the difficulties the student had was understanding the assignments. He avoided writing as much as possible, both within the classroom and on the job, because he had struggled with writing in his earlier educational experiences. Michaud found that this student, like many in the workplace, used assemblage composing, even going so far as to "right-click-steal" to create documents in the workplace (252). This is a difficult habit for adult learners to break when they enter postsecondary institutions. Michaud concludes the essay by asserting that instructors ask adult students about their literacy practices in the workplace and design courses that are useful to adult students. — KKN

92   Miritello, Mary. "Teaching Writing to Adults: Examining Assumptions and Revising Expectations for Adult Learners in the Writing Class." *Composition Chronicle: Newsletter for Writing Teachers* 9.2 (1996): 6–9. Print.

Miritello uses three case studies of graduate students to explore anxieties related to academic writing. From these case studies, Miritello draws some conclusions about adult writers. First, although the students were or had been successful writers in the workplace, they experienced great anxiety when they received their first writing assignments in their courses. According to the students, one reason for the anxiety is that academic writing has gray areas whereas workplace writing is considered more black-and-white. They were helped when they found that they were not alone in experiencing anxiety. Therefore, Miritello suggests that writing centers provide opportunities for adult students to gather and voice their concerns. However, Miritello also found that adult students often are uncomfortable with seeking help in writing centers because they are seen as places for remedial students, as places for undergraduate students, and as a place where younger people are tutors. Therefore, the author suggests that writing centers provide training on tutoring adult learners. Finally, adult students need clear directions and expectations of assignments. The example Miritello uses is journals in the classroom. She ends with the point that we need "to be poised and ready to address the writing anxieties that non-traditional students bring to the classroom" (9). — KKN

93   Navarre Cleary, Michelle. "Anxiety and the Newly Returned Adult Student." *Teaching English in the Two-Year College* 39.4 (May 2012): 364–76. Print.

Navarre Cleary discusses the anxiety that adult learners bring to the writing classroom as she presents her case study of two students in a college program for students 24 years and older. She states, "The main sources of their anxiety were not knowing what to write because they had a hard time imagining the university and not knowing if they were writing well enough" (364). Navarre Cleary argues, "We need to understand how our teaching decisions affect adults' anxieties about writing" (365). She states that instructors need to define concepts for adult students and to be specific in what they are seeking from the students in their writing. A diverse selection of models of writing helps students. Additionally, Navarre Cleary asserts that instructors need to provide "feedback on low-stakes writing" (369) and that useful, timely feedback helps adult learners the most as they want to improve their writing. She ends with suggestions of strategies that work best with adult learners. — KKN

94   Popken, Randall. "A Study of the Genre Repertoires of Adult Writers." *Writing Instructor* 15.2 (1996): 85–93. Print.

Popken examines genre "extrapolation," a process by which writers adapt familiar genres to the unfamiliar genres they want to write. Popken presents case studies of two adult students — John, age 32, and Aletha, age 33 — developed from personal interviews and student writing. John, who has worked for fourteen years in trades, "hates to write" and, other than love letters to his girlfriend, has only written fragmented responses to questions. However, John has developed knowledge of some genres from his reading of novels, new journalism, philosophy, the newspaper, and others. John's college writing lacks sufficient explicitness; he has difficulty with the "point + illustration" structure and cannot extrapolate this genre feature from previous genre knowledge. In addition, the flip, disinterested style of the creative nonfiction he reads displays a voice inappropriate for college writing. Aletha worked for five years in secretarial positions where she wrote many business letters before becoming a full-time parent. She likes to write, writes fiction for fun, and reads varied material, e.g., popular fiction, encyclopedias, cookbooks, and biographies. Her attempts to extrapolate college writing from the genre of the business letter have met with mixed results. Like John, Aletha has difficulty with explicitness; she is confused by how much support an assertion needs. Business letters also lack a strong enough voice or textual authority to serve as an academic model, especially evident in Aletha's use of sources. However, business letters seem to work well as a pattern for her history essay exams, which call for quick assertions with brief, specific support. Popken concludes that adult writers' base of genre knowledge differs from that of traditional-age students, and the attempt to extrapolate past genre knowledge will affect adults' academic writing. Instructors need to consider how previous reading and writing experiences may influence adults' academic writing. — KSU

95   Popken, Randall. "Adult Writers, Interdiscursive Linking, and Academic Survival." *Attending to the Margins: Writing, Researching, and Teaching on the Front Lines.* Ed. Michelle Hall Kells and Valerie M. Balester. Portsmouth, NH: Boynton/Cook Heinemann, 1999. 56–73. Print.

Using Bakhtin's dialogic approach to analyzing discourse, Popken presents his research on how adult writers use the discourses they know to make connections with academic writing. He terms this "interdiscursive linking" (56). Popken argues that adult students have had many discourse experiences throughout their lives, and they use these experiences to connect with and make sense of academic discourse. He argues that by using genres they already know, adult learners are "enlarging their genre repertoires" (58), but instructors do not always see the connections being made. Popken then presents three of his case studies to demonstrate how all three make connections between some aspect of their academic assignments and what they each have already learned in work writing or speaking. Popken suggests that this process may give some adult learners an advantage over traditional students. He also suggests that adult learners may make some incorrect links between the genres they know and academic discourse. Interdiscursive links break as students become more familiar with academic discourse. However, instructors should help adult learners make these connections by designing initial assignments for their courses with this goal in mind. — KKN

96   Purcell-Gates, Victoria. *Other People's Worlds: The Cycle of Low Literacy.* Cambridge, MA: Harvard UP, 1995. Print.

Arguing that poor white Appalachians form a largely understudied culture of people whose children often fail to thrive in US public schools, Purcell-Gates reports on the literacy learning experiences of one urban Appalachian family in a compelling narrative of a family's struggle to acquire literacy. The family included the parents, Donny and Jenny, and their two young sons, Donny and Timmy. Neither Jenny nor Donny had learned to read or write—both having withdrawn from school in 7th grade—and at the beginning of 2nd grade, young Donny could read only his name and the word *the*. While the older Donny had accepted his weak literacy, Jenny wanted to read so she could help her children with their schoolwork and shop without asking friends for help. With these goals in mind, Jenny asked to sit in on tutoring sessions for her son at the university-based Literacy Center where Purcell-Gates served as director. Purcell-Gates proposed an alternative arrangement: she offered to tutor Jenny, her husband Donny, and their oldest child (also named Donny) in exchange for the opportunity to record and take notes on their learning activities. The result of their agreement is a case study focusing primarily on Jenny and young Donny in the contexts of the university Literacy Center and their daily life routines as members of urban Appalachian culture. Framing her analysis of young Donny's learning in emergent literacy theory, Purcell-Gates describes an absence of print materials and literacy activities in Donny's home life: his parents did not use print for everyday activities, so Donny was not learning key lessons about reading and writing (e.g., directionality of print on a page, meaning-making with printed symbols, and uses of environmental print). As a mentor and teacher, Purcell-Gates provided guidance for Donny's parents and tutoring for Donny, who did begin reading and writing during the two years of this study. To help Jenny learn to read and write, Purcell-Gates encouraged Jenny to write routinely in a personal journal. Purcell-Gates would routinely take home Jenny's handwritten journal entries and transcribe them to conventional spelling and punctuation, type them, and then return the transcribed journal entries to Jenny, who then was able to read her own writing. In addition to describing these and additional literacy learning activities, Purcell-Gates records aspects of the family's daily life and living arrangements, which were strongly affected by the parents' poverty. Sadly, Jenny's ability to take advantage of the opportunities afforded her at the Literacy Center were partially stymied by her husband's conviction and imprisonment for selling marijuana during the two years of this study. Using James Gee's sociocultural theory of literacy and language learning, Purcell-Gates argues that literacy is embedded in a discourse that is always culture-bound and that the discourse of this urban Appalachian family simply did not include print literacy. This absence of print literacy at home made it nearly impossible for Donny to learn to read at school, and Purcell-Gates reminds us that many other children suffer a similar fate. Therefore, family literacy programs need strong support, and teachers should be well informed of literacy learning theory and research to offset disparities in children's family literacy experiences. —BJG

97   Ray, Ruth E. *Beyond Nostalgia: Aging and Life-Story Writing*. Charlottesville: U of Virginia P, 2000. Print.

In a study of older adult life-story writers, Ruth Ray analyzes the effects of gender, age, and ethnicity on adult development, narrated self-understanding, and writing group dynamics. Ray's research is based on interviews with older adult writers, observations, and participation in writing groups that convened in urban and suburban areas of Detroit. Her interdisciplinary perspective is informed by the fields of rhetoric, composition, sociolinguistics, anthropology, psychology, women's studies, feminist criticism, and gerontology. While Ray had observed eight writing groups, she focused more narrowly on the writing and the learning of fifty-five continually present individuals in two writing groups. With ages ranging from 58 to 92, participants' socio-cultural backgrounds were varied. The ratio of women to men was five to one, forty-eight participants being women and seven being men. The research is presented in seven research-based thematic chapters and seven "inter-chapters" that profile individual writers and their writing. Chapter 1 integrates theories of adult development, social construction, narrative, and feminist criticism in order to argue that theories of aging must be informed by gender, culture, and other forms of diversity. Chapters 2 and 3 offer examples of individual writers and writing group conversations as illustrations to support the argument presented in chapter 1. In chapter 4, Ray explores relationships between memory and truth, paying close attention to the influence of family scripts and their gendered nature. Chapters 5 and 6 analyze writing groups as interpretive communities. Chapter 7 addresses connections between life-story writing and adult development. Framed by "critical gerontology" (10), this study contributes to the growing field of feminist gerontology. For teachers of adult learners, Ray's research reveals the potential of life-story writing for critical reflection on lived experience and encouragement of new and potentially transformative learning for older adult writers of autobiography. — BJG

98   Rose, Mike. *The Mind at Work: Valuing the Intelligence of the American Worker.* New York: Penguin, 2005. Print.

In this 250-page book, Rose examines common labor and the thinking it requires. He presents six chapter-long case studies of workers: a waitress (based on Rose's mother), a hair stylist, plumbers, carpenters, electricians, construction workers, a welder, and an industry foreman. In these "cognitive biographies" (xxxi), Rose offers vivid, in-depth stories of working lives developed through description, narrative, interview, and analysis, revealing the complex mix of physical, psychological, and cognitive skills that work requires. Waitressing and hair styling represent the service professions with their emphasis on personal assistance in public spaces, while the chapters on trades explore tools, judgment, planning, and problem solving. Throughout the book, Rose asks, "What in this moment does it mean to be smart?" (xxix), and his answers to this question help teachers of adult learners appreciate the abilities that working adults may bring to the classroom and their possible expectations for learning. Rose profiles both expert practitioners and apprentices, as well as their teachers and mentors. He focuses on community colleges, training programs, and the role of education in those institutions, arguing against an easy dichotomy between body and mind and the consequent separation of vocational from academic education. In fact, in a later chapter, Rose describes surgeons and their absolute reliance on the hand/eye/brain connection. Rose frames these profiles with reflection on the connections among physical, mental, and emotional work and education. He challenges our thinking about what work requires and the terms we use to describe it, terms like *skill*, *agency*, *authority*, *perception*, *technique*, and *communication* through images, for instance, blueprints, and communication through text, talk, and gesture. And he considers crucial related educational issues: tracking and vocational education; first-generation college students; race, class, gender, and social mobility; and teaching, training, and mentoring. Ultimately, Rose proposes a democratic educational approach that honors "the fundamental intelligence of a broad range of human activity" (194). —KSU

99   Rosenberg, Lauren. "Retelling Culture Through the Construction of Alternative Literacy Narratives: A Study of Adults Acquiring New Literacies." *Reflections: Writing, Service-Learning, and Community Literacy* 9.3 (Summer 2010): 75–114. Print.

Rosenberg describes case study research on older adult learners who attend an adult literacy program. Having interviewed four adults, Rosenberg writes here of George, a 60-something man who survived World War II and lived to help his mother in her extreme old age. When conducting her interviews, Rosenberg anticipated that study participants would narrate dominant culture literacy narratives — e.g., the view that learning literacy relates to functional skills and economic gain. The older adult study participants did produce these narratives but also told alternate literacy narratives about their reasons for pursuing literacy. Four alternative literacy narratives emerged in this research: "Illiteracy as Social Violence," "Material Conditions," "Pleasure versus Self-Improvement," and "Getting by without Schooling" (85). In telling these alternate literacy narratives, the older adults proved to be critical of the dominant culture and aware of social injustice. For example, one dominant culture literacy narrative views illiterate adults as responsible for their own illiteracy. George does not accept this view of his own weaknesses with reading and writing. George explains his own low literacy by citing scarce material conditions for acquiring literacy and attending school. This research has implications for both teachers of older adults and for teachers of young adults in college. —BJG

100   Selfe, Cynthia L., and Gail E. Hawisher. *Literate Lives in the Information Age: Narratives of Literacy from the United States*. Mahwah, NJ: Erlbaum, 2004. Print.

A study of twenty Americans explores digital literacy by profiling individuals' literacy practices in the contexts of family, school, workplace, and community. Drawn from a corpus of 350 study participants, the twenty profiled individuals represent different generations (ages range from 14 to 60), cultural identities (European Americans, African Americans, mixed-race, and Native Americans), and genders (fifteen females and five males). Their evolving literacy practices are contextualized in cultural narratives chronicling well-known events and relevant technological advances (especially in chapter 3, "Privileging—or Not—the Literacies of Technology," and chapter 4, "Shaping Cultures: Prizing the Literacies of Technology"). Connections between technological innovations, public cultural and social events, and private family environments combine to form "the cultural ecology of literacy," a concept described by the authors as a "complex web of social forces, historical events, economic patterns, material conditions, and cultural expectations within which both humans and computer technologies co-exist" (31). Age, gender, family literacy practices, and race are used to analyze the impact of people's attitudes, opportunities, and material access to computers on study participants' lives. Eight themes emerge from analysis of case studies. Two of these themes are (1) literacies exist in cultural ecologies and have lifespans involving old literacies fading away and new literacies becoming dominant and (2) race, ethnicity, and class have played key roles in literacies evolving between 1978 to 2003, the years identified as bookends for this study of digital literacy.—BJG

101   Sork, Thomas J. "Applied Ethics in Adult and Continuing Education Literature." *Negotiating Ethical Practice in Adult Education*. Ed. Elizabeth J. Burge. Hoboken, NJ: Wiley, 2009. 19–32. Print. New Directions in Adult and Continuing Education 123.

Sork reviews the literature on applied ethics in adult education to see how the field of adult education has addressed ethics until 2009. He discusses a Miami incident with an adult education program and an instructor who invested students' funds poorly when he taught an investment course. The case resulted in the development of *Industry Standards for Classes with Potential Commercial Content* and caused adult educators to reconsider their ethical and legal responsibilities to their students. A debate on the feasibility and interest in a code of ethics for adult education ensued. Some scholars argued that the field of adult education had not developed enough to develop such a code, while others argued that further professionalization of the field was not desirable. Sork notes that early arguments lacked empirical evidence of how specialists felt about ethics of practice and developing a code of ethics. While the debate was ongoing, several organizations developed a code of ethics, and Sork reviews several of these codes. Some groups have developed processes to help practitioners develop sound ethical choices. Sork concludes with a discussion of the lack of developments in ethics in adult education.—KKN

102   Watkins, Audrey P. *Sisters of Hope, Looking Back, Stepping Forward: The Educational Experiences of African-American Women*. New York: Peter Lang, 2009. Print.

Watkins weaves autobiographical narrative into a qualitative study of five participants' lives to explore effects of race, gender, prior education, family, religion, and class on African American girls' and women's experiences. As a speech and language educator in a Midwestern bank, Watkins met five employees, ranging in age from 23 to 47, who later became study participants. Scholarship by African American women (Barbara Omolade, Lisa Delpit, and Jacqueline Jones) provides a cultural perspective that informs Watkins's analysis. Implications for curriculum and instruction are suggested throughout the book and explicitly discussed in chapter 4, "Education at School: Competence and Confidence" (65–94). Of common concern to all study participants are instructor expertise and the rigor of curricula in schools attended primarily by African American children. Study participants agreed that their educational experiences had been negatively impacted by the quality of their public schools. As adults, they try to protect their children from discrimination and attempt to motivate their children to succeed academically. An analysis of study participants' work experiences reveals that all five women report experiencing discrimination in the workplace and all have come to view education and their own competence as keys to success. In addressing social inequities and related impacts on individual lives, Watkins argues that our current efforts to oppose social injustice are insufficient and that informal teaching and learning occasions can elicit changes in attitudes as well as perceptions based on race, class, and gender. — BJG

103   Williams, Mitchell R., and Tracy Southers. "Blurring the Lines between High School and College: Early Colleges and the Effect on Adult Learners." *Adult Learning* 21.1–2 (2010): 26–30. Print.

Traditionally community colleges have educated adult learners who returned to school because they recognized a need to improve their occupational skills. Since the 1950s, these colleges focused on developing successful pedagogical strategies for older teenagers and adults. However, a new trend is changing the demographics of the community college classroom. Several states have formed Early Colleges within the community college setting to educate younger high school students. Students in the ninth grade may concurrently enroll in high school and college. Williams and Southers researched the effects of teaching 14- or 15-year-old students together with adult learners. Specifically, they measured the perceptions of chief academic officers with respect to the way Early College programs create differences in the education of returning adult students. They first used a survey instrument based on a scale similar to Likert; then they followed up with in-depth interviewing. The surveys were completed by twenty-four chief academic officers at community colleges in North Carolina. The findings show that over 90 percent of the respondents felt the Early College programs did not diminish their ability to teach all students. Over 60 percent felt the Early College programs improved the quality of education. However, aside from these positive perceptions, 75 percent of the officers noted that adult students complained about the Early College learners. In addition, space problems arose, creating problems for serving the adult learners. With respect to the adult learner complaints, many of their concerns related to the fact that the younger teenagers were not academically and socially prepared to accept responsibility for achieving their own educational goals. In addition, the presence of these younger students created psychological barriers that too frequently created distractions for adults focused on achieving occupational and personal goals at the community college. Williams and Southers believe that more research is needed to investigate both the positive and negative effects of Early Colleges on adult learners. —LDB

Writing and Reading Curricula

Writing and Reading in the Workplace

104 Belanger, Kelly, and Linda Strom. *Second Shift: Teaching Writing to Working Adults.* Portsmouth, NH: Boynton/Cook Heinemann, 1999. Print.

Belanger and Strom provide a historical perspective of schools that teach working-class adults and then analyze corporate-based and union-based programs. Their research focuses on how well "present writing programs for working adults represent a Freirean approach to teaching critical literacy" (vii). The historical perspective begins with a discussion of worker education from 1820 to 1935, which Belanger and Strom describe as a way to cause social change. Soon after the 1930s, the educational system for workers began to focus on liberal arts education, which these authors argue broadens the worker's experiences to philosophical ideas. Belanger and Strom then analyze the five programs that focus on worker education. The first is the liberal arts program at Alfred North Whitehead College, which has as its "greatest strengths . . . its insistence upon identifying the needs of working adults and putting those needs at the center of the program and curriculum development" (29). Descriptions of the various writing courses, as well as the teaching strategies for the courses at this institution, are provided. A description of the program, courses, and teaching strategies is provided for Empire State College, which focuses on students between 30 and 50 years of age. Queens College Worker Education Program is presented by Belanger and Strom as one that was "developed to serve the research and educational needs of the labor movement and the community" (55). This program was a collaboration between the school and unions and is writing-intensive. Swingshift College at Indiana University Northwest also is aligned with unions and requires intensive writing in the courses. Belanger and Strom focus on their interviews with two instructors in the program. Finally, the authors discuss their experiences of teaching Youngstown University's writing courses that are presented in union halls. They share the changes in their pedagogy and the assignments in their courses. In the conclusion, Belanger and Strom argue that intensive writing is needed in working adult programs and that the writing should focus on "action-oriented writing pedagogies" (102).—KKN

105 D'Amico, Debby, and Emily Schnee. "It Changed Something Inside of Me: English Language Learning, Structural Barriers to Employment, and Workers' Goals in a Workplace Literacy Program." *Changing Work,*

Changing Workers: Critical Perspectives on Language, Literacy and Skills. Ed. Glynda Hull. Albany: SUNY Press, 1997. 117–40. Print.

This essay portrays a four-year history of Education for Education Careers (EEC), a grant-funded worker education program designed to offer literacy and English language instruction to immigrant workers and help them gain new employment opportunities. Strongly contextualized in the occupational hazards, opportunities, and challenges of New York City, EEC tested the assumption that increased literacy and language proficiency would lead to more and better employment opportunities. Supported by unions and the Consortium for Worker Education, a union-based education organization, EEC primarily aimed to teach English language and literacy to immigrant workers in year one. The majority of the 106 workers who initially entered the program spoke Spanish or Spanish and English. All of these workers possessed either a GED or a high school diploma. Because federal funding ran out at the end of year one, two unions offered to sponsor two classes in EEC's second year. During this year, EEC began focusing on helping workers move out of the garment work industry and into paraprofessional education jobs. In year three, EEC administrators began focusing on moving worker-students into daycare employment. Continuing in year four under the auspices of the Consortium for Worker Education (CWE), EEC began coordinating with a newly established CWE Child Care Project and helping worker-students to enroll in college classes. Case studies of two EEC students illustrate the different experiences of workers who either start with a strong educational base and have legal status in the United States or start with weak educational attainments and an undocumented immigrant status. The authors conclude by discussing the varied experiences of immigrant workers and the broader social, cultural, and political contexts in which they seek employment. Employment challenges experienced by EEC students challenge the commonly held assumption that more education and increased language and literacy learning lead to more work opportunities. —BJG

106   Diehl, William A., and Larry Mikulecky. "The Nature of Reading at Work." *Journal of Reading* 24.3 (1980): 221–28. Print. Rpt. in *Perspectives on Literacy*. Ed. Eugene R. Kintgen, Barry M. Kroll, and Mike Rose. Carbondale: Southern Illinois UP, 1988. 371–77.

Diehl and Mikulecky researched how workers use reading skills at their jobs. Previous studies had indicated that many workers did not have the required reading skills to function at their jobs, yet research had not concluded how much literacy was necessary for work situations. Diehl and Mikulecky interviewed and tested (using the Diehl-Mikulecky Job Literacy Survey) various people at a variety of workplaces to discover how they used literacy skills on the job. The authors also reviewed some of the reading material to determine the readability level of these pieces. Diehl and Mikulecky learned that reading that occurs in the workplace occurs everywhere at some level. However, much of the reading that occurred was not seen as vital to the job, although it was deemed helpful. The authors conclude that the reading taught in school differs from that needed to function as an adult on the job.—KKN

See: Stephen Doheney-Farina. "A Case Study of One Adult Writing in Academic and Nonacademic Discourse Communities" [84].

107   Gowen, Cheryl Greenwood, and Carol Bartlett. "'Friends in the Kitchen': Lessons from Survivors." *Changing Work, Changing Workers: Critical Perspectives on Language, Literacy, and Skills.* Ed. Glynda Hull. Albany: SUNY Press, 1997. 141–58. Print.

In the absence of salary increases, a university custodial staff requested educational opportunities as an employee benefit. The requested benefit was provided for entry-level custodial staff, of whom many were women. Literacy classes were taught on campus by two female college instructors—the authors of this essay. These two white female academics were teaching working-poor African American women who had (in some cases) experienced domestic spousal abuse or childhood sexual abuse. The authors describe their own learning about the financial, legal, occupational, and social challenges faced by female victims of spousal abuse and the impacts these experiences can have on educational attainments and on teaching and learning in a literacy class. Citing the work of scholars such as Carol Gilligan (*In a Different Voice*, 1981) and research by the American Association of University Women on unequal treatments of boys and girls in schools, the authors discuss the fact that some female students possess weak rhetorical self-confidence, fluency, and expertise. The authors assert a role for advocacy of female spousal abuse survivors in the context of worker education programs, where spousal abuse might be even more prevalent because it is associated with low educational attainments and low wages. At the same time, they point out the dangers of rhetorical empowerment to women experiencing domestic abuse while attending school: some female literacy students have been raped and even killed by husbands and male friends who cite GED programs, education, and increased rhetorical competence (talking back) as reasons for their anger and abuse. The authors argue that worker education programs should generally become more responsive to female students' spousal abuse histories, and this topic should gain greater prominence in the adult literacy education scholarship.—BJG

108   MacKinnon, Jamie. "Becoming a Rhetor: Developing Writing Ability in a Mature, Writing-Intensive Organization." *Writing in the Workplace: New Research Perspectives.* Ed. Rachel Spilka. Carbondale: Southern Illinois UP, 1993. 41–55. Print.

In a study of adults' workplace writing development, ten college-educated bank employees were interviewed twice about their knowledge of writing, the writing process, written products, and their workplace organization (e.g., departmental structures, chain of command, communication practices). Each interview was scheduled just after the employee had written a significant document at work so that the interviews could focus on specific writing experiences. Managers were consulted about the issues discussed in participants' interviews in order to provide supervisors' perspectives on study participants' writing development. The research revealed that all ten participants learned a great deal about writing and about their workplace organization during the ten- to twenty-month intervals between their two interviews. The author concludes that by learning about the workplace organization, the study participants learned about writing strategies associated with purpose and audience. The writing process was also a key area of learning: participants gained expertise in circulating documents and requesting feedback, clarifying assignments with oral discussions, initiating ad hoc writing projects, and communicating with colleagues about works-in-progress. The participants' knowledge of written products improved in the areas of structure and purpose, context, audience awareness, content, and use of detail. In large part because they were newly hired, the ten study participants learned a great deal about the culture of their workplace during the months this study was conducted; this increased understanding contributed to their self-confidence and to their ability as writers in the workplace. This study challenges the notion that writing development primarily occurs in school when people are children, adolescents, and young adults. In contrast, it promotes the views that writing development often occurs in settings outside of school and that educated adults can significantly develop as writers after they leave school. The research also provides evidence for the theory that both writing products and writing development are context-dependent. — BJG

109   Murray, Donald M. "Don't Profess: Coach." *Worlds of Writing: Teaching and Learning in Discourse Communities of Work*. Ed. Carolyn B. Matalene. New York: Random, 1989. 257–63. Print.

Coaching newspaper writers provides profitable and rewarding part-time work for college writing instructors. Drawing on his prior experience as a writing coach, Donald Murray describes pedagogical strategies that he has used to coach journalists; he then goes on to discuss rewards and challenges of teaching writing in a newspaper office. Rather than teaching traditional classes, Murray conducts participatory workshops and individualized conferences for reporters and editors. Journalists benefit from the opportunity to focus on their writing individually and collectively; writing instructors gain the advantage of observing newspaper writers and editors at work. Murray encourages college writing instructors to consider coaching newspaper writers to gain new perspectives on writing and writing instruction. — BJG

Writing and Reading in Adult Education Programs

110   Baldwin, Yvonne Honeycutt. *Cora Wilson Stewart and Kentucky's Moonlight Schools: Fighting for Literacy in America*. Lexington: UP of Kentucky, 2006. Print.

In chronicling the thirty-year career of Cora Wilson Stewart, Baldwin profiles two competing approaches to adult literacy education in the early decades of the twentieth century. The approach advocated by Stewart was a grassroots, community-based effort that relied primarily on unpaid volunteer tutors and teachers. The alternative, which ultimately prevailed, prioritized professional educators with university degrees and the development of an academic field. After establishing a night school for rural adults in 1911, Stewart successfully campaigned for creating a network of Moonlight Schools for illiterate adults in Kentucky. She enlisted the support of politicians, teachers, preachers, and the press to pass legislation creating the Kentucky Illiteracy Commission, for which Stewart served as the first president. To document adult illiteracy, Stewart organized a group of volunteers to canvass Kentucky residents and create a census report of individuals' reading and writing competencies. Documenting the existence of illiterate white adults was essential in order to combat the dominant view that illiteracy mainly existed in African American and immigrant communities. Stewart also wrote and published primers for rural people, prisoners, soldiers, mothers, and Native Americans. A skilled community organizer and a charismatic orator, Stewart held leadership positions in several state and national organizations, some of which she founded: she was the first woman to serve as president of the National Education Association. Stewart argued that when parents attained literacy skills and adopted positive attitudes toward formal education, their children would benefit, a fundamental principle to the family literacy movement today. Although Stewart did not achieve the recognition accorded to the two women she most admired—Jane Addams and Ida Tarbell—Stewart remains an example of the public leadership roles that women could aspire to and attain during the era when women were seeking the right to vote and to participate in public administration.—BJG

111   Beverstock, Caroline, Shanti Bhaskaran, Jacquie Brinkley, Donna Jones, and Valerie Reinke. "Transforming Adult Students into Authors: The Writer to Writer Challenge." *Adult Basic Education and Literacy Journal* 3.1 (2009): 48–52. Print.

Commenting on many curricula for adult literacy programs, Beverstock et al. argue that lack of attention to writing instruction in adult literacy courses has resulted from an overemphasis on reading and from instructors' uncertainties about how to teach developmental writing to adults. As a consequence of this inattention to writing needs of adult students, program administrators may focus too much on grammar at the expense of critical thinking, whereas instructors may feel their own grammatical skills are inadequate for them to become teachers of writing. To address these issues, Beverstock et al. describe an introductory reading and writing curriculum for adult learner participants in California public library literacy programs. Unlike other programs, the Writer to Writer (WTW) Challenge teaches students to read and write simultaneously. The adult learners are encouraged to read any book they choose, after which they write letters to the authors to communicate how these books changed their lives. WTW is administered as a contest with two

rounds of judging. Developed by Valerie Reinke of the California State
Library, the WTW Challenge follows the model of a national program
called Letters about Literature. Its purposes include helping adult learners learn to read for pleasure and to improve their writing skills. In
addition, the self-confidence of the letter writers seems to improve as
the adult students learn to make connections between the ideas in the
books and their own life experiences. Beverstock et al. provide sample
winning entries as well as a detailed checklist entitled "How to Create
a Writing Challenge Like Writer to Writer." —LDB

112 Beverstock, Caroline, and Sue McIntyre. "Dividing and Conquering:
     Successful Writing Processes for Adult Learners." *Adult Basic Education
     and Literacy Journal* 2.2 (2008): 104–8. Print.

     Using a case-study approach, Beverstock and McIntyre show how lit-
     eracy programs for adults may convince men who have failed in other
     areas of their lives that they can learn to read and write. Their research
     site is Project Read, a residential drug and alcohol recovery program in
     San Mateo, California. Focusing on one of the research participants,
     the authors describe one man's transition from being an illiterate
     participant in the program to being an employed counselor attend-
     ing college as he advances in his career. Alonso McConnell believes
     Project Read saved his life. The authors emphasize the need to break
     the writing process into a series of small steps and to eliminate as many
     distractions as possible because the adult learners can only process a
     maximum of seven thoughts in short-term memory. Working with this
     basic learning theory, they describe strategies and tools to help tutors
     learn to teach adult males who fear writing. The recommended tools are
     commonly used in college writing classes and include "quick-words,"
     yellow highlighting, clustering, and reading backwards. The authors'
     belief in the program is based on statistical evidence indicating that
     the success rate for males enrolled in the addiction recovery program is
     50 percent better for those who also chose to participate in the Project
     Read writing sessions. —LDB

113 Fallon, Dianne. "Making Dialogue Dialogic: A Dialogic Approach to
     Adult Life." *Journal of Adult and Adolescent Literacy* 39.2 (1995): 138–
     46. Print.

     After struggling to use dialogue journals with her adult students in a
     literacy program, Fallon explores the Bakhtinian concept of dialogic
     language in relation to literacy education. Believing that her students
     were remaining distanced from their own use of language, Fallon argues
     that engagement with their language and word choices can empower
     adult learners: "My sense is that this process of individualizing a word
     helps an adult learner to retain the connection between the written
     form of the word, its sound, and its meanings" (140). To achieve this
     goal, Fallon suggests using Paulo Freire's notion of "generative themes"
     that are relevant to the students' lives as opposed to reliance on tradi-
     tional academic topics in order to reduce the intrusion of teachers and

encourage student-to-student dialogue. Writing about subjects that dominated their lives, students were encouraged to explicitly explore their understanding of individual words, defining these words within their own personal and specific contexts. When claiming words and discovering personally relevant meanings, students "experience the transformative moments that give them compelling reasons to speak, to write, and to read" (146).—SFL

114   Glasgow, Jacqueline N. "Accommodating Learning Styles in Prison Writing Classes." *Journal of Reading* 38.3 (1994): 188–95. Print.

Glasgow discusses her experience of teaching a college-level developmental writing course to prisoners. She based her instructional strategies on her research on teaching African American students and on learning styles for adult learners. Knowing that her students were "concrete-experiential learners" (189), Glasgow managed the classroom with a "direct, assertive discipline plan" (190) and set routines for the classroom. The students helped to set the goals for the course, and the writing prompts were based on personal experiences. Glasgow used portfolio assessment to evaluate the students' progress. To accommodate the students' need for social interaction, Glasgow used the buddy system and student models so students could share their work. She argues, "Overall, I conclude that accommodation of learning style preferences is a key to help students become better writers, not merely to produce better texts" (195).—KKN

See: Marianne Mazzei Hanlon and R. Jeffrey Cantrell. "Teaching a Learning Disabled Adult to Spell: Is It Ever Too Late?" [86].

115   Himley, Margaret, Chris Madden, Al Hoffman, and Diane Penrod. "Answering the World: Adult Literacy and Co-Authoring." *Written Communication* 13.2 (1996): 163–82. Web. 2 Dec. 2010.

In working with new adult writers, the authors developed coauthoring as a way to scaffold student writing without squashing student voices. When the authors moved from the familiar context of the university to a community literacy center that serves adult learners, they thought expressivism would both help the students develop fluency and play down the power differential between students and instructors. However, unlike in the academy where students rarely questioned their pedagogy, the adult students at the literacy center did. These students wanted to be taught "correct" writing that would gain them authority in the world. The instructors wanted to respect the students' wishes and help them successfully communicate to audiences who would expect "standard" English. Yet the instructors also saw how self-editing inhibited self-expression and did not want to participate in or further validate the subjugation of the students' discourses. Eventually, by recognizing their differences, students and instructors negotiated a process of coauthoring. Coauthoring enables "critical reflection for both tutor and student about choices in writing, about language and power" (186). In coauthoring, teachers participated in the creation of students' texts. For example, an instructor might lightly edit while taking dictation so the student could focus on fewer issues while revising. Informed by theories of Bakhtin and Foucault, the authors came to understand coauthoring as an acknowledgment and exploration of the dialogic nature of writing and the ways writing, identity, and power are entwined. — MNC

116   Jarvis, Christine A. "Desirable Reading: The Relationship between Women Students' Lives and Their Reading Practices." *Adult Education Quarterly* 53.4 (2003): 261–76. Print.

Jarvis studied the reading practices of women ages 21 to 55 "in a U.K. Access to Education Course" (263), and she used a feminist framework to analyze the results. The data was collected from interviews with the students and their reflections on their reading. Her "argument is that reading is so deeply interwoven with the fabric of people's identities and relationships that examining it critically with others, through dialogue in the classroom, will challenge profoundly held beliefs and values" (265–66). Jarvis states her research supports other research that argues women's reading is seen as leisurely while men's reading is seen as scholarly. She also confirms that women share books to help others escape the monotony of daily life and for friendships. Jarvis argues that women read for pleasure but also to understand different issues in various contexts and to build their own concepts of themselves. — KKN

117   Jones, Jill, Bridgett Brookbank, and Jennifer McDonough. "Meeting the Literacy Needs of Adult Learners through a Community-University Partnership." *Journal of College Literacy and Learning* 35 (Annual 2008–09): 12–18. Web. 16 Apr. 2014.

The authors write about their experience as an instructor and as graduate students in a graduate reading course in which the students tutored adult literacy students. The thirteen students and instructor were required to complete the training offered by the local literacy coalition, but the students were allowed to add to the tutoring materials as needed. The student researchers wrote about their experiences, tutees, and responses throughout the course. The students used a "cyclical process of assessment and planning" (15) to create their lessons, and the students learned to follow the needs of their tutees as the students reflected on what occurred during each meeting. The study's findings included the need for more university interaction with literacy coalitions, the pluses of graduate students working outside of their comfort zones, and the importance of reflection by graduate students. — KKN

118   Kazemek, Francis E. "They Have Yarns: Writing with the Active Elderly." *Journal of Adolescent & Adult Literacy* 40.7 (1997): 516–23. Print.

Kazemek shares her experiences of writing with the elderly, ages 68 to 91, at a community center. The article begins with a review of literature on elderly literacy and then continues with a description of the strategies used in the weekly meetings. Each session began with a conversation that led into writing, and each person developed that piece over the following weeks. Kazemek also offered information on the writer's craft during each session. Finally, the writers shared their pieces at a local bookstore and with elementary children before the works were put together in a published booklet that was sold. —KKN

119   Laughlin, Thomas. "Teaching in the Yard: Student Inmates and the Policy of Silence." *Teaching English in the Two Year College* 23.4 (1996): 284–90. Print.

Teaching literature in a prison classroom leads the author to struggle in a "contact zone," a borderland between prison culture and academic culture. Prison administrators had banned inmates from revealing personal information and from discussing racial tensions, yet the author assigned reader-response writing and twentieth-century fictional stories with allusions to racial prejudice. Having told their instructor they would decide how much personal information they would communicate, a few students did begin alluding to their life experiences as they wrote fictional stories and responses to literary texts. Discussions of racism emerged in the context of reading short stories by Flannery O'Connor and other authors. Students at first resisted discussing race, with some expressing anger at being asked to address a banned topic. Initial resistance then gave way to strong interest in discussing racial prejudice, a process that induced students to differentiate between attitudes of authors and attitudes of characters. Students benefitted from these discussions by developing critical thinking and communication skills. The author concludes that all teaching takes place in highly specific classrooms where differing cultures routinely coexist and sometimes collide. Teachers must develop instructional practices and assignments that account for these cultures and related conflicts in order to ensure effective teaching and learning. —BJG

120   Lynch, Jacqueline. "Print Literacy Engagement of Parents from Low-Income Backgrounds: Implications for Adult and Family Literacy Programs." *Journal of Adolescent & Adult Literacy* 52.6 (Mar. 2009): 509–21. Print.

Lynch begins by reviewing various studies of adult literacy levels and their findings. She then moves to her argument: "It is critical that educators and researchers continue to explore the out-of-school literacy activities of low-income parents to support effective adult literacy teaching and learning as well as to gain a clearer understanding of the print literacy knowledge of children and adolescents" (510–11). Lynch's research included "38 randomly selected parents" (511) ages 20 to 29 from seven counties within one state. Lynch received the names of the parents from Head Start programs, and the participants, categorized as low income, were from urban, rural, and migrant communities. Lynch then interviewed each of the participants, noting that fifteen of them requested the interviews be conducted in Spanish. The interview questions focused on the participants' reading and writing engagements during the previous year. She found that the parents read a variety of items, including newsletters from the schools, calendars, magazines, and labels. Lynch argues that knowing the types of print experiences of adults gives literacy educators a basis for what is meaningful for their students. Once the students' skills improve, then their types of reading will change. She also found that the participants did not recognize the various literacy activities in which they engaged in their daily lives. Thus, reading materials need to be authentic for adult learners. — KKN

121   Massengill, Donita. "The Impact of Using Guided Reading to Teach Low-Literate Adults." *Journal of Adolescent & Adult Literacy* 47.7 (2004): 588–602. Print.

Massengill discusses her research with four low-literacy adults and her use of guided reading to help them improve their reading abilities. The four students ranged in age from 25 to 52 years. Students met with Massengill three times a week for one hour each time for three months. After detailing each student's progress and reading strategies, Massengill argues that guided reading is a good strategy to use with low-literate adults even though she used it with individuals instead of small groups as is done with young students. Even though the time period for the interventions was short, Massengill argues "that time resulted in positive reading gains" (600) and calls for further study of guided reading with low-literate adults. — KKN

122   Padak, Nancy D., and Bryan A. Bardine. "Engaging Readers and Writers in Adult Education Contexts." *Journal of Adolescent & Adult Literacy* 48.2 (2004): 126–37. Print.

Padak and Bardine begin by reviewing definitions of literacy and then argue that literacy is more than skill; it also includes choosing to read and write. They reviewed multiple literacy programs and found that they focused on basic skills, not authentic literacy. The authors then discuss the Recommended Trade Books Project, which promotes authentic literature to be used with adult learners. The books are reviewed and recommended by ABE, literacy teachers, and program directors. Additionally, the group develops a list of ideas on how to use the books with adult learners. Padak and Bardine provide a description of various strategies used with the books and a list of some of the books. They discuss some of the concerns with the book selections, which include children's books and picture books. However, they note that teachers found the students liked the books. Padak and Bardine then discuss the writing aspect of literacy, citing the Language Experience Approach (LEA) as used with adult learners. The authors share several ways in which adult learners can develop their writing skills and include what they have written. — KKN

123   Padak, Nancy, and Gary Padak. "Writing Instruction for Adults: Present Practices and Future Directions." *Lifelong Learning: An Omnibus of Practice and Research* 12.3 (Nov. 1988): 4–7. Print.

Padak and Padak observed GED classes with adult basic literacy students after the writing requirement for the GED test was changed. The classes were held at different sites, including a large city and a semi-rural area. The authors also observed the training of the instructors. Padak and Padak found that less time was spent on writing activities than on reading and math activities, and the writing often focused on grammar and mechanics instead of actual writing. The few writing assignments that were used were related to employment skills or samples for the writing portion of the GED test. Padak and Padak recommend that literacy programs reevaluate their writing curricula to allot time for writing instruction that includes the writing process and actual writing.—KKN

124   Pannucci, Lynnette, and Sean A. Walmsley. "Supporting Learning-Disabled Adults in Literacy." *Journal of Adolescent & Adult Literacy* 50.7 (Apr. 2007): 540–46. Print.

In this study, Pannucci and Walmsley reviewed the records of parents with learning difficulties in an Even Start Family Literacy Program. Then the authors selected a list of ten successful persons with learning disabilities. From these two groups, Pannucci and Walmsley developed a list of characteristics displayed by learning-disabled adults. Based on these characteristics, the authors developed a list of best practices to use with learning-disabled adults. Finally, Pannucci and Walmsley provide a short list of implications that instructors need to remember when working with learning-disabled adults. They remind the readers that learning-disabled adults can be successful if they are in the right environment.—KKN

125   Pfahl, Nancy Lloyd, and Colleen Aalsburg Wiessner. "Creating New Directions with Story: Narrating Life Experience as Story in Community Adult Education Contexts." *Adult Learning* 18.3–4 (2007): 9–13. Print.

Acknowledging the importance of using narration when teaching adult learners, Pfahl and Wiessner argue that adult learners separate themselves from the stories they tell, which allows for critical and reflective examination. They state that when students tell their stories, they are motivated, committed to "new scripts," and learn "to act in different ways" (10). Instructors then need to help students find the relationship or connections between their experiences and interpretations of the experiences, thus making meaning of the experiences. Pfahl and Wiessner argue, "Using storytelling intentionally offers a powerful strategy for helping targeted populations of learners articulate, choose, and commit to more effective life options" (11). They then present six recursive processes of the intentional learning strategy (11). In their summary, Pfahl and Wiessner note that narrative learning helps students to creatively solve problems and stimulate new ways of thinking and acting.—KKN

126   Stino, Zandra H., and Barbara C. Palmer. "Motivating Women Offenders through Process-Based Writing in a Literacy Learning Circle." *Journal of Adolescent & Adult Literacy.* 43.4 (Nov. 1999): 282–91. Print.

This article discusses the experiences of Stino as a GED writing instructor at a rehabilitation center for women convicted of drug or alcohol abuse. The women were court ordered to be in the facility and attend classes. The women's reading and writing abilities varied. Stino used the writing process with the women as they read several books, wrote about their experiences, and discussed their writings with one another. At the end of the course, the students responded to a questionnaire about their learning and their experience in the course. Additionally, the students wrote three essays for the GED: weeks one, nine, and eighteen. These essays then were scored by outside readers who followed the GED guidelines for scoring. Stino and Palmer found that the majority of the women enjoyed their experience in the course and enjoyed the learning circles. The students overall made significant progress between the first two essays, but significant progress was not made between essays two and three. The article ends with ideas for future research. —KKN

127   Winn, Beth, Christopher H. Skinner, Renee Oliver, Andrea D. Hale, and Mary Ziegler. "The Effects of Listening While Reading and Repeated Reading on the Reading Fluency of Adult Learners." *Journal of Adolescent & Adult Literacy* 50.3 (2006): 196–205. Print.

Citing statistics on adult learners with basic skills, the authors discuss the importance of learning more about teaching reading fluency with adult learners. Previous research has shown that repeated reading (RR) and listening while reading (LWR) have been effective in increasing younger students' reading fluency. Therefore, the authors studied a small group of adults using the same reading strategies, and they found that the strategies also work with adults with deficits in their reading skills. However, they note that the study had only a few participants, and it did not focus on long-term results, so instructors should not generalize the results. —KKN

Writing and Reading in Undergraduate and Graduate College Programs

128   Ackerman, John M. "Postscript: The Assimilation and Tactics of Nate." In *Genre and Knowledge in Disciplinary Communication: Cognition/Culture/Power*. Ed. Carol Berkenkotter and Thomas Huckin. Mahwah, NJ: Erlbaum, 1995. 145–50. Print.

Having participated in a case study of one graduate student's writing (Carol Berkenkotter and Thomas Huckin. "Conventions, Conversation, and the Writer: Case Study of a Student in a Rhetoric PhD Program." *Research in the Teaching of English* [1988]), John Ackerman reveals that he was "Nate"—the research subject—and comments retrospectively on the study. Although not credited as an author of this report, he had actually participated in the analysis along with the two authors—a fact not included in the report because at that time, composition and rhetoric researchers "had not yet not published hybrid, collaborative research relationships" (149). Ackerman concludes that even though social science research may be informed by a rationalist/empiricist epistemology, these reports are interpretive, revealing as much about authors' belief systems as they do about the object being investigated. —BJG

129   Aronson, Anne. "Reversals of Fortune: Downward Mobility and the Writing of Nontraditional Students." *Teaching Working Class.* Ed. Sherry Lee Linkon. Amherst: U of Massachusetts P, 1999. 39–55. Print.

The author presents an analysis of student writing produced in an intermediate college writing class that she had taught at a midwestern university. Students enrolled were primarily nontraditional young adult and older adult students, reflecting the university's wider student demographic. Focusing on social class as a class theme, students read two books and wrote four essays. The author's analysis focuses on essays produced for two assignments: (1) an essay presenting the student's own conception of social class and (2) an analysis of how social class has influenced the student's own life. Although upward mobility stories are fairly common in print and are often used in composition classes (e.g., Mike Rose's *Lives on the Boundary* and Richard Rodriguez's *Hunger of Memory*), published downward mobility stories are harder to find and less frequently used in college writing courses. However, downward mobility stories often reflect the lives of nontraditional students. Such stories were incorporated into this course, both because they reflect the experiences of some nontraditional students and because students were being asked to analyze social class inequalities. The author analyzes the writing of three students who have experienced downward mobility. Two of these students—Lisa and Patrick—both recognize and avoid discussion of class inequality in their essays, unable to develop viable analyses. A third student, Charlie, ably presents a strong analysis of social class inequalities. Unlike Lisa and Patrick, Charlie does not possess a strong aspiration to sink a strong foothold in the middle class. On the basis of her analysis of all three students' writing, Aronson hypothesizes that a student's ideological tensions can affect that student's writing performances as strongly as can general writing competencies. In addition, she argues for teaching college students the literacy skills needed to negotiate inside institutions such as hospitals, government agencies, and employment offices—not so that they can avoid downward mobility but so that they can manage the situations they find themselves in when it affects their lives. —BJG

130   Belanger, Kelly, Linda Strom, and John Russo. "Critical Literacy and the Organizing Model of Unionism: Reading and Writing History at a Steelworkers' Union Hall." *Teaching Working Class.* Ed. Sherry Lee Linkon. Amherst: U of Massachusetts P, 1999. 168–78. Print.

The authors report on courses they taught in an associate's degree program established by Steelworkers' Local 1375 and Youngstown State

University. Working class students' needs and interests drove decisions about course schedules, course offerings, and curricula. Classes were offered twice a day in a steelworkers' union hall so that students could choose either an earlier class or a later one, depending on their work shifts. Students co-enrolled in two courses: a labor studies course taught by John Russo and a writing course taught by either Linda Strom or Kelly Belanger. The writing course offered in fall of 1995 involved students in reading and writing about a 1937 strike against Republic Steel Plants in three Ohio towns. Coincidentally, the steelworkers went on strike again in 1995, so students were not only studying a historical strike but were observing a strike unfolding in real time. While participating in strike-related activities, students wrote about their views of current and past strikes and their knowledge of unions. A colloquium hosted by the Ohio Historical Society offered presentations by 1937 steelworkers' union activists, a journalist who had covered the 1937 strike, and community members who felt the impact of that strike. This offering of multiple perspectives reflected the pedagogy students experienced in their courses: they conducted interviews, examined archives, and studied conflicting expert opinions on historical events. They read and worked through exercises in Vincent Ryan Ruggiero's *Beyond Feelings: A Guide to Critical Thinking* (Mayfield, 1995) in order to build critical literacies by starting with their own observations and experiences. Students considered the perspectives of both management and labor activists, engaged in critical analyses of events, and studied the processes by which histories are interpreted and written. What the authors considered most important was the emergence of a culture that valued the empowering influences of critical literacy education. — BJG

131 Coles, Nicholas, and Susan V. Wall. "Conflict and Power in the Reader-Responses of Adult Basic Writers." *College English* 49.3 (1987): 298–314. Print.

The authors describe the learning experiences and the writing of adults enrolled in evening sections of a college basic reading and writing course. Sixteen students were selected as representatives of a much larger pool of students. All identified themselves as workers, although they might not have been employed at the time of this study, and all were first-generation college students. Ten of the students were African American and ten were women. The authors describe these students as being committed to learning even though they often felt powerless in academic settings. The curriculum theme "work" and several books on this subject were assigned (e.g., Studs Terkel's *Working* and Richard Wright's *American Hunger*). In their analysis of students' reader-response writing, the authors note that their adult students often blamed workers for their own failures rather than analyzing larger political and economic contexts. This is one example of how an ideological belief can inform a student's reading. This observation leads the authors to argue that these working adult students' reading and writing difficulties are connected to their ideological beliefs and cannot be explained by their technical literacy competencies alone. The authors suggest that the best approach to helping students become more successful readers is to help students to engage with facts, experiences, and viewpoints depicted in texts. One way to engage students in reading texts is to invite them to identify with people that they are reading about. The authors conclude that existing reader-response theories do not adequately account for the reading experiences of working-class-adult basic readers and writers. Conflicts among cultures and ideologies must be accounted for in a reader response theory that accounts for the reading experiences of students described in this essay. — BJG

See: Richard Courage, "The Interaction of Public and Private Literacies" [81].

132   Ellis, Carol. "Developing Genre Discourse: Graduate Student Writing." Ed. Ben Rafoth. *A Tutor's Guide: Helping Writers One to One*. 2nd ed. Portsmouth, NH: Boynton/Cook Heinemann, 2005. 121–28. Print.

Although relatively few in number, graduate student writing centers are gaining ground in US higher education. Tutors assist graduate students with writing course assignments, dissertations, and journal articles as well as with preparing conference talk proposals. No matter what field they are studying, graduate students must acquire genre knowledge; tutors assist them in this endeavor. Graduate students must learn discipline-specific practices and standards while developing professional and academic identities. As a former graduate student herself, Ellis understands the all-absorbing experience of dissertation writing and the potential anxieties that can befall graduate students; a key role for graduate student writing tutors is to support students with maintaining motivation and developing self-confidence so that they can complete their dissertations. — BJG

133   Fiore, Kyle, and Nan Elsasser. "'Strangers No More': A Liberatory Literacy Curriculum." *College English* 44.2 (1982): 115–28. Print.

Relying on theories developed by Lev Vygotsky and Paulo Freire, Fiore, Elsasser, and two other researchers piloted their "Liberatory Literacy Curriculum" at the College of the Bahamas in 1979. The primary aim was for students to discuss and write about their cultural knowledge so that writing could become a means for intervening in one's own social environment. With support from a Fulbright Scholarship, Elsasser put into practice a new curriculum that is described in this essay. The four researchers believe their curriculum is a success because the adult female students who were at first intimidated by putting any words on a page ended the semester enthusiastically with a broad understanding of writing as a rhetorical practice. Moving beyond a focus on grammar and mechanics, the students decided to summarize their writings about marriage and gender relationships and then publish their work themselves. Elsasser's experiences were summarized and blended with copies of the students' writing in order to show how the students improved their communication skills and developed a new perception of writing, a perspective that gave them the confidence to analyze their relationships with men and to empower themselves. —LDB

134 Gaillet, Lynee Lewis. "Writing Program Administration in a 'Metropolitan University.'" *City Comp: Identities, Spaces, Practices*. Ed. Bruce McComiskey and Cynthia Ryan. Albany: State U of New York P, 2003. 172–88. Print.

A college writing program for Georgia State University (GSU) reflects the mission of "the metropolitan university" by integrating ethnographic research writing and public service into its curriculum. The term *metropolitan university* describes institutions that aim to create ties between college and community; once called "urban colleges," metropolitan universities tend to rely heavily on contingent faculty and commuter students. GSU seeks to establish relationships with the citywide community and to encourage public service while maintaining a traditional focus on research and teaching. GSU's students are older than students at more traditional colleges and universities: the average age of GSU's undergraduate and graduate students is 27. Thus, many students are nontraditional and working in their communities while attending GSU classes. The ethnographic writing project now being piloted in the GSU writing program allows students to choose communities in the city of Atlanta for participant-observer field research projects. This field research writing assignment reinforces the mission of metropolitan universities by fostering permeable boundaries between community and classroom and focusing on public service. It also strengthens students' involvement in their own learning because students are able to spend time researching and writing about communities that they want to learn about. The curriculum is framed by the idea that students can engage rhetorically with their communities to participate in improving them. Concepts such as civic rhetoric and public literacy inform the larger instructional aim of this curriculum. —BJG

See: Alice M. Gillam, "Returning Students' Ways of Writing: Implications for First-Year College Composition" [55].

135 Gleason, Barbara. "Connected Literacies of Adult Writers: Workplace Ethnographies in College Composition." *Multiple Literacies for the 21st Century*. Ed. Brian Huot, Beth Stroble, and Charles Bazerman. Cresskill, NJ: Hampton, 2004. 39–56. Print.

The author describes an ethnographic writing project designed for use in an adult-oriented college degree program and then analyzes three samples of students' workplace ethnographies. These case studies illustrate particular challenges faced by returning adult student writers: writing anxiety, lack of engagement, and lack of recent experience with academic genres and writing practice. They also illustrate the benefits of allowing returning adults to research and write about their own workplace communities: With their insider knowledge of their own workplaces, adult undergraduates can compose longer essays with greater confidence and fluency, use existing knowledge of workplace terms, and exploit prior knowledge of their own workplace communities while learning new research strategies and learning to write academic discourse. Classroom discussions of language form and use are supplemented by readings focusing on dialect, conversational patterns, and linguistic attitudes. Adult learning theory supporting this curriculum includes the claim that adults prefer projects whose practical value is apparent, the idea that student-centered classrooms work best for adults, and the view that adults are more likely to lean toward self-directed learning projects. Unlike young adult students, who practice academic reading and writing in order to develop future careers, older adult learners bring existing workplace literacies and linguistic practices to bear on their classroom-based academic writing development.—BJG

136   Gleason, Barbara. "Returning Adults to the Mainstream: Toward a Curriculum for Diverse Student Writers." *Mainstreaming Basic Writers: Politics and Pedagogies of Access.* Ed. Gerri McNenny and Sallyanne H. Fitzgerald. Mahwah, NJ: Erlbaum, 2001. 121–44. Print.

Arguing that noncredit remedial courses are undesirable for working adult undergraduates, who often attend college while working full-time and aspire to complete college degrees as quickly as possible, Gleason proposes a flexible writing curriculum comprised of writing projects that can accommodate the needs of inexperienced writers and the strengths of experienced writers. Assignments include (1) a language/literacy autobiography, (2) an oral and written storytelling project, (3) a student interview report, and (4) an ethnographic research project. All of these assignments involve both students and their instructors in learning about students' histories as workers, students, family members, neighbors, church members, and self-directed learners. Furthermore, their ages, cultures, languages, and interests all surface when students interview each other and write reports based on the interviews. What instructors can learn directly from their students, Gleason argues, is far more consequential than what they can learn from the numerical scores associated with placement tests and exit exams. To illustrate the value of this curriculum, Gleason presents two case studies of individuals who represent the weakest student and the strongest student in one class. Ultimately, Gleason argues, a flexible, well-designed writing curriculum can serve the needs of both inexperienced and experienced writers, who can learn side by side in one mainstreamed writing course. —BJG

137   Gleason, Barbara. "Something of Great Constancy: Storytelling, Story Writing, and Academic Literacy." *Attending to the Margins: Writing, Research, and Teaching on the Front Lines.* Ed. Michelle H. Kells and Valerie M. Balester. Portsmouth, NH: Boynton/Cook Heinemann, 1999. 97–113. Print.

Inspired by Deborah Tannen's research on oral and literate strategies, Gleason developed a series of three tasks for adult undergraduate writers. The sequenced assignment draws initially on students' oral fluencies and then leads to writing a formal essay. Students first tell short personal or family stories to a small group of their peers, audio-record their stories, write a version of the same story, and then transcribe their oral stories. The assignment culminates with a discussion of the differences between students' oral and written stories and a brief lesson on features of conversational spoken language (e.g., frequent use of *and*, pauses, gap fillers, and the present tense) versus features of formal written language (e.g., use of complete sentences, more descriptive adjectives, and the past tense to report events that occurred in the past). Students then write an analysis of the oral version versus the written version of their stories. In addition to discovering a good deal about their presentational styles and use of language as speakers and storytellers, most students discover that they prefer the written stories and their experiences as writers to the oral versions of their stories and their experiences as storytellers. — BJG

138   Gleason, Barbara. "Urban Literacies and the Ethnographic Process: Composing Communities at the Center for Worker Education." *City Comp: Identities, Spaces, Practices*. Ed. Bruce McComiskey and Cynthia Ryan. Albany: State U of New York P, 2003. 189–202. Print.

Arguing that writing ethnography encourages use of existing rhetorical strengths to acquire academic discourse, Gleason describes a field research project assigned in classes for working adult undergraduates at The City College of New York. Her students select communities, request permission to gain entry, observe and write descriptive field notes, interview informants, and collect primary documents such as newsletters, memos, and reports. Students transform their primary source materials to more formal academic essays that include summary, quotation, analysis, and citation. The City of New York provides a vast network of possible urban communities, one of which is described in this essay. "Audrey" researched a group of patrol volunteers for the Tompkins Housing Project of Bedford-Stuyvesant, Brooklyn. As a volunteer herself, Audrey's rhetorical aim was two-fold: to describe the work of these volunteer patrollers and to honor the good work that they do for their neighbors in a large residential community. Audrey also wanted to produce error-free writing. In a letter of introduction to her instructor, Audrey stated that she was "tired of earning low grades due to poor grammar" (196). This ethnographic research project allowed Audrey and many other students to practice academic writing in the context of familiar neighborhood and work communities. — BJG

139   Hansman, Catherine A., and Arthur L. Wilson. "Teaching Writing in Community Colleges: A Situated View of How Adults Learn to Write in Computer-Based Writing Classrooms." *Community College Review* 26.1 (1998): 21–42. Print.

Although many writing instructors teach composition as a sequential process, Hansman and Wilson argue, "[T]he very processes that are supposed to help adults write may become obstacles to their writing"

(22) because adults need to learn how to write in a context evolving from their activities and social culture. The authors believe other researchers fail to take into account the way computers, activities in the classroom, and cultural structure influence the learning and teaching processes. Too many instructors provide guidelines for writing and expect that students will easily transfer what they have learned from one writing task to another. Those teachers believe the students can learn to write in the same way they would learn to cook: from following the steps in a recipe. After reviewing other pedagogical models, Hansman and Wilson provide a detailed discussion of their own situated learning model, basing it on their study of adult community college students enrolled in a composition course taught in a mediated computer classroom. Their objective is to examine how both the tools and the social interaction influence the learning experience. Their research methodology included classroom observation as well as semi-structured, audiotaped interviews. Major findings indicate that students felt empowered by their use of computers and believed that this technology allowed them to be better writers. The use of computers also motivated them to develop their own individualized writing processes. Finally, learning to use the computers and the word processing programs caused students to interact in a social manner, which caused them to engage in discourse relevant to their writing. —LDB

140   Haynes-Burton, Cynthia. "'Thirty-Something Students': Concerning Transitions in the Writing Center." *The Writing Lab Newsletter* 18.8 (Apr. 1994): 3–4. Print.

The author argues that composition is a field that is essentially marked by change, rather than a field defined by a stable center. One recent change affecting composition is the increased presence of older adults on US college campuses. Writing centers can help these older students by hiring older tutors as well as tutors that reflect a college's student demographics generally. A second way that writing centers can assist older students is to establish tutorials that enable students to practice writing as an alternative to enrolling in first-year composition classes. The author contends that writing centers are particularly well positioned to meet the needs of older returning students and that they should be utilized for this purpose. —BJG

141   Hollis, Karyn L. "Liberating Voices: Autobiographical Writing at the Bryn Mawr Summer School for Women Workers, 1921–1938." *College Composition and Communication* 45.1 (1994): 31–60. Print.

Hollis examines the autobiographical narratives of adult learners attending the Bryn Mawr Summer School for Women Workers from 1921 to 1938. The summer sessions encouraged working-class women to experience college in the way that more affluent teenagers did during the academic year. Recording their perceptions of field trips and lectures with distinguished professors and notable leaders such as Eleanor Roosevelt and Walter Reuther, the adult learners developed detailed memoirs of their experiences, thoughts, and feelings as well as their fears about their emerging aspirations for the future. Hollis's objective is to analyze the discursive subjectivity of the narratives by linking it to contemporary composition research on gender and autobiography. She concludes that a comparison of these historical narratives with similar writing in the twenty-first century may show that women in both time periods focus more on human relationships than men do. She also finds that gender is a social construction that individuals develop through their cultural beliefs, values, and attitudes. —LDB

142   Hollis, Karyn L. *Liberating Voices: Writing at the Bryn Mawr Summer School for Women Workers*. Carbondale: U of Southern Illinois P, 2004. Print.

In this book, Hollis documents women workers of diverse ethnicities who enrolled in a special summer course at Bryn Mawr College during the 1920s and 1930s. They read, wrote, and spoke on domestic themes (e.g., family and childhood) and on public themes (e.g., unions and work). They expressed their viewpoints and described their experiences while composing autobiographical narratives, research reports, essays, and poems. One teacher routinely compiled her students' writing in books. Students were encouraged to publish their work in a magazine called *Shop and School*, on posters, and in scrapbooks. The writing production and publication orientation of this summer school leads Hollis to term the dominant pedagogy "materialist." While acquiring a liberal arts education, the students were also preparing to return to their workplaces with greater self-confidence, critical insight into their social circumstances, and expertise as orators and writers. Their education empowered them intellectually, politically, and personally. —BJG

See: Mary Kay Jackman, "Where the Personal Becomes Professional: Stories from Reentry Adult Women Learners about Family, Work, and School" [88].

143   Johnson, Helen. "The PhD Student as an Adult Learner: Using Reflective Practice to Find and Speak in Her Own Voice." *Reflective Practice* 2.1 (2001): 53–63. Print.

Johnson uses an autobiographical approach to examine her situation as an adult PhD student dealing with life experiences that created writer's block. She analyzes how adult learners may benefit from distinguishing between reflection *in* action and reflection *on* action. In her literature review, Johnson defines reflective practice and shows how PhD students are typically left to set and complete a task, which must then be written up in an omniscient voice. Describing her own life experiences involving catastrophic events in her family, she shows how an inability to write in this required omniscient manner can be overcome by specific reflective strategies. These strategies encourage the adult writer to emerge and move forward with the PhD project. Johnson's research demonstrates that the adult learner participants in this study used reflective strategies successfully both inside and outside the classroom.

Johnson focuses on a conflict between using the omniscient voice and narrating subjective events for adult students who are burdened with personal tragedies. —LDB

144   Kiely, Denis O., and Lisa Swift. "Casualties of War: Combat Trauma and the Return of the Combat Veteran." *Teaching English in the Two-Year College* 36.4 (2009): 357–64. Print.

Kiely and Swift discuss how they use *The Iliad* and *The Odyssey* in their courses as ways for veterans to share their war experiences, which also helps other students understand combat. They discuss the tragic ways some veterans return from the Iraq and Afghanistan wars and how these students need the chance to share their stories. The authors find using *The Iliad* and *The Odyssey* is therapeutic for the returning veterans. The essay includes the parallels between the stories and the experiences of the veterans, and it relates studies and books that discuss the parallels. —KKN

145   Leonhardy, Galen. "Transformations: Working with Veterans in the Composition Classrooms." *Teaching English in the Two-Year College* 36.4 (2009): 339–52. Print.

Relating Victor Villanueva's writings of being a veteran in a college classroom, Leonhardy discusses his experiences as a veteran in college and as a teacher of veterans in college. He notes that the Department of Veterans Affairs estimates the number of veterans receiving education benefits at half a million at the time of this article. Leonhardy proceeds to compare the experiences of veterans from different eras returning to college. Then he notes that many veterans really need basic writing courses, but they passed the composition test when entering college, so they are in first-year composition classes. Following this discussion, Leonhardy discusses the progression of the writing of the veterans in his courses and what instruction veterans need. He urges instructors to work toward inclusion of the veterans and their experiences, even if the veterans initially share their experiences in a journal that is not read by everyone. Leonhardy then shares ideas for instructional strategies, including teachers completing the same course assignments as the students and allowing students, especially veterans, to choose their own writing topics. —KKN

See: Yongyan Li, "Apprentice Scholarly Writing in a Community of Practice: An Intraview of an NNES Graduate Student Writing a Research Article" [90].

See: Michael J. Michaud, "The 'Reverse Commute': Adult Students and the Transition from Professional to Academic Literacy" [91].

See: Mary Miritello, "Teaching Writing to Adults: Examining Assumptions and Revising Expectations for Adult Learners in the Writing Class" [92].

See: Michelle Navarre Cleary, "Anxiety and the Newly Returned Adult Student" [93].

146   Navarre Cleary, Michelle. "What WPAs Need to Know to Prepare New Teachers to Work with Adult Students." *Writing Program Administration: Journal of the Council for Writing Program Administrators* 32.1 (Fall/Winter 2008): 113–28. Print.

Navarre Cleary reviews the literature on adult college composition students. Her goal is to provide Writing Program Administrators (WPAs) with the information they need to prepare new teachers to work with the growing number of adults returning to college. She acknowledges that adult students are diverse, but says the scholarship consistently identifies them as more anxious, motivated, busy, and experienced than younger students. She shows how these four characteristics account for common misconceptions about adult students that can lead to teaching that does not build on their strengths or address their needs. Drawing upon the scholarship and her teaching experience, she offers suggestions for teaching adults that takes these characteristics into account. The "Teaching Writing to Adults: A Handbook for New Composition Teachers" on *CompFAQs* supplements this article. — MNC

147   Navarre Cleary, Michelle, Suzanne Sanders-Betzold, Polly Hoover, and Peggy St. John. "Working with Wikis in Writing-Intensive Classes." *Kairos: A Journal of Rhetoric, Technology, and Pedagogy*. 14.1 (Fall 2009): n. pag. Web. 11 Dec. 2010.

Noting that there is much hyperbole and little research on the value of wikis for teaching writing, particularly to nontraditional students, the authors report on their use of wikis in three writing-intensive, team-taught classes that combined students from a community college with returning adult students at a university. They found wikis very effective as a teaching tool to distribute information, promote collaboration, and build a sense of community in classes initially divided by the students' different life experiences. Using a wiki for collaborative writing projects, instructors observed students engaged in and seeming to learn from metacognitive discussions about their writing on the wiki. However, while student writing skills improved in each of these classes, the authors could not isolate wikis as a cause of this improvement. The authors assess faculty as well as student learning, showing how their use of wikis improved through collaboration and iteration. This wiki text includes a discussion of the authors' context, research methods, and findings as well as an annotated bibliography, each author's reflections on working with wikis, and examples of how students used the wikis, including an annotated group research paper that illustrates the author's findings. — MNC

148   Pies, Timothy. "Reducing Anxiety in the Adult Writer." *Adult Learning* 5.3 (1994): 14–15, 18. Print.

Pies reports that a study at his college confirmed research indicating that adult students tend to be more anxious than younger students and particularly anxious about writing. Motivated by these findings, Pies offers six suggestions for reducing anxiety in adult students: make lessons more engaging by learning about students' interests and experiences; let students leverage their experiential learning through prior learning assessment; similarly, show students how they can use what they know in their courses; assign early low-stakes writing; teach writing as a process; and give feedback that praises strengths, offers constructive criticism, and focuses on a few major issues. His background in adult education and Robert Sommer's *Teaching Writing to Adults* inform his suggestions. —MNC

See: Randall Popken, "Adult Writers, Interdiscursive Linking, and Academic Survival" [95].

149   Prior, Paul. "Contextualizing Writing and Response in a Graduate Seminar." *Written Communication* 8.3 (1991): 267–310. Print.

Reporting on a qualitative study of graduate student writers and their writing in a graduate education seminar, Prior analyzes a professor's communications about his writing assignments and examines graduate students' understandings and negotiations of those assignments, as revealed by their writing, interviews, and responses to questionnaires. The graduate students, mostly in their 30s and 40s, were pursuing either an MA or a PhD. Of fifteen students, eight were writing in English as a second language. Course writing assignments included a research proposal, a written critique of a PhD dissertation or an MA thesis, written critiques of two additional studies, and research on a proposed topic. Prior observes a need for "an expanded research agenda to investigate natural literacy processes, to attend to long-term, self-directed, recursive processes of reading and writing that writers undertake and how those processes contribute to the production of a particular text at a particular time" (296). In their interviews, students reported that factors outside the course partially affected their research proposals, which pointed back to their prior life experiences and forward to future plans to write an MA thesis or a doctoral dissertation. The author concludes that "the emergence of continuity in academic work . . . may be one of the characteristics that distinguishes graduate study, especially at advanced levels, from undergraduate work" (295). Prior concludes that writers compose texts in historical and social contexts with personal meanings and motives, and that in order to learn about writers and their writing, we need to observe writers working in natural contexts rather than relying solely on formal or structural analyses of their texts. —BJG

150   Quinn, Edward. *Responsibilities: A College Reader*. New York: Harper & Row, 1987. Print.

Quinn's college reader is designed for use in college writing classes enrolling both young adult and mature, working adult undergraduates. Dedicated to past and present students of the City College of New York's Center for Worker Education (CWE), the book contains texts written by two former CWE instructors, Leonard Kriegel and Edward Rivera, and seven CWE students whose average age is 41. In an introductory essay, Quinn discusses *adult learners* and *maturity*, calling attention to experience and motivation as two key aspects of learning in adulthood. He advises students to become active readers who write in journals or annotate texts and revise for meaning and style. A collection of essays by published authors and student writers is thematically organized in seven sections titled "Lifelong Learning," "Starting Over," "Modern Times: Past and Present," "The Job," "Male/Female," "Parenting," and "Cultural Contexts." A short editor's introduction presents the collected essays for each section. In his introduction to "Lifelong Learning," Quinn writes, "We learn more from experience than from the classroom, but what we learn in a formal school setting can add depth and dimension to the practical knowledge we acquire in everyday life" (9). — BJG

151   Smith, Beatrice Quarshie. "Genre, Medium, and Learning to Write: Negotiating Identities, Enacting School-Based Literacies in Adulthood." *Journal of College Reading and Learning* 34.2 (2004): 75–96. Print.

Focusing on technology and adult learners, Smith expands the concept of literacy narratives to include a sub-genre she dubs "technology autobiographies" (79). She studied eighteen community college students, ages 20 to 54, using technological literacy surveys and the technology autobiographies. The survey introduced the technology autobiography assignment, the first major project in a freshman-level reading/writing course taught within a networked environment. Smith analyzes these technology autobiographies thematically, focusing on three categories: how students engage and write about memory, construct identities of self to negotiate authority in both the social and academic world, and represent technology and its relation to literacy. Her discussion of these categories applies not only to technology autobiographies but also to literacy narratives generally and the value and purpose of the larger genre. Three conclusions emerge from Smith's thematic analysis: (1) The technology autobiography is useful for adult learners because it requires them to represent themselves in a technological environment. (2) The narratives suggest ways of thinking about teaching with technology and suggest the importance of considering three areas where technology is present in students' lives: recreation, education, and daily life on or off the job. In fact, the student work Smith discusses expands our definition of "technology" to include not only computers, video games, and cell phones, but also television, home appliances like refrigerators, electricity, photographs, and even reading, writing, and education itself. (3) And, perhaps most important, students' stories help teachers "interrogate the social, cultural, and economic interests . . . [that] construct the cultural narratives about literacy education and technologies in the new economy" (93). — KSU

152   Sommers, Nancy. "Revision Strategies of Student Writers and Experienced Adult Writers." *College Composition and Communication* 31.4 (1980): 378–88. Print. Rpt. in *Landmark Essays on Writing Process*. Ed. Sondra Perl. New York: Routledge, 1995. 75–83. Print.

Sommers presents her case study of student writers and experienced adult writers. First, she discusses how revision has been defined by various compositionists. Then she summarizes the revision strategies of each group of writers. Sommers found that student writers were more concerned with vocabulary and finding the best word when revising and that they think of revising as "redoing" (79). They want to avoid repetition. Student writers also revise their introductory paragraphs and thesis statements. Sommers argues that student writers focus on these aspects of writing because they are what the students have been taught to focus on. In contrast, experienced adult writers revise to shape their writing and to connect with their readers. Sommers states that the focus of this revising is to "resolve the dissonance they sense in their writing" (82). She also argues that the experienced writers' revising process demonstrates that writing is not linear as some instructors present it, but student writers attempt to stay within the guidelines presented to them. —KKN

See: Merle O'Rourke Thompson, "The Returning Student: Writing Anxiety and General Anxiety" [67].

153   Uehling, Karen S. "Older and Younger Adults Writing Together: A Rich Learning Community." *The Writing Instructor* 15.2 (1996): 61–69. Print.

Uehling begins by examining Malcolm Knowles's theory of "andragogy," the teaching of adults, and "pedagogy," a term Knowles argues derived historically from the teaching of children. Uehling compares andragogy with pedagogy, focusing on Knowles's six assumptions about learning: (1) the need to know, (2) the learner's self-concept, (3) the role of experience, (4) readiness to learn, (5) orientation to learning, and (6) motivation. Uehling notes that ultimately Knowles linked andragogy with a student-centered approach and pedagogy with a teacher-directed approach, maintaining that neither model is inherently good or bad, adult or childlike, but rather that the two models represent a range of teaching/learning choices. Uehling then describes the natural affinity between writing theory and adult learning theory; she characterizes a beginning writing course based on adult learning theory as a "process-oriented writing workshop or a reading/writing seminar emphasizing invention, revision, and final editing for mechanics" (65) and applies Knowles's six andragogical principles to teaching beginning writing instruction. Uehling supports mixed-age writing classrooms, arguing that younger and older students are more alike than different, especially in community colleges or urban universities where most students balance many responsibilities, such as work, family, and school, and asserts that mixed-age classes offer a richness missing when traditional-age students are segregated from older learners. —KSU

154   Uehling, Karen S. *Starting Out or Starting Over: A Guide for Writing.* New York: HarperCollins, 1992. Print.

A composition textbook designed for nontraditional students and adult learners, *Starting Out or Starting Over* simultaneously presents practical advice for students enrolled in college classes and a developmental writing curriculum for teachers of introductory college writing courses. In the ten chapters comprising this book, Uehling integrates adult learning theory and practical considerations for adult learners with writing strategies and projects informed by composition scholarship, rhetorical theory, and linguistics. A bibliography of cited works at the end of the book reveals a well-informed textbook drawing from scholarship in adult learning, writing pedagogy, composition research, linguistics, and rhetoric. Although designed for use in a college writing class for undergraduates, the book presents a clear and carefully explained overview of composing process theory and pedagogy equally useful for readers who are learning about composition and rhetoric as a professional discipline and those who wish to teach writing to adults. Each chapter contains multiple samples of writing produced by nontraditional young adult students and mature adult learners, all of which illustrate specific writing strategies, topics, and issues of concern to writers and readers in introductory college classes. Also common to all chapters is a section titled "Angles of Vision," which invites readers to explore topics from multiple perspectives. Collaborative learning and writing activities appear alongside individual writing projects in every chapter. While most of the book's ten chapters focus on writing, chapter 2 addresses specific issues faced by college students who are starting college as nontraditional students (working while attending college) and adult learners who are either starting college for the first time or reentering college classrooms. Several chapters include sections on grammar and style useful for editing language and punctuation. A strong focus on invention, revision, and editing strongly situates this textbook in the tradition of 1970s and 1980s composing process scholarship. — BJG

Writing and Reading in ELL Programs

155   Auerbach, Elsa. *Adult ESL/Literacy from the Community to the Community: A Guidebook for Participatory Literacy Training.* Mahwah, NJ: Erlbaum, 1996. Print.

Both a report on the challenges and successes of a community-based adult ESL and literacy program and a guide to creating a participatory program of this nature, this handbook approaches its topic with deep enthusiasm. "Community" is more than a descriptive term for Auerbach and her collaborators; it is a way of viewing the teachers, interns, and learners who engaged in teaching and learning. Auerbach describes an adult literacy curricular model with four key features: "A meaning-based culturally variable view of literacy; a participatory approach to literacy instruction and training; a native language literacy for adult learners with little prior schooling; [and] training and leadership development of community instructors" (8). The adult literacy program model involved training interns, who then also led classes. Content for the classes came in part from the students; thus, their participation was central to the curriculum and to their learning. Citing Paulo Freire's theories on the potential to empower learners, Auerbach and associates argue for the participatory process: "In participatory education, transforming teacher-learner roles is central to enabling learners to assume more control of the direction of their lives. Education becomes a context for understanding and challenging the forces that maintain their powerlessness" (55). Resistance from interns and students is also documented: learned expectations of classrooms and curricula sometimes conflicted with the participatory educational model. —SFL

156   Baitinger, Katerina. "Engaging Adult Learners in the Writing/ESL Classroom." *College Quarterly* 8.1 (Winter 2005): n. pag. Web. 14 Dec. 2010.

The author contends that many students today do not take responsibility for their education and are passive learners. Nevertheless, educators must try to find creative means to engage their students. There are two basic groups of students: traditional students and nontraditional students. Traditional students have little life experience, while nontraditional students have a wealth of life experience and often are accustomed to holding positions of power. Since these students are more likely to walk away if the courses don't meet their expectations, educators must become more learner-centered in their approaches to teaching. Syllabus negotiation is one approach that instructors can use to partner with students and take their life experiences into consideration. Group work also should be included since many adults don't have the time to pursue traditional forms of study. Group work "may develop positive peer relationships among learners, which in many cases are more important and have a much greater influence on learning than teacher-learner relationships." Instructors also should consider holding class meetings outdoors and providing snacks since this will help create relationships between students and teachers. A related consideration is that many adult students lack confidence, so care should be taken to make them feel safe in the learning environment. Writing activities ideally will be highly structured in order to reduce students' anxieties and increase success. Teachers also can ease student anxiety by using journal writing and other informal approaches to writing. In this context, minilessons on grammar issues evident in students' writing can be offered. Baitinger further argues that reading and writing activities should be situated in recognizable contexts. Students will perform better if they are reading and writing about, for example, a cultural event with which they are familiar. The principle of learning in context also applies to the study of students' areas of academic interest. —TBP

157   Currie, Pat, and Ellen Cray. "ESL Literacy: Language Practice or Social Practice?" *Journal of Second Language Writing* 13.2 (2004): 111–32. Print.

Working with teachers and learners in the Language Instruction for Newcomers to Canada program, Currie and Cray studied how teachers and learners understand what writing means and what it means to be literate. Their study included interviews with teachers and students, as well as classroom observations. The adult learners ranged in age from 19 to 50 and were from various countries with varying levels of education. Currie and Cray asked the learners what types of writing they did outside of class so as to establish their real-world writing practices. The writing tended to be basic—notes for children's absences from school, completion of forms, and writing notes, for instance. The writing they did in the classrooms—grammar skills, reading comprehension, and copying other writings—did not relate to the writing the students did outside of the classroom. Therefore, the literacy practices of the students in their real-world writing was not taught in the classroom but was learned in the community and at home. In interviews with teachers, Currie and Cray found that the teachers believed that learning to write meant control over morphology and spelling. The teachers saw writing as language practice, and they did not know the types of writing the students did outside the classroom. Their instructional strategies were based on preconceived ideas of what the students needed and how language is taught. Interestingly, most of the teachers disliked how they were teaching writing, so they did not focus on it in the classes. Another important note is that the program has set requirements for each level of language learning, and these requirements support a traditional approach to language learning, such as the approach that the teachers use. Currie and Cray call for literacy education that emphasizes the social so that students understand why and for whom they are writing.—KKN

158   DelliCarpini, Margo. "Early Reading Development in Adult ELLs." *Academic Exchange Quarterly* 10.2 (2006): 192–96. Print.

DelliCarpini researched the skills that adult English language learners (ELLs) need to learn to read in English. Studies on ELLs have focused on phonological awareness (PA) with children, but few have researched PA of ELLs with low or nonexistent reading skills. DelliCarpini argues that most adult ELL programs focus on helping ELLs learn to read and speak for work or life skills but not on teaching them how to decode. She continues to argue that PA skills take time to develop, and these skills are directly related to decoding. She states that adult ELLs expand their reading skills in a similar manner as children do. DelliCarpini also argues that adult ELL programs need to reevaluate their curriculum to address the time needed for adult ELLs to learn and to develop teaching strategies to lessen the learners' frustrations.—KKN

159   Jungkang, Kim. "A Community within the Classroom: Dialogue Journal Writing of Adult ESL Learners." *Adult Basic Education* 15.1 (2005): 21–32. Print.

The instructional practice of using dialogue journal writing as a collaborative tool to teach adult ESL learners to write is the focus of a research study conducted by Jungkang. Journal writing is commonly used in adult literacy programs. Research studies show that it is beneficial because it creates authentic learning as well as student engagement. Jungkang's goal in performing her research study was to show other educators that dialogue journal writing can help teachers and learners to create a sense of community within a classroom. Her focus is unique because she uses journal writing to be shared with classmates, whereas journals are more often read by teachers. Learner-centered dialogue journal writing in a diverse classroom can cause adult students to improve their writing skills because they are more eager to share experiential dialogues with people challenged by similar problems. Jungkang emphasizes that dialogue writing in this study was not simply one method of learning. It instead provided "a meaningful living and learning context of the learners in the classroom" (29).—LDB

160   Larrotta, Clarena. "Inquiry in the Adult Classroom: An ESL Literacy Experience." *Adult Learning* 18.3–4 (2007): 25–29. Print.

Larrotta illustrates the effectiveness of what she terms "inquiry cycles," in which students "ask questions that are relevant to them, collect data to answer their questions, present findings, and start a new cycle by formulating a new question derived from the original question" (25). Based on Knowles's principles of andragogy and Freire's dialogic approach to fostering literacy, inquiry cycles engage students by allowing them to pursue authentic learning through gathering information relevant to their own lives and interests. Larrotta implemented inquiry cycles in an adult ESL literacy class of seventeen students and studied four students in particular to determine how this ability to guide their own course of study enhanced their learning. Students reported at times being overwhelmed by all of the information they found but were more engaged and worked beyond the assignment requirements, reporting that reading had become "fun" (28).—SFL

161   Pappamihiel, N. Eleni, Takayuki Nishimata, and Florin Mihai. "Timed Writing and Adult English-Language Learners: An Investigation of First Language Use in Invention Strategies." *Journal of Adolescent & Adult Literacy* 51.5 (Feb. 2008): 386–94. Print.

Noting that many universities and colleges require English language learners (ELLs) to pass English competency tests to enter school and that many of these tests require timed writing, Pappamihiel, Nishimata, and Mihai's research considered whether it was better for ELLs to write their inventions in their native languages, or if it was better to use English during the entire writing process. The authors' research was based on Cummins's Common Underlying Proficiency Hypothesis and on their own belief that writing is a generative process. They argue that the writing process taught in the classroom is difficult to use in timed writing situations, but the invention step is an important one in these situations. The authors then review past studies on the use of a first language in the invention stage of writing. A key finding is that these studies did not focus on timed writings. In this study of participants in an intensive English language learning program, adult ELLs wrote two different samples for two different timed essays in English. For one essay, they wrote the brainstorming in their native language, and for another, they wrote the brainstorming in English. The completed essays then were scored by two different instructors who used an analytic method. Samples of the writing are provided in the article. The research revealed that lower-level English language learners did better when they used English rather than a native language in the invention stage while those with higher levels of English proficiency were not affected positively or negatively by using a native language in the invention stage of a timed writing task. The authors recommend that instructors encourage lower-level English language learners to complete all phases of writing in English during timed writing situations and that all practice topics be embedded in real contexts. —KKN

Instructors of Adults and Instructional Approaches

Instructors and Instructor Preparation

162 Aronson, Anne, Craig Hansen, and Brian Nerney. "Introduction to the Special Issue of *The Writing Instructor*: Undergraduate Learners and the Teaching of Writing." *The Writing Instructor* 15.2 (1996): 51–58. Print.

This essay introduces a special theme issue of *The Writing Instructor*, edited by Aronson, Hansen, and Nerney, on adult learners and writing instruction. The issue focuses on how adults challenge assumptions about learners and writing pedagogy and includes both research articles and brief narratives by adult students. The editors ask, "How would the questions compositionists ask change if we threw age differences into the mix?" (52) After summarizing basic adult learning theory, Aronson, Hansen, and Nerney discuss key issues that adult learners bring to the classroom. These include mainstreaming and basic writing; possible inexperience with technology and resulting anxiety; awareness of the importance of revision from work experience; textbooks that largely address younger students' concerns; desire for instruction that allows for varied learning styles and uses varied media, not just text; and motivation for learning that may be vocational and pragmatic, particularly within the mixed-age classroom.—KSU

See: Alisa Belzer, "What Are They Doing in There? Case Studies of Volunteer Tutors and Adult Literacy Learners: Volunteer Tutors and Adult Literacy Learners Face a Number of Challenges as They Work Together" [70].

163 Brookfield, Stephen. "Through the Lens of Learning: How the Visceral Experience of Learning Reframes Teaching." *Using Experience for Learning*. Ed. David Boud, Ruth Cohen, and David Walker. Berkshire, UK: SRHE and Open UP; New York: McGraw, 1993. 21–32. Print.

Arguing that educators can gain meaningful insights about their own teaching practices by engaging in self-reflective discussions with other teachers, Brookfield outlines an instructional approach that encourages adult educators to scrutinize their informal theories of teaching in a collective learning experience. While working in small groups, instructors identify assumptions about teaching that they most agree on and then test these assumptions by talking about their own relevant experiences. They then analyze the degree to which the assumptions are context-bound and whether the assumptions about teaching can transfer to other contexts. In so doing, teachers work toward developing and revising their own theories of teaching. — BJG

164 Clarke, Lauren E., and Trent E. Gabert. "Faculty Issues Related to Adult Degree Programs." *Developing and Delivering Adult Degree Programs*. Ed. James P. Pappas and Jerry Jerman. Hoboken, NJ: Wiley, 2004. 31–40. Print. New Directions in Adult and Continuing Education 103.

Arguing that incongruences exist between adult student needs, institutional norms, and faculty preparation, Clarke and Gabert discuss andragogical points of view, trends in teacher training, professional development, and hiring practices affecting faculty roles in both traditional higher education and adult degree programs. The teacher-centered model is part of the wider philosophical orientation underpinning views of traditionally educated faculty members. In contrast, successful adult educators are often characterized as facilitators of transformational learning, a reflective practice that conflicts with the model prescribed by traditional institutions of higher education. The student-centered model features decentralized, collaborative learning environments and incorporates adults' background knowledge and experiences into instruction and course design. Studies cited by the authors suggest that formal postsecondary education for adult educators does little to inspire student-centered views of teaching and practice. Rather, many adult programs within traditional institutions favor normative practices over transformational approaches. The focus in traditional institutions is mainly on research and teaching traditional students, and mentoring by tenured and more experienced faculty serve to maintain this status quo. Citing other studies, the authors report that new teachers receive minimal teaching preparation and minimal professional development related to methods for instructing adult and nontraditional students. The authors argue that adjunct and part-time faculty may be good candidates for teaching nontraditional students due to their flexible work schedules. Part-time faculty may also view retraining in adult education theory and practice as an opportunity to gain more professional experience. Clarke and Gabert argue that ideal faculty candidates possess terminal degrees, teaching experience, interest in facilitating collaborative learning, and knowledge of adult education research. Teachers with these credentials help schools meet accreditation standards and help students mesh academic knowledge and life experience. Both the demand for adult programs and a need for appropriately prepared faculty are likely to increase, as many adults view these programs as directly related to career development and advancement. At the same time, factors such as shifts in educational funding, teacher supply-and-demand, reorganization of American universities, tenure, and other faculty incentives are likely to come under close scrutiny. — TS

165 Fleming, Cheryl Torok, and J. Bradley Garner. *Brief Guide for Teaching Adult Learners*. Marion, IN: Triangle, 2009. Print.

As a concise teachers' guide, this book synthesizes scholarship on adult learning theory and suggestions for teaching adults. Case studies of classroom scenarios invite readers to respond to provocative situations and consider theories of andragogy, self-directed learning, experiential learning, transformational learning, and constructivism in chapter 1. After reporting criteria used to identify nontraditional students by the National Center for Educational Statistics, Fleming and Garner introduce the concept of learning outcomes as statements of desired changes in students' knowledge, skills, and dispositions and present questions that adult learners tend to ask. For example, adult learners want to know why they are required to learn particular topics or to engage in learning activities, which suggests that instructors can motivate students by discussing rationales for their curricula. Recommended instructional approaches include the bookshelf model, which scaffolds learning by dividing class time into carefully constructed sequential segments, and the ten-plus-two model, which suggests that for every ten minutes a teacher talks, students should be allowed two minutes to process information. Adult learners tend to experience heightened motivation when participating in decision-making about curricula, yet they are sometimes unprepared to engage in curricular design. Fleming and Garner note that teachers can address adult learners' need to have some degree of influence on their own learning by embedding structured opportunities for making learning choices in syllabi. Furthermore, use of narrative and personal stories can provide powerful incentives for adult learners, whether presented via conversation, writing, television, film, music, or poetry. Internet technologies can also be exploited—e.g., via class blogs or a college-supported online Blackboard. The final chapter presents specific instructional strategies that connect classroom learning to adults' life experiences and circumstances. — BJG

166   Hashimoto, Irvin Y. "Adult Learning and Composition Instruction." *Journal of Basic Writing* 4.1 (Spring 1985): 55–68. Print.

Although adult enrollments in college have grown significantly in recent years (the 1980 US Census reports that about 34 percent of higher education participants are over the age of 25), writing instructors and scholars have yet to account for adult learners' needs and experiences. One reason may be a failure to notice distinctions between child and adolescent learners and adult learners. A second reason could be the lack of a widely accepted theory of adult learning. However, Hashimoto claims that enough is known about adult learners that their needs can and should be incorporated into basic writing curricula. For example, adult learners have a stronger sense of self-direction than younger learners and, as K. Patricia Cross argues, adults might therefore be able to take on more responsibility for their learning. In addition, adult learners tend to be pragmatic, strongly goal-oriented, and less likely to accept instructors' and textbook authors' rationales for learning activities and assignments. In addition, because they tend to value writing conventions and understand the importance of their own writing improvement, adults often prefer direct grammar instruction instead of the more indirect approach offered by sentence combining practice. Finally, the author notes that adults may not respond well to materials addressed primarily to young adult college students, but this lack of response should not be interpreted to indicate a lack of interest in learning. Differences between younger and older adult learners are significant and therefore should be acknowledged in basic writing teaching materials, curricular design, and instructional strategy. —MW

167   Heimlich, Joe E., and Emmalou Norland. "Teaching Style: Where Are We Now?" *Contemporary Viewpoints on Teaching Adults Effectively*. Ed. Jovita M. Ross-Gordon. Hoboken, NJ: Wiley, 2002. 17–25. Print. New Directions for Adult and Continuing Education 93.

Heimlich and Norland begin by distinguishing between teaching style and teaching method or technique, with a focus on the former. They define teaching style as "the beliefs, values, and behaviors of educators as they relate to the way the elements of the exchange function" (17). While educators know that learning styles are important to know and address in the classroom, the authors argue that few educators reflect on their own beliefs and values or on how their classroom practices are affected by their beliefs and values. Once educators understand how these work together, the interchange between students and teachers is more successful. One concern that Heimlich and Norland note is that adult educators are not viewed as lifelong learners in most studies. The methods an educator uses reflect his or her philosophy. To attain congruence between philosophy and style, educators need to explore changing behaviors, changing beliefs, or a change in both or neither. The authors then discuss each of these changes and what educators should consider within each of these areas. —KKN

168   Herman, Lee, and Alan Mandell. *From Teaching to Mentoring: Principle and Practice, Dialogue and Life in Adult Education*. New York: Routledge, 2004. Print.

In higher education, mentoring offers instructors opportunities to teach by conversing in mentor-mentee dialogues rather than by delivering lessons with preplanned curricula. Drawing on their experiences at Empire State College, SUNY, authors Herman and Mandell define mentoring by offering six principles, beginning with "act so that what you believe you know is only provisionally true" (26). Challenges and rewards of mentoring (addressed in chapters 3 and 4) include learning how to ask different kinds of questions (e.g., initial questions, open questions, informational questions, and leading questions) and learning to listen patiently for mentees' responses. Potential instructor rewards resulting from careful listening are learning about mentees' interests and goals and developing mentor-mentee relationships. The notion of developing curricula collaboratively in exploratory conversations is discussed in chapter 5. When this practice is applied to prior learning assessment conferences, mentors are often challenged to consider all kinds of prior learning that students may have acquired, including knowledge of areas not commonly addressed in traditional college courses. Referring to Socrates' dialogic learning practices and principles, Herman and Mandell examine mentor-mentee relationships and the learning experienced by mentors (chapters 6 and 7). Issues concerning student access to higher education are also addressed (chapters 8 and 9), focusing mainly on the topics of online conferencing and interrogations of existing institutional structures. In every chapter, the authors advocate for new, adult-oriented ways of teaching and learning in institutions of higher learning. — BJG

See: Marian L. Houser, "Expectancy Violations of Instructor Communication as Predictors of Motivation and Learning: A Comparison of Traditional and Nontraditional Students" [87].

See: Jill A. Jones, Bridgett Brookbank, and Jennifer McDonough, "Meeting the Literacy Needs of Adult Learners through a Community-University Partnership" [117].

169   Marshall, Brigitte. *Preparing for Success: A Guide for Teaching Adult English Language Learners.* McHenry, IL: Ctr. for Applied Linguistics, 2002. Print.

Within a multilevel frame of workplace requirements, adult English language learners' needs, and grant-funding agencies' assessment tools, pedagogical approaches, and classroom strategies are described alongside sample worksheets useful for teaching adult English language learners. Background information on adult education legislation and worker education is provided in the first section and referred to repeatedly in the books' five subsequent sections. In 1990, the US Department of Labor invited adult educators, business leaders, and union representatives to determine workplace needs that can be addressed inside educational institutions. The commission agreed upon a set of five competency areas and three basic skills, referred to as the Secretary's Commission on Achieving Necessary Skills (SCANS). The SCANS model describes skills (basic skills, thinking skills, personal qualities) and competency areas (finding and using resources, interpersonal skills, acquiring and using information, understanding systems, and technological expertise) needed by employers of their workers. Proposed as a basis for adult education curricula, SCANS can readily be translated into adult education curricula. Similarly, in 1998, the US Department of Education's Division of Adult Education and Literacy developed a National Reporting System (NRS) for collecting and reporting adult education programs' learner outcomes. And in 1994, the National Institute for Literacy established its new Equipped for the Future (EFF) model of adult education, which focuses on learners' needs. Taken together, SCANS, NRS, and EFF provide a complex model of education that is explained and applied to classroom teaching along with concrete strategies for engaging adult learners. Marshall concludes with a commentary on relating education to needs of all stakeholders, and especially to the needs, interests, and goals of adult learners. —BJG

See: Patricia J. McAlexander, "Mina Shaughnessy and K. Patricia Cross: The Forgotten Debate over Postsecondary Remediation" [20].

170   McKay, Heather, and Abigail Tom. *Teaching Adult Second Language Learners*. New York: Cambridge UP, 2000. Print.

This book provides curricular structures, instructional strategies, and theme-based units for teaching adult English language learners. An introductory section presents characteristics of adult learners, descriptions of learning styles, and techniques for acquiring student information—e.g., questionnaires, interviews, and formal tests. The second section offers suggestions for building class community, including conversational scripts for beginning each class and strategies for forming students in small groups. Thematically unified curricula are described in each of nine chapters. Proposed curricular themes include personal identification, community, food, clothing, housing, health, work, and money. The authors strongly endorse integrating students' views of their own learning needs and interests into courses and establishing learning-centered classrooms. — BJG

171   Navarre Cleary, Michelle, Ed. "Teaching Writing to Adults: A Handbook for New Composition Teachers." *CompFAQs from CompPILE*. Web. 11 Dec. 2010.

Part of the "Adult Learners" section of the *CompFAQs* wiki, this site is intended as an evolving, collaborative handbook in which composition teachers share knowledge about teaching adult students. It currently includes pages on what we know about adult students and the implications of this knowledge for practice, useful reading for adult students, ideas for writing assignments for adult students, suggestions for preparing to teach adult students, cases for discussion, and readings for new teachers of adult students. Navarre Cleary started this handbook to supplement her article on teaching adults in the *WPA Journal*. A number of her colleagues have added and discussed cases on the "cases for discussion" page. — MNC

172   Orem, Richard A. *Teaching Adult English Language Learners*. Malabar, FL: Krieger, 2005. Print.

This book offers a well-constructed synthesis of adult learning theory, second-language acquisition theory and research, and English as a second language curricula and instructional strategies for teachers of adult English language learners. Designed for use in adult education and TESOL (Teaching English to Speakers of Other Languages) programs, *Teaching Adult English Language Learners* offers six thematic chapters on topics that range from teaching oral language (chapter 2) and teaching literacy (chapter 3) to teaching cross-cultural communication skills (chapter 5) and planning for a future in which teachers of adult English language learners will be better prepared and more sufficiently recognized as professional educators by their own employers. Integrated into the academic passages are Orem's reflections on his own lived experience as an English teacher, first in Tunisia—where he served as a Peace Corps Volunteer—and later in the United States, where he taught adult literacy and adult ESL while pursuing a doctoral degree in adult education at the University of Georgia. As Orem was developing his career as an ESL educator from the 1960s through the 1990s, the professional field of TESOL was evolving from its infancy in 1966, when the TESOL organization was founded, to the 1990s, when the TESOL organization was developing a set of standards for the TESOL profession. Significantly, Orem served as Chair of the 1989 TESOL convention in San Antonio and as Executive Director of TESOL in 1989–1990. In chapter 1, "Getting Started," Orem defines terms (TESL, TEFL, TESOL, ELL), explores profiles of adult English learners, discusses various types of adult ESL programs, and summarizes adult learning theory. This introductory chapter offers a valuable synthesis of concepts and research in adult education and TESOL. A valuable survey of historical and contemporary adult literacy education models is offered in chapter 3, "Teaching Literacy Skills." A special feature of the book is chapter 6, "Looking Forward," where Orem discusses the developing standards movement within the TESOL organization and describes specific TESOL-recommended standards for hiring and employing adult English language instructors and program administrators. Two appendices provide models for assessing English language learners' skill levels and competencies.—BJG

173   Parrish, Betsy. *Teaching Adult ESL: A Practical Introduction.* New York: McGraw, 2004. Print.

This book provides theoretical knowledge and practical advice for teachers of adult English language learners. In the first section, Parrish argues that educators can teach more effectively by learning about their students—a practice that should be routinely integrated into curricula—and then offers an overview of dominant second-language acquisition theories. Section 2 presents summaries of dominant instructional models and descriptions of program structures—for example, citizenship classes, workplace curricula, pre-academic English, and distance learning. Approaches to contextualized language teaching and explanations of how adults learn speaking and listening skills are described in sections 3 and 4. Issues in learning to read and write English are discussed in section 5, along with practical suggestions for teaching. A series of effective teaching practices is described in section 6, while classroom management issues are covered in section 7. Advice on selecting teaching materials, especially textbooks, is provided in section 8. Assessment strategies for both adult learners and teachers are covered in section 9, while models for teaching literacy (e.g., Equipped for the Future [EFF] and Secretary's Commission on Achieving Necessary Skills [SCANS]) and assessing educational standards are presented in section 10. Each section integrates theory and research with practical activities for instructors planning to teach English to adults.—BJG

174   Rose, Mike. *Lives on the Boundary: A Moving Account of the Struggles and Achievements of America's Educationally Underprepared*. New York: Penguin, 1989. Print.

Rose looks at how the educationally underprepared deal with the American education system by telling his story. He discusses his experiences as a student in the K–12 system, in college, and in graduate school. He then moves through his experiences as a teacher in the Teacher Corps and later a teacher of veterans, and finally his experiences as a tutor in a college. He explains how as a child and teenager, he struggled with the requirements in his educational system, learning more from those outside the classroom or teachers who invested in him. When he went to college, he was at a deficit because he did not know the language of the academy. When he became part of the Teacher Corps, he worked with children who were labeled as remedial, but he found success with them through the literacy strategies he used. When he began teaching in the Veteran's Program housed at UCLA, he found many of the students struggled with the requirements of the courses and with being students. Through creative instruction and tying the class work to the students' knowledge base, Rose helped the students to move beyond what was expected. He did this because he discovered "why the men had come to the program. . . . The men wanted to change their lives, and . . . they still held onto an American dream: Education held the power to equalize things" (137). He immersed them in literacy activities so that they could find their way through the academic world. He learned that the students did not have the background knowledge needed for the reading that was required, so he had to put the readings in context and help the students to make meaning. Rose then discusses his experiences as head of a tutoring program at UCLA. He says that students, particularly traditional students, enter academia lacking critical literacy and most remedial students are "competently literate" (188). Because underprepared students are crossing the boundaries into higher education, they tend to try to write as they think an academic should write, resulting in errors, which Rose argues instructors should welcome so that education can take place. Rose concludes by presenting his findings from his study of students taking placement exams, showing that students have difficulty with the concepts of the test, but they really have skills at figuring out the answers based on their experiences. He argues, "We need an orientation to instruction that provides guidance on how to determine and honor the beliefs and stories, enthusiasms, and apprehensions that students reveal" (236).—KKN

175   Schwarzer, David. "Best Practices for Teaching the 'Whole' Adult ESL Learner." *Bringing Community to the Adult ESL Classroom*. Ed. Clarena Larrotta and Ann K. Brooks. Hoboken, NJ: Wiley, 2009. 25–33. Print. New Directions for Adult and Continuing Education 121.

Schwarzer describes a curriculum developed for volunteer adult ESL instructors who have nonteaching careers in "the real world." This curriculum introduces novice instructors to best practices for teaching adult ESL learners within the frameworks of communicative language teaching and whole language principles of education. After reviewing SLA research on teaching English, Schwarzer defines concepts key to whole language teaching, which "implies that we look at adult learners as whole persons rather than just ESL learners" (28). These concepts include a holistic perspective, a community of learners, authentic learning, curriculum negotiation, inquiry based lessons, alternative assessment, and language learning as a developmental process. Relying on this conceptual base, Schwarzer describes a set of best practices for teaching English to adults—e.g., creating classroom communities, establishing clear routines that are repeatedly used, connecting the classroom to the wider world via field trips and other activities, and promoting student use of new literacy habits (e.g., Internet searches, pleasure reading, and newspaper reading). The curriculum described in this essay aims to prepare volunteer ESL instructors for teaching and developing their own curricula within the combined framework of communicative language teaching and whole language education.—LDB

176   Villanueva, Jr., Victor. *Bootstraps: From an American Academic of Color.* Urbana, IL: NCTE, 1993. Print.

Villanueva narrates a memoir of his formal education and experiential learning from childhood through adulthood. After growing up in Brooklyn, Villanueva and his parents moved to Los Angeles, where he entered one high school and then another, only to withdraw from school before graduating. He later earned a GED while serving in the military and eventually went on to college as an adult in his late twenties. His parents having come to the United States from Puerto Rico, Villanueva was conversant in Spanish, Spanglish, African American Vernacular, and Standard American English. Never quite fitting into one cultural identity exclusively, Villanueva tried on different cultural identities at various points in his life, including an identity he calls racelessness: "Racelessness . . . is the decision to go it alone. And it is most clearly marked linguistically . . . by asserting that one is choosing to speak 'correct' English" (40). Relying on a wide range of scholarship in linguistics, rhetoric, sociolinguistics, sociology, and literary theory, Villanueva summarizes his education and interprets his experiences as a bilingual Puerto Rican American negotiating social and linguistic experiences. Villanueva's description of the economic challenges he faced while beginning his academic career as a young married man with children also calls attention to a changing US economy that requires dual-income households. The story of this GED-holder from a community college who eventually earned a PhD concludes with a professional narrative that includes depictions of administering a basic writing program, becoming a college instructor, and writing a dissertation on the language and literacy learning experiences of basic writing and college composition students.—BJG

177   Wlodkowski, Raymond J. *Enhancing Adult Motivation to Learn: A Comprehensive Guide for Teaching All Adults.* 3rd ed. San Francisco: Jossey-Bass, 2008. Print.

In a practical guide for adult educators and staff developers, Wlodkowski offers an argument for integrating motivational concepts and strategies into courses designed for adults, with a special focus on nontraditional college students, working adults (age 25–64), and older adults (65 and older). Wlodkowski states the book's objective as contributing "useful means for creating unity among worth, meaning, and joy in adult learning . . . through motivationally sound instruction" (437–38). A biological explanation for motivation, grounded in the neurosciences, is provided in chapter 1, with subsequent explanations of connections to emotional and cultural influences. Chapter 2 addresses the effects of aging and culture on adult learners, while chapter 3 provides instructional strategies that motivate adults and describes attributes of motivational teachers. Chapter 4 articulates a complex profile of adult learning—e.g., commentary on the possibility that human brains continue to develop until age 25 to 30 and how this might affect motivation. Chapters 5, 6, 7, and 8 describe four motivational conditions: inclusion, attitude, meaning, and competence, along with strategies teachers can use to promote these conditions. Chapter 9 suggests concrete measures for integrating motivational strategies into curricula, and in an epilogue, Wlodkowski emphasizes the importance of creating and maintaining institutions offering access and support for low-income adults.—BJG

178   Worthman, Christopher. "The Positioning of Adult Learners: Appropriating Learner Experience on the Continuum of Empowerment to Emancipation." *International Journal of Lifelong Education* 27.4 (2008): 443–62. Print.

Worthman studied two instructors of adult learners in ESOL (English Speakers of Other Languages) programs. The author collected data to determine how each instructor empowered his or her students through the instruction provided. Each instructor used a different methodology to meet the goal of helping students learn English. Worthman argues that the type of instruction the instructors offered reflects how they valued their students' learning experiences. One instructor used the students' experiences to design the lessons while the other one focused on semantics and syntax for the lessons. Worthman argues that the second instructor attempted to empower students by teaching them the discourse of the mainstream while the first instructor allowed students the opportunity "to critique the Discourses they encountered" (461). He concludes that understanding empowerment will help instructors develop their practices so that they can change the power structure of the institution.—KKN

Theoretical Frameworks and Instructional Approaches

See: Caroline Beverstock and Sue McIntyre, "Dividing and Conquering: Successful Writing Processes for Adult Learners" [112].

179   Brewer, Susan A., James D. Klein, and Kenneth E. Mann. "Using Small Group Learning Theories with Adult Re-entry Students." *College Student Journal* 37.2 (2003): 286–97. Print.

In a study of 109 adult reentry business majors in a bachelor's degree completion program, Brewer, Klein, and Mann investigate the impact of cooperative small group learning and motivation to affiliate with others on achievement, attitude, and interaction. Brewer et al. found that after completing an affiliation questionnaire, fifty-three students reported having high motivation to affiliate with others while fifty-six students reported low motivation to affiliate. One important finding is that "the need for affiliation is likely to influence students' preference for small group strategies and how they perform in these settings" (287). After accounting for this affiliation motive factor, Brewer et al. divided the 109 adult students into four treatment groups: individual learning and low motivation to affiliate; group learning and low motivation to affiliate; individual learning and high motivation to affiliate; and group learning and high motivation to affiliate. A study of learning achievement revealed no significant difference among students in these four groups. However, students in high affiliation groups (who were assigned either to individual learning or to group learning) stayed on task longer than students assigned to low affiliation groups. Additionally, a study of interaction among the variables being investigated showed that students who showed a high affiliation motive and who worked in small groups enjoyed their learning experience more than students assigned to all three other treatment groups. In discussing implications of their research findings, Brewer et al. conclude that while small group learning strategies did not yield gains in achievement, students who worked in small groups rated their motivation, confidence, enjoyment, and belief in ability to learn more highly. These gains suggest to the authors that cooperative small group learning strategies merit further research and should continue to be explored by instructors of reentry adult students. —SFL

180   Brookfield, Stephen D. *The Skillful Teacher: On Technique, Trust, and Responsiveness in the Classroom.* 2nd ed. San Francisco: Jossey-Bass, 2006. Print.

Drawing on thirty-five years of experience teaching college classes and leading seminars for teachers, Brookfield offers a comprehensive guide for teachers of college students at all levels. Useful concepts, teaching techniques, practical advice, and inspirational comments appear in every chapter of this second edition of a book that first appeared in 1990. Writing from a perspective of adult teaching and learning theory, Brookfield notes that while college students are adult learners, teachers are also adult learners, continually reflecting on teaching practices and making discoveries. He also advises readers that diverse student populations and unpredictable human behavior require teachers to be responsive to unexpected situations and to become acquainted with their students rather than relying on formulaic, prepackaged teaching approaches. Fourteen chapters offer commentary on a variety of topics, including "experiencing teaching," "core assumptions about skillful teaching," "lecturing creatively," "getting students to participate in discussions," "teaching online," "responding to resistance," and "surviving emotionally" (ix). An example of a helpful instructional technique (offered in chapter 3, "Understanding Our Classrooms") is the critical incident questionnaire: students are asked to respond to three questions in writing and to submit their responses without identifying themselves by name. The questions invite students to comment on a moment in the class session when they felt most engaged, a moment when they felt distanced, and an action taken by either a teacher or a student that was helpful. The final chapter ("Surviving Emotionally") advises teachers to develop a philosophy of practice that will define a teacher's role, describe a good class, and explain successful teaching. — BJG

181   Brown, Judith O. "Know Thyself: The Impact of Portfolio Development on Adult Learning." *Adult Education Quarterly* 52.3 (2002): 228–45. Print.

As students participate in prior learning assessment for college credit, they create portfolios, either electronic or conventional, to express and demonstrate their life learning. Brown explores the affective aspects of this process and its transformational power for students who had otherwise undervalued their own experiences. Through in-depth interviews with students who had completed an "Autobiographical Learning Essay" (based on the Kolb model) and developed portfolios with documentation, Brown found that the process shaped their understanding of themselves and their prior experiences: "Students expressed (a) increased recognition of all they had accomplished in the course of their careers, and (b) a new sense of self-discovery and personal empowerment to achieve future goals" (235). Brown also found that students gained a much greater appreciation of the learning they experienced in their workplaces and of their guidance by mentors in those settings. Portfolio development also strengthened the students' writing and organizational skills, while enhancing their appreciation of reflection as a way of learning. — SFL

182   Brumagim, Alan L. "Using the Experiences of Nontraditional Students in the Classroom." *Journal of Management Education* 23.4 (1999): 444–52. Print.

Brumagim discusses an exercise he used for an entire semester in a management course. The class had an equal number of traditional (20–21-year-old juniors) and older, nontraditional students. The exercise had three stages, including applying for positions within an organization, a team project, and the wrap-up stage. In his reflections on the exercise, Brumagim notes that traditional students realized that the nontraditional students had knowledge, experience, and skills that the traditional students sought. Additionally, the nontraditional students became engaged in the activity, often applying their work experience to the situations in the exercise. The nontraditional students shared their company documents with the classroom to add to the information of the course. Brumagim lists a couple of drawbacks of the exercise because of student reaction. His final recommendation is for instructors to make use of adult students' expertise. —KKN

See: Gregory Clark and Stephen Doheny-Farina, "Public Discourse and Personal Expression: A Case Study in Theory-Building" [80].

183   Dallmer, Denise. "Collaborative Test Taking with Adult Learners." *Adult Learning* 15.3–4 (2004): 4–7. Print.

Dallmer describes her experiences of using collaborative test taking with her graduate students, who are teachers in elementary and secondary schools. She began using collaborative test taking for midterm and final exams to help relieve her adult students' test-taking anxiety, which has resulted from negative experiences with test taking throughout their educational experiences. Students were questioning the idea at first, but they reported positive experiences with collaborative test taking. Grades in the courses were not inflated as the A's and A-'s continued as in previous courses. Students also felt that the experience taught them to work collaboratively as they do in the workplace. —KKN

184   Dominicé, Pierre. *Learning from Our Lives: Using Educational Biographies with Adults*. San Francisco: Jossey-Bass, 2000. Print.

While introducing the concept of educational biographies, Dominicé guides his readers to better understanding these learning narratives and the adult learner. Like Stephen Brookfield, Malcolm Knowles, and Jack Mezirow, Dominicé breaks new ground as he explores the adult learner's "needs, motivations, and desires." Recognizing educational biographies as a method for students to learn about themselves, Dominicé views this approach as potentially emancipating for students, who may "[find] autonomy" in relation to "family, education, and the sociocultural environment" (81). In an Educational Biography, adult learners trace their educational paths while reflecting on formal and informal learning experiences and interpreting these experiences, a process that can be subjective yet revelatory. This learning narrative may be shared, and the sharing itself may be part of the reflective process. Creating these learning narratives can prompt individuals to explore a "personal life history as a whole" and may allow for new understandings of experiences that might not have been originally recognized as learning (26). Dominicé acknowledges both the utilitarianism of many adults who seek further education for practical purposes, such as career advancement, and the marketplace of institutions. Dominicé also suggests that educators can benefit from using educational biographies to promote critical self-reflection and experiential learning. —SFL

See: Thomas Flint & Associates, *Best Practices in Adult Learning: A CAEL/APQC Benchmarking Study* [6].

185   Holyoke, Laura, and Erick Larson. "Engaging the Adult Learner Generational Mix." *Journal of Adult Education* 38.1 (2009): 12–21. Print.

Holyoke and Larson studied how the three main generations found in classrooms—Baby Boomers, Generation-X, and Millennial—learn and what strategies work best for each one. In their research, the authors used three assumptions of andragogy as developed by Knowles: readiness to learn, orientation to learning, and motivation to learn. Within each of these areas of assumptions, Holyoke and Larson share responses from selected participants in each generation. The authors argue that instructors "of adult learners need to be aware of generational characteristics when developing lesson plans and training materials" (20). They then provide strategies for instructors to use in classrooms with students from multiple generations. —KKN

See: Marian L. Houser, "Are We Violating Their Expectations? Instructor Communication Expectations of Traditional and Nontraditional Students" [57].

See: Carol Kasworm, "What Are They Thinking? Adult Undergraduate Learners Who Resist Learning" [13].

186   Kenner, Cari, and Jason Weinerman. "Adult Learning Theory: Applications to Non-Traditional College Students." *Journal of College Reading and Learning* 41.2 (Spring 2011): 87–96. Print.

Focusing on students ages 25 to 50, Kenner and Weinerman discuss several strategies to use with nontraditional students in developmental courses. They review some adult learning theories, such as those developed by Knowles and Horn, and then proceed to highlight needs of older students in the classroom and ways to meet those needs. Kenner and Weinerman argue, "Because integration into the academic environment is a challenge for adult students, developmental educators must understand the background of adult students and develop a curriculum that addresses their particular needs" (90). They also argue that if instructors and institutions do this, then the attrition rate of adult students may decrease. Adult students must be able to connect their everyday lives to what they are learning in the classroom, and instructors need to help the students overcome their frustrations. Finally, Kenner and Weinerman argue that instructors of developmental courses need to "embrace the adult learners' differences and see them as people who will actively embrace the concept of higher education" (94). —KKN

187   Largent, Liz, and Jon B. Horinek. "Community Colleges and Adult Service Learners: Evaluating a First-Year Program to Improve Implementation." *Linking Adults with Community: Promoting Civic Engagement through Community-Based Learning.* Ed. Susan C. Reed and Catherine Marienau. Hoboken, NJ: Wiley, 2008. 37–47. Print. New Directions for Adult and Continuing Education 118.

Largent and Horinek discuss what they learned about the effects of service-learning projects in first-year courses on adult learners. Creators of service-learning projects in courses need to consider the demographics of all students, but age, in particular, affects one's learning and approach to the projects. In the pre-study survey, the authors found younger students (18–22 years old) were more satisfied with their service-learning experiences than older students, so Largent and Horinek interviewed adult students to learn why the difference in satisfaction existed. They found that adult learners who were dissatisfied wanted the experiences to have significance to them and their communities, and they wanted interaction with staff at the agency. Additionally, adult learners needed to understand the mission of the organization. Dissatisfied adult learners also noted that they felt the experience "devalue[d] their life experience" (41). As a result of Largent and Horinek's study, the program they studied was redesigned so that faculty using service-learning projects in their classrooms were trained on alternate reflective practices. Agency representatives were trained on the expectations of the service learning, the students, and the agency. The study also developed suggestions for service-learning projects that involve adult learners. After the changes were made in the program, the authors again administered the survey to students and found that the changes met the adult students' needs. —KKN

See: Galen Leonhardy, "Transformations: Working with Veterans in the Composition Classrooms" [145].

See: Donita Massengill, "The Impact of Using Guided Reading to Teach Low-Literate Adults" [121].

188   Materna, Laurie. *Jump Start the Adult Learner: How to Engage and Motivate Adults Using Brain-Compatible Strategies*. Thousand Oaks, CA: Corwin, 2007. Print.

Educational research over the past two decades has revealed a greater understanding of how the brain builds neural pathways to store and recall learning, and how specific techniques used during learning experiences can foster the development of these neural connections. Other research, building on the work of Howard Gardner, has emphasized the idea of "multiple intelligences," the view that individuals can take advantage of different forms of knowing (e.g., mathematical, verbal, or spatial), which Gardner describes as "intelligences" (58). By incorporating various learning theories and Bloom's Taxonomy of Higher Level Thinking into a broad conception of adult learning, we can move away from the traditional lecture or "sage on the stage" model of curriculum delivery to a more active approach, which may more successfully account for multiple learning styles and varied student needs. Materna presents both the theoretical framework for this approach as well as a guide to developing and implementing new methodologies into the adult learner classroom. She creates what she terms "The Materna Method," which she describes as "a guide for educators designed to help in the process of selecting supplemental classroom activities to facilitate this natural flow of learning" (138). This method includes warm-up mental exercises for the openings of classes, the inclusion of visual matrices for organizing of material, multiple forms of reflective writing, and the inclusion of movement and musical stimuli in the classroom. The method is documented in an extensive chart. —SFL

189   Mazurek, Raymond A. "Running Shoes, Auto Workers, & Labor: Business Writing Pedagogy in the Working-Class College." *Teaching English in the Two-Year College* 29.3 (2002): 259–72. Print.

Arguing that service courses are rich contexts for teaching critical thinking, Mazurek describes a research writing project he developed for teaching business writing at Penn State (Berks-Lehigh Valley College), where many students are nontraditional individuals from working-class families. Drawing on a project described by Linda Flower in *Problem-Solving Strategies for Writing* and relying on interviews provided by Studs Terkel (published in *Working*), the author assigns students a project where they assume the role of trouble-shooters in a Ford auto plant. Students read two interviews by spot-welders and one interview by a plant manager in order to become familiar with the perspectives of both labor and management. Students then wrote two reports to two different audiences: one to a militant United Auto Workers union president and one to a plant manager, an experience that forced them to become familiar with two different perspectives. Since many of the students were working full-time while enrolled in a summer session writing course, they had little time outside of class to write. Thus, much of the writing and related discussion occurred inside the classroom, where students worked collaboratively. The assignment brings to light rhetorical issues of audience and social context while inducing students to learn about business problems from both union and management perspectives. The project is accompanied by discussions of changes in the US economy brought on by globalization, multinational corporations, and associated human rights concerns. Mazurek uses this discussion to argue that nontraditional students deserve the same opportunities to learn critical thinking skills as middle-class traditional college students enrolled in literature courses. —BJG

190   McShane, Susan. *Applying Research in Reading Instruction: First Steps for Teachers.* Washington, DC: NIFL and The Partnership for Reading, 2005. Print.

McShane's accessible teacher's guide presents principles, concepts, research findings, and pedagogical techniques for reading instruction in adult basic education classes. In chapter 2, five components of reading (phonemic awareness, decoding, fluency, vocabulary, and comprehension) and related published research are introduced. Reading assessment is addressed in chapters 3 and 8. In chapter 3, a discussion of contrasts between standardized reading tests and curriculum-based tests is accompanied by descriptions of performance-based assessments,

portfolio assessment, and self-assessment. The author suggests that limitations of a single test of reading require that multiple types of assessment be used to evaluate one person's reading abilities. Definitions of
phonemic awareness and decoding are followed by an explanation of
phonics instruction in chapter 4. Reading fluency skills, instruction,
and assessment are described in chapter 5. Vocabulary development
and comprehension strategies are presented in chapters 6 and 7. Course
design for beginning adult readers is discussed in a final chapter, with
attention to structuring and sequencing classroom activities and
teaching groups of adults who read at different levels. Four appendices
provide introductions to research design, phonics instruction, formulas
for calculating readability, and an approach to teaching summary writing. — BJG

191   Mohammed, Methal R. "Don't Give Me a Fish; Teach Me How to Fish:
      A Case Study of an International Adult Learner." *Adult Learning* 21.1–2
      (2010): 15–18. Print.

      Learning contracts can be used to motivate students who are classified
      as "lifelong learners." Mohammed defines learning contracts as plans
      for learning in an orderly progression. He doesn't view these agree-
      ments as being content- or outcome-oriented. The contracts should
      help to provide an academic environment encouraging collaboration in
      a manner that empowers adult students. The purpose of these contracts
      is to enable students to structure their own course work. Using his own
      experiences, Mohammed develops a case study to show how an inter-
      national adult learner can benefit by signing a contract to limit the role
      of the professor to that of a facilitator. — LDB

See: Michelle Navarre Cleary, "What WPAs Need to Know to Prepare New
      Teachers to Work with Adult Students" [146].

192   Nixon-Ponder, Sarah. "Using Problem-Posing Dialogue in Adult Lit-
      eracy Education." *Adult Learning* 7.2 (Nov./Dec. 1995): 10–12. Print.
      Rpt. in *Teaching Developmental Writing: Background Readings.* 3rd ed.
      Ed. Susan Naomi Bernstein. Boston: Bedford, 2007. 206–13.

      Nixon-Ponder clarifies the sometimes abstract "problem posing" dia-
      logue method advocated by Dewey, Piaget, Freire, and Shor. In this
      form of critical pedagogy, the instructor identifies a topic significant
      to class members, and then students engage in a five-step process:
      (1) *Describe the content* of the problem through a "code" or text, such
      as written dialogues, role plays, stories from students' lives, public texts,
      (newspapers, pamphlets, government forms, others), or images — dis-
      cuss/write about what the text is about. (2) *Define the problem* — through
      discussion or writing, identify one specific problem the class will
      focus on. (3) *Personalize the problem* — discuss/write about students'
      experience with the issue and how it makes them feel. (4) *Discuss the
      problem* — discuss/write about economic reasons for the problem and
      economic effects on class members. (5) *Discuss alternatives to the prob-
      lem* — discuss/write about solutions and the consequences of particular

actions (208–10). Then Nixon-Ponder provides case studies demonstrating how she has used the method. In an adult basic education (ABE) literacy class, students focused on childcare; they read varied materials, wrote journal entries, oral histories, and letters, and "learned they had the answers to their problems and they learned the steps to . . . arrive at solutions" (211). Nixon-Ponder also describes problem-posing in general equivalency degree (GED) classes: In a writing class, Nixon-Ponder focused on what correct writing is and who sets the standards, while in a history class, she focused on what history is and how it should be studied.—KSU

See: Nancy Lloyd Pfahl and Colleen Aalsburg Wiessner, "Creating New Directions with Story: Narrating Life Experience as Story in Community Adult Education Contexts" [125].

193   Pratt, Daniel D. "Good Teaching: One Size Fits All?" *Contemporary Viewpoints on Teaching Adults Effectively*. Ed. Jovita M. Ross-Gordon. Hoboken, NJ: Wiley, 2002. 5–15. Print. New Directions for Adult and Continuing Education 93.

Pratt discusses five perspectives of teaching and how they affect adult learners. First, he defines a perspective as "an interrelated set of beliefs and intentions that gives direction and justification to our actions" (6). He argues that most teachers do not know their perspective because they look at teaching through their perspective, not at it. He also notes that perspectives on teaching are not the same as methods since methods may be part of all the perspectives. His research found that 90 percent of teachers have only one or two perspectives on teaching but may identify with a couple of other perspectives. The five perspectives he discusses are as follows: The transmission perspective views learners as containers who need to be filled with knowledge. The developmental perspective, based on constructivist theory, states that educators need to develop complex "reasoning and problem solving within a content area or field of practice" (8). The apprenticeship perspective helps learners work on authentic tasks so that learning transfers to the workplace. In this perspective, teachers help adult learners "adopt the language, values, and practices of a specific social group" (10) and enter communities they want access to. The nurturing perspective features teachers helping students learn without fear of failure. Because adult learners often come to the classroom with fears from previous schooling, this perspective builds students' confidence and self-sufficiency while setting challenging goals. Pratt argues that the fifth and final perspective, the social reform perspective, is difficult to describe because it consists of multiple characteristics and strategies. This perspective is found in settings such as community development, AIDS awareness, Native American education, and environmental education. The teachers work toward a set of ideals and changing the world in view of these ideals. Students adopt these ideals as they learn. Pratt concludes by arguing that all of these five teaching perspectives are legitimate views if used correctly (14).—KKN

194   Rivera, Klaudia M., and Ana Huerta-Macías. "Adult Bilingualism and Biliteracy in the United States: Theoretical Perspectives." *Adult Biliteracy: Sociocultural and Programmatic Responses*. Ed. Klaudia M. Rivera and Ana Huerta-Macías. New York: Erlbaum, 2008. 3–28. Print.

Unequal access to goods and services is particularly high in the United States (compared to other countries), with immigrants being especially vulnerable economically. Immigrants are a fast-growing population: three times as many immigrants were residing in the United States in 2000 as in 1970. The majority of US immigrants come from Latin America, with the second largest population having come from countries in Asia. As for educational attainments, about 33 percent of US immigrants have not completed high school. Both lack of English language proficiency and low educational attainments are barriers to employment as well as to future educational attainments. Consequently, adult education programs are providing significantly more courses in English language and literacy, adult basic education skills, and GED preparation. Too often, adult education programs rely on an English-only model of instruction and an autonomous model of literacy. Citing Brian Street, the authors define the autonomous model of literacy as focusing on "discrete elements of reading and writing skills . . . conceptualize[d] . . . in technical terms, which are independent of social context" (12). Use of the autonomous model restricts educators' motivation to learn about how language and literacy function in a wide variety of cultures, and thus impedes their ability to develop effective curricula and instructional approaches for bilingual adults. More inclusive is the ideological model—a view that situates literacy practices in concrete situations, sociocultural scenes, and power structures. The ideological view of literacy aligns closely with sociocultural models, which embed literacy in cultural practices, and the concept of multiliteracies (a view that one language can accommodate different literacies). Rivera and Huerta-Macías argue that adult educators can better serve the needs of bilingual adults by employing a sociocultural model of literacy and by recognizing the diverse linguistic expertise and cultural knowledge that adult learners bring to their experience of learning English language and literacy. — BJG

195   Shaughnessy, Mina. "Some Needed Research on Writing." *College Composition and Communication* 28.4 (1977): 317–20. Print. Rpt. in *Teaching Developmental Writing: Background Readings*. 4th ed. Ed. Susan Naomi Bernstein. Boston: Bedford, 2013. 7–12.

Shaughnessy argues that because inexperienced adult writers have become such a strong presence in higher education, new pedagogies must supplant traditional teaching. Unlike academically prepared college students, unprepared adult learners have not acquired reading and writing competencies incrementally since childhood and must rapidly catch up, often with just one or two semesters of direct writing instruction. For instructors to facilitate unprepared adults' writing development, new forms of research are necessary. Shaughnessy poses four questions to frame needed research. She first suggests inquiry into "signs of growth among [unprepared] adults" exposed to intensive writing instruction (318). More specifically, she proposes longitudinal case studies to investigate inexperienced adult writers' learning over time. Secondly, teachers need to identify literacy skills that can be taught directly in first-year writing courses. These literacy skills might include spelling, vocabulary, and syntax. Areas of research that can usefully be explored include adult learning, children's spelling, and vocabulary development. A third area of need is linked to writing assessment: In addition to focusing on language errors in student writing, instructors should pay attention to other aspects of crafting text—e.g., forming arguments and employing persuasive strategies. A fourth area of need involves teaching practices and styles: Shaughnessy proposes classroom-based observational studies of both traditional and experimental writing classes. While calling for research on inexperienced adult students' writing development, Shaughnessy reminds readers of existing inequities in public schools that have produced inexperienced adult writers.—BJG

See: M. Cecil Smith, "Does Service Learning Promote Adult Development? Theoretical Perspectives and Directions for Research" [37].

196   Sommer, Robert F. *Teaching Writing to Adults: Strategies and Concepts for Improving Learner Performance*. San Francisco: Jossey-Bass, 1989. Print.

Sommer targets both the adult learning professional who knows nothing about writing theory and the writing professional new to adult learning ("andragogy"). In this interdisciplinary synthesis, Sommer weaves concise summaries of theory with specific recommendations for practice, including many step-by-step sample assignments. A 250-page book, *Teaching Writing to Adults* contains thirteen chapters divided into three sections—the distinctiveness of adult learners, adult-centered techniques for writing instruction, and adult learners in varied settings—and six resource appendices. Sommer identifies writing anxiety as especially characteristic of adult learners and argues that "the writing classroom for adults ought to be a place where judgments are subordinated to supportive activities" (31), such as short, informal practice writing not evaluated in detail, setting goals to solve particular writing problems, and writing groups that reveal the value of reader response. In a key chapter on andragogy and writing theory, Sommer describes the assumptions and practical components of andragogy, followed by suggested writing assignments. Writing topics, for instance, should allow adults not only to describe and narrate experience but also to reflect on it thoughtfully; topics also should encourage students to explore change, especially the college reentry transition. Instruction should address immediate applications for writing, including writing to learn in all subjects and survival writing strategies for college and the job. Assignments should be functional with reference to real-world situations, written to real audiences. The book also offers specific chapters on teaching adults in workplace writing workshops, college composition, and GED centers with their mixed ability levels. The role of the instructor is critical; early on Sommer describes a range of teacher roles: "an environmentalist who enables students to discover their own resources and to challenge themselves; a consultant who can answer direct questions about concrete issues of language usage, rhetorical situations, formats, audiences, procedures; a professional whose experience with writing can help her anticipate the frustrations and anxieties of inexperienced writers" (14). In the final chapter, Sommer summarizes fifteen strategies for teaching writing to adults and recommends that the andragogical writing instructor continuously reflect on teaching and the roles an instructor might play. The bibliography contains key writing and adult learning materials up to 1987. — KSU

197   Sticht, Thomas G. "Swords and Pens: What the Military Can Show Us about Teaching Basic Skills to Young Adults." *American Educator* 24.3 (Fall 2000): 8–10. Print.

The author examines two approaches to reading and writing instruction provided by the US Army, finding that one approach is more effective than the other. The two approaches were used by the US military in the 1940s through the 1960s and again in the 1970s. Having relied on a general functional literacy educational approach in the past, the Vietnam-era US Army educators narrowed the educational focus to a concentration on specific jobs soldiers were required to perform. For example, soldiers assigned to kitchen duty would read recipes, dishwashing machine manuals, field kitchen instructions, and guidelines for running cafeteria-style services. This jobs-related curriculum proved to be more compelling for the soldier-students and more likely to lead to improved literacy abilities than the general literacy education approach used previously. Lessons can be learned from this military education case study and applied to contemporary adult literacy instruction. First, adult literacy students often do not want to participate in courses labeled "remedial" because of the implied stigma. Second, adults frequently want to improve their literacy skills in order to achieve a specific goal, often related to seeking a new job or being promoted in a current position. — BJG

See: Kathleen Taylor and Annalee Lamoreaux, "Teaching with the Brain in Mind" [29].

198   Zacharakis, Jeff. "Extension and Community: The Practice of Popular and Progressive Education." *Adult Education in the Rural Context: People, Place, and Change.* Ed. Jeffrey A. Ritchie. Hoboken, NJ: Wiley, 2008. 13–23. Print. New Directions for Adult and Continuing Education 117.

Extension education has a long history in the United States, dating back to George Washington, who discussed creating educational programs that would reach rural citizens. Extension education began to flourish with the passage of the first Morrill Act (1862), which created land grant colleges, and the passage of the second Morrill

Act (1890), which helped to establish historically black colleges by forbidding racial discrimination in admissions policies, except in cases where states established higher-education institutions for African Americans. Extension education also has roots in the early-twentieth-century Progressive movement. Today, the term *extension* refers to the Cooperative Education Service (CES), a "national, publicly funded, nonformal education system that links the educational and research resources and activities of the US Department of Agriculture (USDA) with over one hundred land grant institutions in every state, territory, and the District of Columbia" (14). CES staff members work together with land grant colleges and with people living in rural communities to offer services and help solve local problems: collaborative learning, lifelong learning, and need-based education are fundamental concepts for extension education. One example of extension work in the early twentieth century is support for forming local cooperatives and gaining economic independence. Popular education concepts (described by Paul Freire in *Pedagogy of the Oppressed*) and Progressive ideals have been important influences on extension education. — BJG

199   Zachary, Lois. J. "The Role of Teacher as Mentor." *Contemporary Viewpoints on Teaching Adults Effectively.* Ed. Jovita M. Ross-Gordon. Hoboken, NJ: Wiley, 2002. 27–38. Print. New Directions for Adult and Continuing Education 93.

Noting that teachers who mentor students are more successful with helping students grow and learn, Zachary provides a look at the mentoring process for both students and other instructors, whom she describes as adult learners also. Mentoring is now viewed as process-oriented instead of product-oriented, which is how mentoring previously was viewed. She defines mentoring as "a reciprocal and collaborative learning relationship between two or more individuals who share mutual responsibility and accountability for helping a mentee work toward achieving clear and mutually defined learning goals" (28). The key to good mentoring is a relationship between the two parties. Zachary notes that good mentoring practice fits with Knowles's theory on andragogy. She then discusses the four phases of the mentoring journey, which include preparing, negotiating, enabling, and coming to a closure. According to Zachary, behaviors are what help mentors and mentees negotiate each phase, and none of the phases should be skipped. Preparing requires that the right teacher meets the right student. Negotiating is when the mentor and mentee agree on the learning goals and parameters of the relationship. Enabling, which is the longest phase of the mentoring, requires an open and supportive atmosphere so that learning goals are met. Coming to closure begins when the partners get to know one another in the negotiating phase, then develop their relationship in the enabling stage, and then implement the exit strategy in the coming to closure phase. During this last phase, the two partners evaluate and reflect on the learning that has occurred. A celebration of the learning is important. Zachary ends with a summary of what she has discussed, noting that mentoring adult students can have a great impact on learners. — KKN

Curricula and Assessment

200   Askov, Eunice N., Barbara L. Van Horn, and Priscilla S. Carman. "Assessment in Adult Basic Education." *Assessment in Adult Basic Education Programs*. Ed. Amy D. Rose and Meredyth A. Leahy. Hoboken, NJ: Wiley, 1997. 65–74. Print. New Directions for Adult and Continuing Education 75.

Askov, Van Horn, and Carman discuss the value, types, and alternative models of assessment in Adult Basic Education (ABE) programs. Assessment is necessary in these programs as they help to place students, follow their progress, and prove the worth of the program. The authors argue that instructors and administrators of ABE programs need to think about the function of the assessment, what information each stakeholder requires, and the strengths, weaknesses, and limitations of each type of assessment. Based on these concerns, the authors then discuss several reasons why programs use assessments and why programs should or should not use standardized assessments. Various types of alternative assessments are then reviewed. Askov, Van Horn, and Carman argue that the environment for testing adult students has special requirements, which they then list. — KKN

201   Beaman, Ronda. "The Unquiet . . . Even Loud, Andragogy! Alternative Assessments for Adult Learners." *Innovative Higher Education* 23.1 (1998): 47–59. Print.

Beaman argues that with increasing enrollments of adult undergraduates in college classrooms, teaching styles and curriculum development have been reimagined, but assessment of learning has been largely overlooked. In recent years, instructors' approaches to facilitating adult learning have more frequently emphasized participatory and self-directed learning; however, assessment has remained teacher-directed and summative. After studying the implementation of various innovative formats for assessment, Beaman suggests several alternative approaches, including "praiseworthy grading," which calls attention to those aspects of an assignment where students have demonstrated strength and skills; peer assessment, which echoes the collaborative nature of adult learning; and self-assessment, which capitalizes on the self-directed nature of adult learners. While all of these methods have their drawbacks, Beaman aptly concludes: "In view of what we know of andragogy . . . traditional grading of adult learners cannot be defended and should be amended" (58). Included are many suggestions for implementing alternative assessments. — SFL

202   Brady, E. Michael. "Redeemed from Time: Learning Through Autobiography." *Adult Education Quarterly* 41.1 (1990): 43–52. Print.

Using a Hasidic tale of four generations of rabbis who guide a village through its crises through ritual and remembrance as his point of departure, Brady examines the way in which autobiography facilitates learning. He posits that autobiography allows students to recover three aspects of their selves: "the remembered self, the ordered self, and the imagined self" (44). Autobiography, he argues, allows for the recovery of memory and of one's multiple past selves, it allows for a greater understanding and sorting of memories and knowledge, and it allows for a metaphoric envisioning of one's possible self. As he says, "Every autobiography is a work of art, and at the same time, a work of enlightenment. It does not show us the persons from outside their visible actions, but as they are in their inner privacy; not as I am, not as I was, but as I believe and wish myself to have been and to be" (49). The goal of autobiography in an adult learning focus is not necessarily to recover or report the entire life so much as it is to draw together pivotal moments and to create new insights into the ways in which a learner has arrived at the current moment. Students thus learn best when allowed to integrate the new self that has been created with students' autobiographical constructions of their earlier selves. — SFL

203   Cercone, Kathleen. "Characteristics of Adult Learners with Implications for Online Learning Design." *AACE Journal* 16.2 (2008): 137–59. Print.

Cercone analyzes various learning theories about adults and how they relate to the development of online courses and curricula. She begins with the idea that most adults have learned in "instructor-designed and instructor-led" classes (138), but online learners come with different expectations of learning design. After reviewing common characteristics of adult learners, Cercone discusses learning styles and their importance in the design of online courses and then notes, "There is no one theory that explains how adults learn, just as there is no one theory that explains all human learning" (142). Instead, the theories help instructors to be aware of who their students are and how to design their courses for these learners. Cercone then discusses the assumptions, criticisms, and concerns of andragogy, concluding that andragogy simply tries to recognize how adults learn differently from children. A discussion of the relationship between andragogy and experiential learning, self-directed learning, and transformative learning theory follows. Cercone then applies all of these theories to the development of courses and curricula in the online environment. — KKN

See: M. Carolyn Clark and Marsha Rossiter, "Narrative Learning in Adulthood" [49].

204   Crawley, Kristy Liles. "Renewing Our Commitment to Connecting to Student Veterans." *Teaching English in the Two-Year College* 41.1 (2013): 20–25. Print.

Noting that English instructors read articles on many aspects of diversity in the classroom, Crawley argues that instructors need to research articles on veterans so that the course materials meet the needs of veterans in the college writing classroom. Crawley not only read articles about veterans' needs, but she also found articles that complemented the works her students were reading. Adding these articles to the curriculum aided the discussion and the transition process the veterans were making to college and their nonmilitary lives. Crawley then addresses the development of student veteran organizations on college campuses and how instructors need to respond to veterans' essays as they read stories that often contain despair. —KKN

205   Fiddler, Morris, and Catherine Marienau. "Developing Habits of Reflection for Meaningful Learning." *Linking Adults with Community: Promoting Civic Engagement through Community-Based Learning.* Ed. Susan C. Reed and Catherine Marienau. Hoboken, NJ: Wiley, 2008. 75–85. Print. New Directions for Adult and Continuing Education 118.

Many assignments request that students reflect on their lives and experiences in order to provide context for current circumstances. However, as Fiddler and Marienau so aptly note, "for many adult students reflection does not happen easily on command" (76). Thus, they offer a model to facilitate the incorporation of reflection into the learning process, defining reflection as "inquiry into one's experience" to allow "meaningful learning." Fiddler and Marienau focus on "attention"; that is, they focus on the idea that we perceive only part of a specific experience, and it is what we perceive that shapes our memories, understanding, and learning. Being aware of where and how that attention is focused can change the way we understand an experience. They caution that there is a difference between experiential learning and learning from experience; it is reflection that allows what has been experienced to become learning. Adding specific, dedicated time for the practice of reflection, providing a rubric to both guide and assess the students' evaluation of their experiences, and making plain the difference between experience and learning can encourage authentic reflection. Fiddler and Marienau offer specific and concrete recommendations to facilitate this process. —SFL

206   Fiddler, Morry, Catherine Marienau, and Urban Whitaker. *Assessing Learning: Standards, Principles, & Procedures.* 2nd ed. Dubuque, IA: Kendall Hunt & CAEL, 2006. Print.

Fiddler, Marienau, and Whitaker provide guidelines for assessing both "sponsored learning" (guided by a person other than the learner, e.g., a teacher) and "unsponsored learning" (guided by a learner). Since the authors' focus is on assessing higher-order thinking, their guide to assessing learning pertains mainly to adults. Ten standards for prior learning assessment (PLA) are described in chapter 3. Approved by the Council for Adult and Experiential Learning, these ten standards provide a foundation for the book's seven chapters. Because these principles apply (at least in part) to course-based sponsored learning, the book's contents are useful for assessment in traditional teacher-directed classes as well as for assessing self-directed and undirected (unsponsored) learning experiences. Key definitions and distinctions appear throughout the book; for example, the authors distinguish between assessing the learning achieved by an organization and assessing the learning acquired by an individual. A series of appendices provides a glossary of terms, concrete suggestions for articulating learning outcomes, and principles and procedures for assessing learning in both sponsored and unsponsored learning contexts. By avoiding discussion of any specific learning theory, learning activity, or instructional approach, the authors offer a guide to learning assessment that has wide applications to all academic disciplines and forms of professional expertise. — BJG

207   Freiler, Tammy J. "Learning through the Body." *Third Update on Adult Learning Theory.* Ed. Sharan B. Merriam. Hoboken, NJ: Wiley, 2008. 37–47. Print. New Directions for Adult and Continuing Education 119.

Freiler discusses various types of embodied learning in relation to knowing one's self. She states that the terms *embodiment, embodied learning,* and *somatic learning* are all interrelated, as they deal with how bodily experiences are "a source of constructing knowledge through engaged, lived body experiences" (39). She then presents different types of body-centered activities that promote bodily awareness. Freiler follows this discussion with a presentation of research on embodiment in various contexts, including miners and female student-athletes. Freiler presents her own study on how students in a nursing course experienced bodily awareness and summarizes the various discussions by arguing that embodied learning is "an alternative way to construct knowledge" (43). She then presents a brief discussion on why it is important to give attention to the body as it relates to adult learning. — KKN

208   Gadbow, Nancy F. "Teaching All Learners As If They Are Special." *Contemporary Viewpoints on Teaching Adults Effectively.* Ed. Jovita M. Ross-Gordon. Hoboken, NJ: Wiley, 2002, 51–61. Print. New Directions for Adult and Continuing Education 93.

Basing her study on learner-centered approaches for teaching adult learners, Gadbow argues that instructors need to become learners along with their students, considering the special needs and situations for learning. She then provides examples of types of special needs and situations that adult learners bring to various learning environments, from adult education to graduate school programs. Gadbow argues that adult educators need to help each student identify his or her learning style and special needs. She states that traditional education focuses on content, but this focus does not provide for students with disabilities who may need alternate learning methods. This does not mean that standards are lowered. Teachers can match creative learning strategies with learners' needs, but first instructors need to get to know their students individually. This can be done through small group meetings or individual meetings. Instructors then can adjust the approaches used with the class content. Teachers need to encourage students to try different learning approaches also. Gadbow notes that many adult learners "do not know what they do not know" (58). Therefore, teachers need to provide individual resource information to students so that they can find the particular help they need. —KKN

209   Holzman, Michael. "Evaluation in Adult Literacy Programs." *The Writing Instructor* 7.1 (Fall 1987): 8–20. Print.

Relying on commentary by A. H. Charnley and H. A. Jones in *The Concept of Success in Adult Literacy* (Huntington Publishers Limited, 1979), Holzman explores issues and questions surrounding evaluation of adult literacy education. Defining *literacy* is an essential starting point, a process that must answer two questions: "literacy for whom?" and "literacy for what?" (8). Holzman argues that by answering these questions, we will reach a consensus that there are multiple literacies, not just one type of uniform literacy. One longstanding and widely used approach has been the use of primary and secondary school grade levels to identify adult students' literacy competencies. This approach is not viewed as appropriate for describing adults' literacy abilities by Charnley and Jones or by Thomas Sticht, and Holzman agrees. He points out that while a child's developing literacy abilities matches the child's age with a grade level, no such equivalency exists for adults, who often make as much progress in one month as a child can make in one full year. Holzman adds that adults' learning processes are not necessarily the same as children's learning processes. Two alternative bases for evaluation are considered: performative and functional literacy. Performative evaluations of literacy are exemplified by the University of Texas Adult Performance Level (APL) scale, which Holzman views as highly problematic. Functional evaluations of literacy, first introduced by UNESCO, are characterized by assessing specific functional tasks and have yielded the lesson that literacy activities must be useful to individuals and supported by societies. While functional and performative approaches to adult literacy evaluation start with the needs of a society, the intentions of the individual are discussed as an important starting point by Charnley and Jones. Holzman observes that this focus on individual adults' expressed learning interests and emotions is a particularly valuable contribution to discussions of adult literacy evaluation by Charnley and Jones. Holzman concludes by observing that direct methods of assessing are more valid than indirect methods, that assessments should be tied to the specific goals of educational programs, and that adult literacy evaluations are best used to serve the needs of adult learners. —BJG

210   Karpiak, Irene. "Writing Our Life: Adult Learning and Teaching through Autobiography." *Canadian Journal of University Continuing Education* 26.1 (2000): 31–50. Web. 26 Sept. 2010.

Drawing upon the work of Stephen Brookfield and Jack Mezirow, Karpiak explores the capacity of autobiography to facilitate critical reflection and transformative learning in adults. She argues that "autobiography involves not only recounting memories and expressions but also finding their larger meaning, and to the extent that activity expands the individual's knowledge of self and the world, it constitutes learning" (35). In her adult learning class, Karpiak allowed students to substitute "five chapters of their life" for a traditional final assignment, encouraging them to look for larger meanings, metaphors, and patterns as they wrote, rather than strictly reporting a chronology of events. These central metaphors created greater coherence for students and allowed them to contextualize their experiences. When interviewed six months after the course ended about the efficacy of the assignment, students reported that the course had provided many benefits, including "validation and self-acceptance" (42). While Karpiak cautions that not all autobiographical writing is as effective in fostering learning, she offers a set of guidelines to help students create meaningful learning experiences through autobiography. — SFL

211   Kasworm, Carol E., and Catherine A. Marienau. "Principles for Assessment of Adult Learning." *Assessing Adult Learning in Diverse Settings: Current Issues and Approaches.* Hoboken, NJ: Wiley, 1997. 5–16. Print. New Directions for Adult and Continuing Education 75.

Kasworm and Marienau propose five principles to use when developing "adult-oriented assessment practices" (6). The principles were developed because most postsecondary institutions develop assessments based on younger, traditional students. However, these traditional assessment principles do not fit adult learners with different characteristics and experiences. Additionally, as adults age, they become even more differentiated. The principles were developed according to the principles of adult learning, based on several researchers' work. Summing up, the authors state, "Assessment . . . centered in adult learning will consider the community of social practice, critical reflections on applications of knowledge, and knowledge that contributes to meaning-making in the context of various adult roles" (15). — KKN

See: Denis O. Kiely and Lisa Swift, "Casualties of War: Combat Trauma and the Return of the Combat Veteran" [144].

212   Lees, Elaine O. "Building Thought on Paper with Adult Basic Writers." *The Writer's Mind: Writing as a Mode of Thinking.* Ed. Janice N. Hays, Phyllis A. Roth, Jon R. Ramsey, and Robert D. Foulke. Urbana, IL: NCTE, 1983. 145–52. Print.

A sequence of two basic writing courses offers reentry adults opportunities to gain practice in constructing knowledge and shaping meaning. As an instructor in the evening division at the University of Pittsburgh, Elaine Lees observed that her basic writing students experienced difficulties with generalizing and with writing effective conclusions. Drawing on published research by James Moffett and David Bartholomae, Lees designed sequenced writing assignments that start with narrative writing about particular cases and end with generalizations and theory-building. A first basic writing course focuses on the subject of writing while a second course addresses the topic of changing versus preserving, with specific reference to adjustments made by adults. These writing assignments encourage students to practice a key cognitive strategy associated with academic discourse: moving back and forth between particular cases and generalizations.—BJG

213   Mansfield, Margaret A. "Real World Writing and the English Curriculum." *College Composition and Communication* 44.1 (1993): 69–83. Print.

Investigating possible benefits of professional writing to college writing courses, Mansfield analyzes graduate students' learning in a course titled Writing for the Public. Graduate students were asked to develop a survey questionnaire and conduct interviews in order to explore faculty and student perceptions of a college writing proficiency exam. A faculty senate committee inquiry was already underway to address student complaints, so these graduate students were encouraged to view themselves as a subcommittee of an active faculty senate committee. The graduate students were engaged in "real-world" writing, as opposed to the artificial construct of writing for a teacher and a course grade. They learned about concepts of collaborative authorship and the practice of writing for multiple audiences as they crafted questions for a survey questionnaire. As current or future secondary school teachers, these students would be able to apply their learning to their own teaching of writing. Mansfield concludes that professional writing assignments have a legitimate place in academic writing courses. Her students practiced new forms of writing, learned about collaborative writing, wrote for multiple audiences, deepened their understandings of professional writing, and challenged their perceptions of what counts as "real" writing. Similarly, these same lessons can be taught to students enrolled in first-year college composition courses.—BJG

214   Mueller, Julie, Eileen Wood, and Jen Hunt. "Assessing Adult Student Reactions to Assistive Technology in Writing Instruction." *Adult Basic Education and Literacy Journal* 3.1 (2009): 13–23. Print.

In a research study conducted at a community-based adult literacy program, Mueller, Wood, and Hunt analyze the results of implementing assistive technology so that adult learners can use computers to improve their communication skills. Several key findings have emerged. When choosing software and instructional methods for adult learners enrolled in writing classes, instructors should consult adult students about their selections to ensure that these students' needs will be met. Tutors must be available to encourage and instruct adult learners so that they develop independent critical thinking skills with respect to both writing and computers. Outcomes must be measured according to the objectives and requirements of the adult students. In general, the study showed that students reacted positively to the assistive technology, which helped them to improve their writing skills.—LDB

See: Julie L. Ozanne, Natalie Ross Adkins, and Jennifer A. Sandlin, "Shopping [for] Power: How Adult Literacy Learners Negotiate the Marketplace" [25].

See: Nancy D. Padak and Bryan A. Bardine, "Engaging Readers and Writers in Adult Education Contexts" [122].

215   Wright, Melissa, and Adelia Grabowsky. "The Role of the Adult Educator in Helping Learners Access and Select Quality Health Information on the Internet." *Adult Education for Health and Wellness.* Hoboken, NJ: Wiley, 2011. 79–88. Print. New Directions for Adult and Continuing Education 130.

Wright and Grabowsky provide statistics on Internet searches for health information, and then they argue that adults' health literacy is poor. The authors note that most adults read at an eighth grade level, but most health care materials are written at a tenth grade level. Therefore, their work is focused on how adult educators can aid learners with identifying and evaluating good health care information sources online. Referring to Knowles's five steps for self-directed learning, Wright and Grabowsky discuss the steps adult educators can use to help learners locate, access, and understand health information on the Internet. They then provide specific guidelines to help adult learners evaluate reputable online sources of health information. Suggestions for questions to teach students to ask about Web sites are provided, and the questions are the common journalist questions of who, what, why, where, when, and how. Noting the number of hits simple health terms may get on the Internet, Wright and Grabowsky discuss how adult learners may be overwhelmed with the amount of information. Therefore, the authors note examples of reputable, professional health information sites. Because of the vast amount of health information on the Web, some of which is not reputable, Wright and Grabowsky call for adult educators to help adult learners learn how to evaluate the information. — KKN

Diverse Contexts for Teaching and Learning Reading and Writing

English Language Learner Classes

See: Elsa Auerbach, *Adult ESL/Literacy from the Community to the Community: A Guidebook for Participatory Literacy Training* [155].

216 Guth, Gloria J. A. "Profiles of Adult ESL Literacy Programs." *TESOL Quarterly* 27.3 (1993): 533–37. Print.

Guth explains that adult ESL literacy programs vary by organizational sponsor, approach to literacy instruction, and learner needs. Common organizational sponsors of adult ESL literacy programs are community-based organizations, community colleges, workplaces, and adult schools—all of which are briefly described in this essay. Adult ESL programs housed in community-based organizations often attract staff and students from local neighborhoods where people are likely to come from similar cultures and speak the same language. Community college adult ESL courses usually serve the academic needs of students who aspire to enter college, though this is not always true for all programs or all students. Workplace literacy programs serve the specific literacy needs of individuals who are employed to perform particular tasks for their employers. Adult schools attract a more culturally diverse population than community-based organizations and are therefore more challenged to meet students' needs. Approaches to literacy instruction are often determined by funding sources; for example, state-funded adult ESL literacy programs are usually held accountable by test scores, so a competency-based curriculum is commonly required. Alternatively, the International Institute of Rhode Island employs a learner-centered curriculum based on student writing about topics that students know or care about, which then can become reading material for the course. El Barrio Popular Education Program in New York City relies on a participatory approach to produce biliterate graduates who can serve as leaders in their communities. Learners' needs sometimes form the foundation for adult ESL literacy curricula, as is true for The Refugee Women's Alliance in Seattle, where refugee women's common experiences create a foundation for curricula based on storytelling and oral histories. Guth argues that learners' needs and community needs are particularly important for creating adult ESL literacy programs that best serve the students who seek out these programs. — BJG

217   Hillard, Van E. "A Place in the City: Hull-House and the Architecture of Civility." *City Comp: Identities, Spaces, Practices.* Ed. Bruce McComiskey and Cynthia Ryan. Albany: State U of New York P, 2003. 111–27. Print.

Hillard presents the mission and services of settlement houses as a useful model for integrating civic engagement and distinctly urban concerns into contemporary urban college writing classes. Established by Jane Addams and her colleagues in 1889, Hull-House provides the most well-known example of US settlement houses. It addressed the social, educational, cultural, and legal needs of recent immigrants and other city residents who inhabited poor neighborhoods while promoting middle-class values and socioeconomic benefits. An extension of the 1880s urban charitable movement, Hull-House evolved from a social service organization to a multipurpose institution offering public speaker events, a labor history museum, theater performances, special exhibits, sponsorship of a branch of the public library, legal services, and free classes. Clients and volunteer employees were encouraged to create a geographically anchored community by living in the same neighborhood and coming together in spaces where they could dine, engage in sports activities, and use public baths. Hull-House writing classes invited students to write about their observations of places, organizations, and issues in their communities—for example, street cleaning, garbage collection, and trade unions. Critical literacy was promoted by reading civic documents, such as the Declaration of Independence or naturalization manuals, rather than by reading grammar handbooks or educational textbooks. The model represented by Hull-House and other settlement houses offers a rich framework for developing critical literacy and civic engagement in contemporary urban university college writing classes.—BJG

See: Yongyan Li, "Apprentice Scholarly Writing in a Community of Practice: An Intraview of an NNES Graduate Student Writing a Research Article" [90].

218   Lvovich, Natasha. *The Multilingual Self: An Inquiry into Language Learning.* Mahwah, NJ: Erlbaum, 1997. Print.

Portraying her complex language learning and acculturation experiences as a young, multilingual adult, Lvovich narrates her experiences learning French, Italian, and English. After immigrating from the Soviet Union to Paris, where she felt very much at home, Lvovich lived briefly in Italy and then arrived in Brooklyn, New York, where she and her parents ultimately settled. Her first reaction to New York City was profoundly negative: "I walk along New York streets—and they are prison to me" (61). However, after finding work as an English language teacher, Lvovich challenged herself to love American culture. In the end, she learns more about her own multilayered identity "as a teacher, a person, an immigrant, and a language learner" (67). As a Jewish woman, she was a political refugee from the Soviet Union, a factor which may have affected her motivation to learn English and to integrate into US culture. As a teacher of English language learners, Lvovich speculated on the applications of language learning theories to her own experiences. She expresses the view that her autobiographical account is designed to inform students who are learning a new language, graduate students studying language learning and teaching, and language instructors. — BJG

See: Brigitte Marshall, *Preparing for Success: A Guide for Teaching Adult English Language Learners* [169].

See: Heather McKay and Abigail Tom, *Teaching Adult Second Language Learners* [170].

See: Methal R. Mohammed, "Don't Give Me a Fish; Teach Me How to Fish: A Case Study of an International Adult Learner" [191].

See: Richard A. Orem, *Teaching Adult English Language Learners* [172].

See: Betsy Parrish, *Teaching Adult ESL: A Practical Introduction* [173].

See: David Schwarzer, "Best Practices for Teaching the 'Whole' Adult ESL Learner" [175].

219   Weinstein-Shr, Gail. "Overview Discussion: Directions in Adult ESL Literacy: An Invitation to Dialogue." *TESOL Quarterly* 27.3 (1993): 517–28. Print.

In reviewing other authors' contributions and her own experiences for a special issue of *TESOL Quarterly*, Weinstein-Shr provides a platform for future discussions of adult literacy teaching, learning, program planning, and research. Three areas are proposed for future dialogues: (1) a need for shifting the focus from individuals and institutions to families and communities; (2) emphasis on the value of existing knowledge for acquiring new learning; and (3) fostering collaboration for everyone involved in adult literacy education. Weinstein-Shr describes examples of adult learners to illustrate these specific areas of need. One of these adult learners is Maria, a literacy student who knew only three letters of the Spanish alphabet, yet had full responsibility for the literacy-related needs of her family (e.g., purchasing groceries, handling bill payments, and filling prescriptions). One implication from Weinstein-Shr's discussion is the need for teachers to look beyond student performance inside classrooms. Research must also expand beyond classroom boundaries to include family and community contexts for literacy use and literacy acquisition. — BJG

See: Christopher Worthman, "The Positioning of Adult Learners: Appropriating Learner Experience on the Continuum of Empowerment to Emancipation" [178].

Online Environments

220   Blair, Kristine, and Cheryl Hoy. "Paying Attention to Adult Learners Online: The Pedagogy and Politics of Community." *Computers and Composition* 23 (2006): 32–48. Print.

Blair and Hoy argue that private, one-on-one communication, particularly e-mail, offers an important tool for responding to the unique needs and learning styles of adult students in online classes. When teaching an online writing course for adult students working on prior learning assessment portfolios, they found that e-mail allowed student-teacher and student-student coaching relationships that became "among the most powerful tools in teaching and learning" (33). These private exchanges supported students by creating connection, establishing an ethic of caring, and accommodating the varying levels of academic preparation and life circumstances of adult students. The exchanges involved more intimacy and more mixing of the personal with the academic than face-to-face office hours and individual conferences. In making their argument, the authors are responding to critiques that "too much" e-mail can turn an online class into a "correspondence course," to the privileging of community building in public discussion boards, and to the lack of recognition for the hidden labor of teachers engaged in these private exchanges. They argue that the important role of one-on-one communication needs to be considered in preparing online instructors and that the labor-intensive practices associated with one-on-one communication should be taken into account by administrators who are making decisions about faculty workload. —MNC

See: Lauren Marshall Bowen, "Resisting Age Bias in Digital Literacy Research" [74].

See: Jennifer Calvin and Beth Winfrey Freeburg, "Exploring Adult Learners' Perceptions of Technology Competence and Retention in Web-based Courses" [46].

See: Kathleen Cercone, "Characteristics of Adult Learners with Implications for Online Learning Design" [203].

221   Collins, Royce Ann. "The Role of Learning Styles and Technology." *International Journal of Web-Based Learning and Teaching Technologies* 4.4 (2009): 50–65. Print.

Collins investigates the connection between the way students learn and the technologies developed to teach them. She analyzes why adult learners in particular must have constructive feedback and encouragement from their instructors if they are to perceive technological advances in a positive manner. Since technology has changed the way students seek and respond to data, more research is needed to develop effective virtual classrooms in which students' learning styles help to determine the curriculum. In her article, Collins begins with a discussion of learning styles, specifically connecting styles with a variety of instruments involved in learning style research. She analyzes the styles within the context of a discussion involving online course development. Experiential approaches, social interaction approaches, personality models, multiple and emotional intelligences, perception models, and conditions and needs are the six categories of learning styles upon which the article is based. Collins includes suggestions for using blogs, wikis, chats, and video conferencing, depending on the learning styles of adult students. However, she believes more research is needed to explore the link between learning styles and the needs of US and international adult students. Advancements in global knowledge exploration have increased the demands placed on these older students, and many of them are uncomfortable with technology. She concludes that this research should be a priority because more adult learners are selecting online classes due to their convenience and rising gas prices. —LDB

222   Cornelius, Sarah, and Carole Gordon. "Adult Learners' Use of Flexible Online Resources in a Blended Programme." *Educational Media International* 46 (2009): 239–53. Print.

Examining the effectiveness of online learning, Cornelius and Gordon report on a study of adult students enrolled in the Teaching Qualification (Further Education), or TQ(FE), program. The study was intended to "illustrate how learners engage with flexible online materials" (242). The TQ(FE), delivered by the University of Aberdeen, is taken by about 130 lecturers each year. It is taken by small groups of lecturers (fifteen to twenty) and facilitated by one university tutor. Two of the four courses in the TQ(FE) follow an alternative model that includes full-day workshops and online learning. The authors note that online "materials form the core of the content for each course" and that the "major feature of each course is a 'Learning Lexicon.' . . . This is a flexible set of activities and resources organized under a set of key terms" (242). The Learning Lexicon encourages adults to be self-directed learners and allows faculty to address students' needs at various levels. It also offers several advantages to students: The activities are always accessible and can be used flexibly, either for group or individual study. To study adult students' use of the Learning Lexicon, the researchers collected data through focus groups with the program's tutors, reviewed artifacts, examined students' reports on their use of the "Learning Lexicon," and interviewed students. One finding is that students report a "generally positive attitude towards the flexibility provided by the programme" (245). Students also described "a range of roles and strategies adopted . . . for working with online resources" (245). The authors note that most study participants expressed a positive response to the flexibility offered by the curriculum. They also adopted a variety of learning strategies, including the "universalists," who studied everything available to them; the "butterflies," who touched lightly upon multiple subjects of interest; the "changelings," who changed from one strategy to another; and the "minimalists," who did as little as possible. The authors suggest that an online learning environment is helpful to most students because of the flexibility it provides, but also note that students continue to need support in order to be successful. Since returning students are likely to be more comfortable with a lecture-based model of education, it's important for there to be clear guidelines and expectations for online learning, and students should have regular opportunities to reflect on their learning experiences. Finally, online course delivery changes the relationships between learners and instructors since it isn't lecture based. In these courses, the instructor functions more in the capacity of a "guide on the side" (251).—TBP

223   Crow, Angela. "What's Age Got to Do with It? Teaching Older Students in Computer-Aided Classrooms." *Teaching English in the Two-Year College* (May 2000): 400–6. Print.

Crow argues that older students may have difficulty moving from the traditional classroom to one that is computer aided, and once instructors understand the challenges that older students face in computer-aided classrooms, they can "make that integration feasible and maintain older students' authority and dignity" (400). She says that we need to address the issues of access as well as difficulty with learning and remembering technology with older students. Crow reviews theories on working memory and capacity of the brain, which deteriorate with age, and literature on the slowing-down process people experience as they age. For students with little to no computer skills, navigating material in a computer-aided classroom is learning a new literacy. She notes that some younger students have similar difficulties, but her experiences show that older students have more difficulties and younger students learn the new material more quickly. After providing suggestions for instructors to help older students in computer-aided classrooms, she concludes by stating that instructors need to be sensitive to students' age-related challenges.—KKN

224   DePew, Kevin Eric, T. A. Fishman, Julia E. Romberger, and Bridget Fahey Ruetenik. "Designing Efficiencies: The Parallel Narratives of Distance Education and Composition Studies." *Computers and Composition* 23.1 (2006): 49–67. Print.

DePew et al. warn that valuing Distance Education (DE) primarily because of its potential to reduce costs might encourage composition faculty to adopt a pedagogy of Current Traditional Rhetoric (CTR) since both DE and CTR are perceived as efficient methods of information transfer. The authors examine "the parallel historical narratives of DE and CTR and discuss some disturbing trends toward mechanization of DE instruction along with promising instances of dialogic practices" (50). Marketing of DE mirrors the marketing of nineteenth-century correspondence courses, which offered "the benefit of flexibility to schedule learning and the efficient use of time for education that could be integrated into an already busy life" (51). The same ideology of efficiency is readily apparent in contemporary scholarship on DE. Similarly, CTR highlighted "communicative efficiency" at the expense of meaning-making and audience awareness. DE instructional methods require smaller class sizes than do courses that rely on CTR and are therefore more expensive. Furthermore, the focus on cost-efficiency always has had an impact on hiring decisions. In the nineteenth century, holders of PhDs in English were considered too valuable to assign to composition instruction. Now, teaching assistants and contingent faculty are the most likely to take on DE courses for many reasons, including the likelihood that these courses will continue to need faculty. Using the least powerful faculty, however, will not lead to the strongest program. A successful DE program will rely on frequent writing assignments and dialogic exchanges between the student and faculty and the students with each other. Over time, a well-regarded DE program will attract more students. — TBP

225   Grabill, Jeffrey T. "Utopic Visions, the Technopoor, and Public Access: Writing Technologies in a Community Literacy Program." *Computers and Composition* 15 (1998): 297–315. Print.

Grabill investigates an adult learning center that he calls the Western District Adult Basic Education program. Reporting on access to computers and online networks, he frames his "discussion in terms of writing with computers outside composition classrooms" (298). This discussion is important because though the question of access to computers and networks has been comprehensively addressed (if not answered) within university settings, these questions have not been addressed in the multiple contexts for learning that exist in other locations. Since "access to writing technologies is unequal, the literacy learning of students and workers suffers" (298). Grabill presents a model of access based on work by James Porter. The model consists of "infrastructural access" (computers connected to a wide area network), literacy (computer skills and expertise), and community or social acceptance (299). Grabill then cites surveys showing that the higher one's income and level of education, the more likely one is to make use of networked computers. The failure to provide adequate equipment to adult basic education programs contributes to the widening gap between the technological haves and have-nots, the "technopoor" of the title (302). Grabill's study of the Western District Adult Basic Education program confirms the survey findings. Having observed a "Computers and Communication class," Grabill found that the computers at the program hardly worked, the network was frequently out of service, the software was out of date, the instructor was inadequately trained, and the students were frustrated. As a result of this study, Grabill concludes that "computers and *composition*" as a field should change its focus to "computers and *writing*." Such a change, he writes, would force us "to consider the public and civic uses of computers for writing" (311). Computers and composition faculty are ideally suited to take on this work since they already have addressed these questions in academic contexts. — TBP

226 Halio, Marcia Peoples. "Teaching in Our Pajamas: Negotiating with Adult Learners in Online Distance Writing Courses." *College Teaching* 52.2 (2004): 58–62. Print.

Because online learning involves the more informal genre of e-mail, Halio analyzes the way in which adult learners often fail to organize their time and their writing styles in response to college course require-ments. Instead, they may rely on frequent e-mails to the instructor. Halio analyzes the content of 423 e-mails, about half of which were written by her to her own adult students. The other half were written by her students, many of whom needed personal attention to understand the assignments. They also required frequent attention due to esteem issues and lack of confidence, even though they were well-qualified in their professions. Proposing a series of eight questions designed to encourage critical thinking about how online learning differs from that of traditional learning, Halio focuses on the way students use e-mails to connect with instructors and thus receive the type of attention they could expect in a traditional or hybrid classroom. This leads to an inter-esting discussion about adult students helping to construct the courses they attend so that these classes meet career and personal requirements. Halio emphasizes the need to recognize both the strengths and weak-nesses of adult learners, who may bring to the classroom unique skills and knowledge but also the burdens of adult career and family respon-sibilities and issues of low self-esteem. —LDB

See: Catherine A. Hansman and Arthur L. Wilson, "Teaching Writing in Community Colleges: A Situated View of How Adults Learn to Write in Computer-Based Writing Classrooms" [139].

227 Huang, Hsiu-Mei. "Toward Constructivism for Adult Learners in On-line Learning Environments." *British Journal of Educational Technology* 33 (2002): 27–37. Print.

Informed by the work of Dewey and Vygotsky and also by adult learning theory, Huang posits ways for online learning to become constructivist through the active use of synchronous and asynchronous discussion and other online resources. Because adult learners are highly motivated and embrace ownership of their learning, they can play an active role in determining the direction of their education if empowered to do so. This involves shared power and agency between instructor and students. Huang identifies seven crucial issues in developing a construc-tivist approach to online learning, including the need for changed roles for both students and teachers in the creation of learning and learning environments, and the acknowledgment that this is an inten-sive process for both students and teachers. Assessment of knowledge in a constructivist approach also involves collaboration between teacher and student. To overcome these issues, she suggests that interactive, collaborative, and authentic learning can be facilitated by an instruc-tor who creates a "safe environment for learners to express themselves freely in appropriate ways" (33). —SFL

228   Inman, James A., and Dagmar Stuehrk Corrigan. "Toward a Doctoral Degree by Distance in Computers and Writing: Promises and Possibilities." *Computers and Composition* 18 (2001): 411–22. Print.

Inman and Stuehrk Corrigan begin this essay by noting that as access to the Web became more commonplace, distance education programs proliferated. These programs are particularly attractive to nontraditional students, who often have responsibilities that prevent them from pursuing degrees at residential campuses. The authors argue that because of these dynamics, the time has come to offer a fully online PhD program. The field of computers and writing has many experienced teachers of composition without doctoral training who are place-bound. Many of these are returning adult learners who would fit into a distance learning doctoral program. The authors then turn to the results of their survey of 150 degree-granting institutions. Half of these are four-year institutions, and the other half have graduate programs. Among the responses received from the four-year institutions, seven implied that "they do not believe computers and writing is a reasonable specialty" (415). The authors interpret these responses and others that reflected the same sentiment to mean that the field of computers and writing "does not fit well into all contemporary institutional and departmental cultures" (416). In terms of the assessment of applicants, many of the respondents did not feel that the applicants were strong candidates for a number of reasons — e.g., the candidates' lack of balance between technical and pedagogical issues, the failure to look at the new forms of writing that the technology created, and the weak records of publication. In their conclusion, the authors propose a PhD program that would exist fully online. The program would be administered by a consortium of institutions, and no course work would be required. Instead, students would complete four research projects overseen by any member of the consortium of the student's choice. The program of study would culminate with a dissertation. — TBP

229   Kim, Kyong-Jee. "Motivational Challenges of Adult Learners in Self-Directed E-Learning." *Journal of Interactive Learning Research* 20 (2009): 317–35. Print.

Kim reports on a study of adult students' motivations for completing online course work. The research included in-depth interviews with twelve students who had completed "self-directed e-learning courses in either academic . . . or workplace settings" (317). Study participants had taken self-paced, stand-alone courses developed by an e-learning vendor that offers over "3,000 e-learning courses to 20 million learners per year" (318). One finding was that students were motivated by the high level of interactivity associated with learning activities "such as animations and simulations" and "control over the pace and sequence of instruction" (317). Although the effectiveness of e-learning has been demonstrated, courses and programs that use this technology are plagued by high dropout rates. This condition warrants the continued study of student motivation, which is often conceptualized as either "intrinsic" or "extrinsic." Little is known about how these types of motivation affect e-learners, and few studies provide practical guidelines for motivating students. Some research has shown, though, that a "systematic approach to the design of motivational components in instruction can enhance or sustain learner motivation in online settings" (320). Individual student preferences also have an impact on motivation. Several studies conclude that a high level of interaction—both a large number of online activities to complete and animated demonstrations—motivates students. A high level of learner control has a positive impact on motivation. Students in the study took courses on a variety of subjects, including desktop applications, computer and Internet programming, and soft skills. About half the students had prior experience with e-learning. Instructors were available to only two students in the study. Six themes emerged from the interview. Of primary importance is the interactivity of course content, including "animations (movement of objects in response to the user's action), simulations (users responding to a set of different situations in conversation with others), and drag-and-drop quiz activities" (324–25). Another motivator is the ability to apply what they learn to real-world situations. Students were very motivated by the control they had over the course; they controlled both the pace and the sequence. Some participants noted that the lack of extrinsic motivators, such as instructor feedback and grades, drained their motivation.—TBP

230 Knightley, Wendy M. "Adult Learners Online: Students' Experiences of Learning Online." *Australian Journal of Adult Learning* 47.2 (2007): 264–88. Print.

In this study, the author "aimed to investigate the potential of online learning to overcome barriers to participating in education by socially disadvantaged adults" (264). Knightley surveyed seventy-nine students taking online learning courses at the Open University in the UK. While the study's sample is too small for generalized claims, the study does provide some insight into students' experiences. Knightley begins by defining "social exclusion." People can be considered socially excluded if "they are unable to participate in the basic economic and social activities of the society in which they live" (266). Indicators of social exclusion might include "financial difficulties, lack of basic necessities . . . poor housing conditions, lack of consumer durables, poor health, limited social contact or perceived dissatisfaction" (266). Though she acknowledges that the two concepts are used interchangeably, the author distinguishes between e-learning, which is "conceived of as learning that is supported and delivered through the use of ICT" (information and communication technology) and online learning, which is "delivered and supported through the internet" (268). Both e-learning and online learning are attractive to students because they offer flexibility in terms of study time. Online learning has the additional value of allowing students to interact with each other. Both forms of learning mask personal characteristics such as disabilities, which promote the sense of an egalitarian learning environment. The study demonstrates that many students (46 percent) chose the Open University because of it offered "part-time, distance learning with high quality resources and support," and another 10 percent chose it because of "the potential to dovetail Open University study with childcare or other caring responsibilities" (79). Many students (21 percent) were not sure what was meant by the phrase "online learning," but 46 percent thought online learning provided "a more convenient way of accessing information and people, through the use of technology" (276). Overall, over half of the survey respondents (53 percent) reported a preference for studying online while only 11 percent preferred offline learning. — TBP

See: Julie Mueller, Eileen Wood, and Jen Hunt, "Assessing Adult Student Reactions to Assistive Technology in Writing Instruction" [214].

See: Michelle Navarre Cleary, Suzanne Sanders-Betzold, Polly Hoover, and Peggy St. John, "Working with Wikis in Writing-Intensive Classes" [147].

231 Pandey, Iswari P. "Literate Lives across the Digital Divide." *Computers and Composition* 23.2 (2006): 246–57. Print.

Pandey draws attention to social and political dimensions of literacy learning. He complicates the concept of the "digital divide" to include not just relative poverty and wealth but also how literacy itself, including digital literacies, is deployed by the government to reproduce or undermine political ideologies. To achieve this goal, Pandey writes a literacy narrative. He begins the narrative in 2005 with the writing of this essay. At that time, he was living in the United States and pursuing graduate studies. His home country of Nepal, however, was experiencing both political and social turmoil. Pandey then describes his literacy education from his early years in "order to give [his] readers a fuller view of the ways the external contexts condition (digital) literacy learning" (247). Pandey was born in a rural area of Nepal in 1968, eight years after the king of Nepal successfully toppled a democratically elected government. The king specifically was concerned that increased levels of literacy would lead to popular discontent, so he strictly controlled education and access to mass media. During this period, the author learned to read and write under his father's guidance. At 5, he entered a Sanskrit school; at 10, he entered a public school at which he studied, among other things, English. Learning English laid the groundwork for the digital literacy that would one day facilitate his ability to cross the digital divide. During this period of his education, two curricula emerged: the state-sponsored curriculum and an alternative curriculum based on protest literature. As he finished his MA in 1993, the writer became aware of the value of digital literacy as he sought to complete his thesis. His access to computers is an important part of his literacy narrative because it demonstrates that "state ideology . . . shapes not only the course of learning as carried out in schools and colleges but also the technology of literacy" (250). It was only the change in politics that was not dominated by nobility that made technology available. Describing the history of technology in Nepal and his own personal history as a learner of technology, Pandey reports overcoming many obstacles to becoming literate and warns against interpreting his story as a "hero narrative." The politics of use and place both "undercut the prevailing myths about computer and the Internet as neutral and world-wide medium" (253). Literacy practices across the digital divide, then, do not take the form of a linear narrative but involve an "ongoing negotiation" (254). — TBP

232   Park, Ji-Hye, and Hee Jun Choi. "Factors Influencing Adult Learners' Decision to Drop Out or Persist in Online Learning." *Educational Technology and Society* 12.4 (2009): 207–17. Print.

The authors review a number of studies that have tried to identify the reasons for high dropout rates among online adult learners. They note, however, that very few of these studies have included empirical research and that "no consensus has been reached for which factors have definite influences on the decision" to drop out (209). The researchers collected quantitative data from "147 learners who had dropped out of or finished one of the online courses offered from a large Midwestern university" and found that dropouts and persistent learners "showed statistical differences in perceptions of family and organizational support, and satisfaction and relevance" (207). The dropout rate in the courses the researchers studied had increased from 47 percent to 54.2 percent. Of the 147 students who participated in the study, 66.7 percent completed the course and 33.3 percent dropped out. The majority of these students (85.7 percent) were 30 or over. Through surveys of students, the researchers concluded that individual characteristics have little or no impact on a student's decision to drop out of an online course. Students' perceived lack of family and job support does have an impact on their decision to drop out. It is important for instructors to try to be aware of students' perceived lack of support since instructors might be able to compensate by providing extra attention to these students and helping the students to remain motivated. If possible, administrators and instructors also should try to build family and organizational support by explaining the relevance of the course. Students are also much less likely to drop out "when they are satisfied with the courses, and when the courses are relevant to their own lives" (215). The authors suggest that course work be centered around activities that can be applied and that the subject be centered around subjects that are relevant to students' interests and goals. An online course needs to be designed to stimulate interaction. These results are consistent with previous studies on this subject. — TBP

233   Rodriquez, Frank G., and Susan Smith Nash. "Technology and the Adult Degree Program: The Human Element." *Developing and Delivering Adult Degree Programs.* Ed. James P. Pappas and Jerry Jerman. Hoboken, NJ: Wiley, 2004. 91–96. Print. New Directions for Adult and Continuing Education 103.

Adult degree programs rely heavily on computers and online learning for delivery of courses and related services to students. While online instruction provides more educational opportunities, online courses also pose new challenges. At the University of Oklahoma's College of Liberal Studies, Frank Rodriquez and Susan Smith Nash have created the college's first online undergraduate degree option. The greatest challenge faced was not with the technologies themselves but within the space where humans and technology intersect. For instance, students sometimes changed their e-mail addresses and then lost contact with their instructors. Use of the more reliable college e-mail accounts instead of personal accounts solved this problem. Professors also had to transition from teaching in a classroom to teaching online. To facilitate this transition, Rodriquez and Smith Nash provided specialized training in online teaching for faculty. In so doing, they identified four faculty responses to online teaching, which ranged from complete acceptance to total rejection of online instruction. For adult degree programs offered entirely online, there is also a significant online customer service component. The lack of opportunity for in-person interaction caused college administrators to question the value of a completely online learning experience. In the end, Rodriquez and Smith Nash concluded that although technology is advancing and increasingly present within many colleges and universities, the experience of face-to-face interaction continues to be valued by faculty, staff, and students.—MAR

234   Ruey, Shieh. "A Case Study of Constructivist Instructional Strategies for Adult Online Learning." *British Journal of Educational Technology* 41.5 (2010): 706–20. Print.

Ruey discusses using constructivist theory in online courses at a national university in Taiwan. Ranging in age from 20 to 49, students met face-to-face at the beginning, middle, and end of the two classes that were studied. Most students were new to online learning. Ruey found that the adult learners, especially those in the 30–39 age group, became "more responsible, self-controlled learners" (715). Sharing life experiences and reading what others thought of a topic helped the students the most. Some students appeared to lack interest in "making more effort throughout the course" (715). Ruey suggests that instructors' lack of feedback and vague assessment policies might account for the lack of interest in making an effort observed in some students. In order to foster an adult-oriented collaborative learning environment featuring shared inquiry, Ruey recommends a "mutual learning relationship" (718) among adult students, teaching assistants, and instructors and careful attention to assessment of student learning.—KKN

235   Stine, Linda. "The Best of Both Worlds: Teaching Basic Writers in Class and Online." *Journal of Basic Writing* 23.2 (2004): 49–69. Print.

Stine argues that a basic writing course should, for multiple reasons, incorporate online learning. Acknowledging that there are many possibilities for how this might be accomplished, she presents one model for a hybrid course that she finds effective. Stine developed this model for adult students (age 25 to 64) who were enrolled in a pre-master's degree program in order to prepare for entry into a Master of Human Services program at Lincoln University (in Pennsylvania). These students attended a face-to-face (f2f) class every other week and on alternate weeks submitted reading responses and essays via a course delivery platform such as Blackboard. Stine begins by acknowledging that there are many good reasons why basic writing students should not be expected to complete their work online. Basic writing students might have less access to technology, so the requirement for online learning might have an extremely negative impact on them. Moreover, even if students do have access to computers, they also must learn to use them for specific applications while they are learning to write. Others note that the online environment is not as rich as the f2f environment, and this lack of richness might diminish student involvement. In addition, many of the features of good online reading—filtering, skimming, and pecking—are exactly the qualities that make basic writing students poor readers. Finally, the online environment forces students to work in a text-rich environment that might be overwhelming for them, and it asks even more of instructors since they must do additional work to prepare their courses for online delivery. Stine concludes that in spite of these legitimate concerns, there are many reasons to pursue a hybrid course. Online learning allows some students who might be unwilling to talk in f2f classrooms the opportunity to participate in online conversations. Stine also notes that "students learn by doing something worth doing" and that writing in online environments is perceived as something worth doing (55). The hybrid course also dramatically increases access to education and "can double the number of students who can use a school's scarce computer laboratories and, at the same time, halve these students' commuting costs" (50). Citing Evan Davis and Sarah Hardy, Stine notes that online learning helps students build their academic skills, which includes "organizing and tacking documents, participating in a community discussion, sharing work with peers, [and] claiming a voice through writing" (56). Instructors should teach students how to participate in online learning since so much meaningful interaction happens on the Web. If basic writing students are to participate fully in contemporary culture as writers, they need to understand communication in a Web context. Stine concludes by noting that online learning encourages and enhances student/faculty contact, cooperation among students, active learning, and time on task. —TBP

Prior Learning Assessment and Accelerated Degree Programs

See: Susan A. Brewer, James D. Klein, and Kenneth E. Mann, "Using Small Group Learning Theories with Adult Re-entry Students" [179].

236   Colvin, Janet. *Earn College Credit for What You Know*. 4th ed. Chicago: Kendall Hunt/CAEL, 2010. Print.

Colvin introduces prior learning assessment (PLA) practices to current and prospective adult undergraduates. PLA allows students to accelerate progress toward degree completion by earning credit for knowledge acquired outside classrooms. Students earn credits for learning they have acquired at work, in the military, at home, in volunteer organizations, and in certificate programs. Common pathways to earning PLA credits include College Learning Exam Programs (CLEP), Advanced Placement exams, transcript evaluation for transfer credits, institutional challenge exams, and portfolio evaluation of documented experiential learning. Complete chapters are devoted to earning credit by transcript evaluation, examination, and portfolios compiled to document learning acquired outside college. Colvin provides concrete guidelines for portfolio development, together with information about how portfolios are evaluated and how to challenge a portfolio credits award. Colvin also offers research practices and writing advice in chapters 9 and 10, while providing resources for students seeking information about PLA throughout the book and in an appendix. —BJG

237   Kasworm, Carol E. "From the Adult Student's Perspective: Accelerated Degree Programs." *Accelerated Learning for Adults: The Promise and Practice of Intensive Educational Formats*. Ed. Raymond J. Wlodkowski and Carol E. Kasworm. Hoboken, NJ: Wiley, 2003. 17–27. Print. New Directions for Adult and Continuing Education 97.

Kasworm reviews findings from her prior study of student experience in an accelerated bachelor's degree program, presents a model of student engagement, and discusses reasons for adult learners' attraction to accelerated degree programs. Previous research reveals four areas in which twenty students were satisfied with one accelerated degree program: a student-centered supportive structure, strong interpersonal bonds among students, adult learners' views of their identities as learners and successful college students, and adult learners' views of engagement as college students. These students reported appreciation for supportive structures that facilitated college applications, course enrollments, and conveniently delivered student services. Cohorts of twelve to twenty students were encouraged to develop friendships and a strong learning community, which students viewed as very beneficial to their learning. Interviews with these students revealed their attitudes and beliefs about successful versus unsuccessful strategies for academic learning and degree completion. For example, successful adult students developed attitudes and time schedules that allowed them to complete course assignments and meet other academic demands. A three-pronged model of adult student engagement presented by Kasworm focuses on (1) adult competence —i.e., the belief that adult students bring experience and knowledge to their college learning, (2) adult action (a program's commitment to students' active participation in work and community and attempts to situate learning in these existing structures), and (3) adults' identities as workers, including their motivations to find new jobs or advance in current jobs. Kasworm concludes that adult learners' involvement in their academic experiences and their persistence toward degree completion can be strengthened by their participation in well-designed accelerated degree programs. — BJG

238   Leaker, Cathy, and Heather Ostman. "Composing Knowledge: Writing, Rhetoric, and Reflection in Prior Learning Assessment." *College Composition and Communication* 61.4 (2010): 691–717. Print.

As Prior Learning Assessment (PLA) gains currency in colleges and universities, students are increasingly being asked to write in sophisticated academic discourse about their experiential learning. Leaker and Ostman see this writing practice as a culture clash of sorts, a "contact zone between the unauthorized writer, institutional power, and the articulation of knowledge claims" (693). When students successfully navigate this divide through a process of critical reflection, they acquire not only a greater understanding of their learning, but also knowledge of the academic discourse that is required of them to express that learning. They become more capable in their new educational setting while reclaiming their experiential learning. However, the model is not always successful. Through excerpts from the narratives of students whom they taught at Empire State College, Leaker and Ostman illustrate the difficulties the students experienced translating their subject knowledge into rhetorically accepted forms. Ultimately, they argue that the current model of the narrative essay for PLA is inadequate to contain the experiential learning adult learners possess, and that the insistence of compliance with a hegemonic academic discourse disempowers these learners once again. — SFL

239   Michelson, Elana, and Alan Mandell. *Portfolio Development and the Assessment of Prior Learning: Perspectives, Models and Practices.* Sterling, VA: Stylus, 2004. Print.

Michelson and Mandell present a historical overview of prior learning assessment (PLA) by portfolio evaluation, together with pedagogical challenges, curricular innovations, and six approaches to PLA course design. There were three major goals of PLA pioneers during the 1970s: creating access to higher education for disenfranchised groups, creating second chances for adult learners, and establishing more inclusive and diverse college student populations. A discussion of curricula is illustrated by twelve case studies of programs located in the United States, England, South Africa, Australia, and Canada. Descriptions of PLA portfolio designs and supportive courses include suggested class activities, instructional techniques, and assignments. The authors explain how innovative PLA programs can result from workplace-college partnerships, Web-based courses, and programs situated in colleges for disenfranchised groups. They also describe challenges that can result from budgetary constraints, changing student populations, and evolving educational environments. — BJG

240   Walvoord, Barbara E. "Assessment in Accelerated Learning Programs: A Practical Guide." *Accelerated Learning for Adults: The Promise and*

Practice of Intensive Educational Formats. Ed. Raymond J. Wlodkowski and Carol E. Kasworm. Hoboken NJ: Wiley, 2003. 39–50. Print. New Directions for Adult and Continuing Education 97.

Walvoord argues that accelerated learning programs should focus on student performance, relationships between performance and external factors, and performance improvement in order to assess programmatic strengths and weaknesses as well as factors that impact student success. Program administrators need to know how well the students are doing within the current program structures and how student performance is related to the knowledge and resources currently available. The author suggests that learning programs have clearly defined mission statements or sets of learning outcomes that can be used as benchmarks in program assessments. These goals can be either program-based or created by individual instructors. As is true of other scientific studies, a program assessment needs to be valid and reliable in its ability to locate strengths and weaknesses. Additionally, the program ought to articulate the nature of particular strengths and weaknesses. Therefore, performance(s) must be measurable by either direct or indirect measures. Examples of direct measures include exams, projects, and papers; indirect measures can include surveys. Assessments should also take into account the external factors (income, ethnicity, motivation) that affect student performance. The program can create the assessment criteria and adjust for external factors by testing experimental and control groups. Results should be used to inform future departmental and program decisions. Aggregated results can be discussed at regular meetings in order to offer encouraging critiques and implement decisions and actions over time. Effective assessment and improvement is a collaborative effort. While external factors cannot be controlled, they can be accommodated for within the program. Walvoord concludes that program changes should accommodate student needs and contribute to improved student performance. —RNR

241   Wlodkowski, Raymond J. "Accelerated Learning in Colleges and Universities." *Accelerated Learning for Adults: The Promise and Practice of Intensive Educational Formats.* Ed. Raymond J. Wlodkowski and Carol E. Kasworm. Hoboken, NJ: Wiley, 2003. 5–15. Print. New Directions for Adult and Continuing Education 97.

Since 1975, some colleges have started offering adult-oriented programs that accelerate degree completion by offering fewer hours of instruction than traditional programs and convenient class schedules. In addition, locating classes at the workplace or online makes it possible for adult learners to complete degrees more rapidly. In fall 1998, 41 percent of college students were age 25 or older; during the ten years following publication of this essay, at least 25 percent of all adult students are expected to enroll in accelerated degree programs (also called intensive programs). However, because less time is spent in learning and teaching than in traditional programs, and because accelerated degree programs often dispense with full-time tenured faculty in favor of part-time contingent faculty, these programs are controversial. Derisive terms such as "Drive-thru U" and "McEducation" underscore potential reductions in value. Research on learning indicates that while time spent on task is an important factor, this factor alone does not determine successful learning. Other important factors are "student capability, quality of instruction, and personal motivation" (8). One study reveals that older adult students in accelerated courses fared better as learners than younger adult learners in conventional courses, suggesting that factors such as "motivation, concentration, work experience, self-direction" (9) may explain the superior learning achieved by adults. Additionally, adults fare slightly better compared with younger college students in the area of retention: nationally, 38 percent of all US undergraduates complete degrees within six years whereas 40 percent of all US adult undergraduates complete degrees within six years. Research is needed on persistence and graduation rates and on potential benefits of conventional college structures as compared with accelerated degree programs. — BJG

Prison Education

242   Genisio, Margaret Humadi. "Breaking Barriers with Books: A Fathers' Book-Sharing Program from Prison." *Journal of Adolescent & Adult Literacy* 40.2 (1996): 92–100. Print.

Genisio shares her experiences of working with fathers in prison who read to their children and then write about their experiences through a program called Breaking Barriers with Books. The fathers/prisoners participated in weekly classes, family visits, and a family support program. They selected books from a collection offered by Genisio and then read the books with their children when they came for family visits. Fathers wrote in journals after the visits, and the children often wrote to or drew pictures for their fathers. During class sessions, Genisio shared reading strategies and responded to the fathers' journal entries. Additionally, the prisoners wrote an in-house publication of their poetry to their children. Genisio states that she hopes to follow the parents and children after the fathers are released from prison. — KKN

See: Jacqueline N. Glasgow, "Accommodating Learning Styles in Prison Writing Classes" [114].

243   Jacobi, Tobi, and Patricia E. O'Connor. *Prison Literacies, Narratives and Community Connections.* Spec. issue of *Reflections: A Journal of Writing, Service Learning, and Community Literacy* 4.1 (Winter 2004). Print.

A special thematic issue of *Reflections* focuses on prison literacy and education. Issue editors Jacobi and O'Connor offer essays on tutoring, teaching, and service-learning courses written by both instructors and college students alongside autobiographical narratives, poems, and reflections composed by incarcerated adults. Several multimodal compositions juxtapose photographs and text. Jacobi's introductory essay provides background on incarcerated adults' literacy competencies, reading and writing practices, and educational experiences. Citing a 1994 US Education Department report on US adults' literacy competencies (*Literacy Behind Prison Walls*), Jacobi notes that literacy competencies of incarcerated adults are significantly lower than literacy competencies among the general adult population. Despite controversy surrounding systematic, funded educational opportunities for convicted criminals, it is clear that incarcerated adults want and need to learn writing, reading, and math skills. Many educational opportunities have been created for imprisoned adults, some documented in this journal; however, prison education programs have recently been systematically defunded by state legislatures and, subsequently, by colleges and universities, making it necessary for prison education programs to rely heavily on private donations and volunteers. A special area of need is General Equivalency Diploma (GED) and Adult Basic Education (ABE) instruction. Another particular challenge is the high rate of learning disabilities among prison populations, a subject explored by Terra White in "Learning Disabilities among the Incarcerated" (51–60). An appendix offers print and online resources on prison education and incarcerated adults' literacies. —BJG

See: Thomas Laughlin, "Teaching in the Yard: Student Inmates and the Policy of Silence" [119].

244   Maher, Jane. "Raw Material." *The Hudson Review* 63.4 (2011): 599–624. Print.

Maher describes her experiences and observations as a college instructor at the Bedford Hills Correctional Facility for women in Westchester, New York. Maher's students are primarily African American, with many having been educated in the poorest of New York City's public schools. Although very few students have documented learning disabilities, Maher suspects that many more have undocumented learning disabilities. In addition to her teaching responsibilities, Maher established a precollege program and assumed special responsibility for inmate-students who have physical and learning disabilities. The college at Bedford Hills is sponsored by Marymount Manhattan College and supported by many individuals who donate their time and money. Although public funding was previously offered to prison inmates in the form of student grants and loans, in recent years this financial support has been eliminated by federal and state legislators. Among the many challenges faced by Maher are a need to avoid discussing personal matters with students, which restricts class discussions, and a need to avoid writing assignment topics that might lead to revelations of inmates' personal information. Despite the general mandate to avoid discussions of inmates' personal histories, some of these inmate-students occasionally leak personal information in correspondence and private conversations. When applying for the precollege program, they are required to write application essays with accounts of their prior educational experiences.

From these limited opportunities to learn about her students, Maher has discovered that they are likely to have come from unstable or poor families and to have experienced sexual or physical abuse. Their educational attainments are generally lower than educational attainments of the wider population; however, many of the women students enrolled in college courses are often "very smart" and "a few are truly brilliant" (620). By earning an associate's degree or a bachelor's degree, these women can increase their chances of attaining employment when released from prison. — BJG

245   Maher, Jane. "'You Probably Don't Even Know That I Exist': Notes from a Prison College Program." *Journal of Basic Writing* 23.1 (2004): 82–100. Print. Rpt. in *Teaching Developmental Writing: Background Readings*. 3rd ed. Ed. Susan Naomi Bernstein. Boston: Bedford, 2007. 56–72.

Incarcerated women benefit substantially from opportunities to learn reading and writing at precollege and college levels. As a college teacher at Bedford Hills Correctional Facility in Westchester, New York, Maher has firsthand knowledge of women prisoners' experiences behind bars, about the importance of educational programs for these women, and about the potential impact that educational experiences can have on incarcerated women's lives. While debates persist about whether prisoners deserve educational opportunities and funding remains a significant challenge, many educational programs allow incarcerated women (and men) to acquire basic literacy skills, study for the GED, or earn college credits. In addition to formal classes on reading and writing, Bedford Hills offers legal counseling sessions, puppy training practice, and church participation opportunities for women prisoners — all to prepare them for reentering their communities. Finding common ground and also differences, Maher compares the prison population she teaches at Bedford to the basic writing students she also teaches at a community college. Her reading/writing curriculum involves asking students to write notes to her about their educational interests and then creating courses that are responsive to student statements about their own literacy needs. Having been deprived of good educational opportunities and safe home environments, women prisoners generally appreciate and take advantage of educational opportunities when such programs are offered. — BJG

246   Pompa, Lori. "Disturbing Where We Are Comfortable: Notes from Behind the Walls." *Prison Literacies, Narratives and Community Connections*. Spec. issue of *Reflections: A Journal of Writing, Service Learning, and Community Literacy* 4.1 (2004): 24–34. Print.

Temple University students and incarcerated men enroll together in a college course titled "The Inside-Out Prison Exchange Program: Exploring Issues of Crime and Justice Behind Walls." Course participation requires Temple University students to attend classes inside Philadelphia Correctional Center. Readings about criminal justice texts and the lives of incarcerated people provide topics for class discussion and writing assignments—multiple reflection essays and a longer essay. The unique combination of student populations and class content contributes to a highly participatory learning experience in which students learn from hearing each other's perspectives. The class can induce transformative learning for incarcerated students, who are encouraged to understand their prison experiences in a larger context, and for Temple University students, who learn that metaphorical "prisons" can constrain their thoughts and actions.—BJG

See: Zandra H. Stino and Barbara C. Palme, "Motivating Women Offenders through Process-Based Writing in a Literacy Learning Circle" [126].

Workplace Writing, Worker Education, and Labor Unions

247   Agnew, Eleanor. "Basic Writers in the Workplace: Writing Adequately for Careers after College." *Journal of Basic Writing* 11.2 (Fall 1992): 28–46. Print.

Agnew reports on the workplace writing requirements of twenty-one former basic writing students five to ten years after they had completed a freshman writing course. This research was inspired by Agnew's discovery that many of her nontraditional college students were writing at work while struggling in their college writing classes. After these students informed Agnew that their work-related writing was satisfactory, Agnew began to question the writing experiences and genres that former basic writing students would encounter in their workplaces after graduation. Most of the twenty-one former basic writing students reported that their workplace writing was short, routine, and repetitive. As such, the writing differed substantially from college writing assignments. Another difference was that while they had to meet deadlines for college assignments, study participants were allowed flexible deadlines or no deadlines at work, which allowed them to feel greater control and autonomy. Other features of their workplace writing experiences included (1) strong motivation to write well, (2) collaboration with coworkers, (3) knowledge of subject matter, (4) familiarity with audience, and (5) a work-related writing persona. In addition, these twenty-one individuals reported that their work-related knowledge and expertise was highly valued, which tended to strengthen their confidence as writers at their workplaces. As a consequence of these findings, Agnew recommends several pedagogical strategies for basic writing classes—e.g., collaborative learning opportunities, reality-based writing assignments, and increasing the presence of writing across the curriculum programs on college campuses.—BJG

248   Alamprese, Judy. "The Worker, Work, and Workplace Literacy: Missing Links." *TESOL Quarterly* 27.3 (1993): 553–55. Print.

Workplace literacy programs aim for two principal goals: (1) increasing workers' skills and knowledge and (2) improving their productivity.

Two factors that influence these goals are the fit between an instructional program and a workplace and support offered to individuals who participate in workplace literacy programs. Alamprese suggests that managerial sponsorship of a workplace educational program is likely to be stronger when the program aligns well with the mission of that organization. Employees are more willing to participate when the educational program addresses tasks that they must master to perform well in their particular roles as workers. Some scholars argue that workplace literacy programs will be more successful if they offer instruction in skills that can be used in current work-related tasks as well as in other work and life contexts. Moreover, workplace literacy curricula should account for employees' own educational goals in order to be maximally effective at recruiting and retaining participants in workplace literacy classes. — BJG

See: Kelly Belanger and Linda Strom, *Second Shift: Teaching Writing to Working Adults* [104].

See: Theresa M. Castaldi, "Adult Learning: Transferring Skills from the Workplace to the Classroom" [78].

See: Debby D'Amico and Emily Schnee, "It Changed Something Inside of Me: English Language Learning, Structural Barriers to Employment, and Workers' Goals in a Workplace Literacy Program" [105].

249 Fenwick, Tara. "Workplace Learning: Emerging Trends and New Perspectives." *Third Update on Adult Learning Theory*. Ed. Sharan B. Merriam. Hoboken, NJ: Wiley, 2008. 17–26. Print. New Directions for Adult and Continuing Education 119.

Fenwick reviews the concepts and perspectives of workplace learning. She states that adult educators have tended to look at the processes people use to solve workplace difficulties and how groups learn in the workplace. However, workplace professionals are interested in how people use creativity and learn entrepreneurial practices in their workplaces. This discrepancy is important for adult educators to note as they work with adult learners. Fenwick then defines the relevant terms (e.g., *learning* and *workplace*) and explains how these terms have changed over time. Following a discussion of the history of workplace learning research, Fenwick describes a practice-based orientation in relation to workplace learning, arguing that these organizational studies "bypass questions of politics and power relations" (21) in the workplace. In a discussion of how identities and learning in the workplace are related to language and literacy, Fenwick argues, "People's sense of whom they are and what they know and can do at work is embedded in the language and textual practices they use" (22). The author calls for more research on how power and politics are linked to learning in the workplace. — KKN

See: Barbara Gleason, "Connected Literacies of Adult Writers: Workplace Ethnographies in College Composition" [135].

See: Cheryl Greenwood Gowen and Carol Bartlett, "'Friends in the Kitchen': Lessons from Survivors" [107].

See: Karyn L. Hollis, "Liberating Voices: Autobiographical Writing at the Bryn Mawr Summer School for Women Workers, 1921–1938" [141].

See: Karyn L. Hollis, *Liberating Voices: Writing at the Bryn Mawr Summer School for Women Workers* [142].

250   Holzman, Michael. "Teaching Is Remembering." *College English* 46.3 (1984): 229–38. Print.

Holzman describes a two-month grant-funded worker education literacy program for sixty young adult members of the California Conservation Corps (CCC). Classes were offered on the University of Southern California (USC) campus in the summer of 1983. Holzman had provided leadership for this program, together with CCC employee Bruce Saito and CCC consultant Olga Connolly. USC Writing Center Director Irene Clarke had provided the needed institutional space. Instructors were hired from a pool of graduate students employed in the USC Freshman Writing Program. Sixty participating CCC members were young adults whose ages ranged from 18 to 23. Classes were part of their workday schedule and conveniently located near CCC offices. Reporting on his observations of CCC members, Holzman notes that once students were grouped with particular instructors, they refused to be regrouped—even when redistribution would even out the numbers. After talking with a secondary school teacher, Holzman realized that CCC members had probably been shuffled around from place to place in public schools and had been absent from school so often that teachers could not remember them. Forgotten by their teachers in previous schools, they refused to be forgotten now. In his analysis of these young adults' prior educational experiences, the author discusses the fact that while tuition-free literacy classes exist, many young adults similar to this group of CCC workers choose not to participate. These courses and their possible benefits may seem too remote from these young adults' everyday experiences of street violence and magical thinking (based on film and television versions of sudden success experienced by celebrities). One important response to these students' possible disconnect from everyday realities was to inform them of how institutions work and to introduce them to a variety of people and situations. Most important of all was a need for these literacy students to form and sustain bonds with their instructors as well as with each other. Holzman argues that teaching adult literacy is not essentially a technical problem: successful adult literacy instruction starts and ends with encouraging and supportive interpersonal relationships. — BJG

251   Hull, Glynda. "Hearing Other Voices: A Critical Assessment of Popular Views on Literacy and Work." *Changing Work, Changing Workers: Critical Perspectives on Language, Literacy, and Skills*. Ed. Glynda Hull. Albany: State U of New York P, 1997. 3–39. Print.

Three commonly expressed views of government officials, literacy educators, and employers are (1) too many US workers are illiterate; (2) low-literate workers can cause harm at their places of work; and (3) US jobs increasingly require higher levels of literacy. Challenging these commonly held assumptions, Hull advocates a broader, more complex, and highly context-dependent view of workplace literacy—a view that incorporates workers' voices, stories of actual worker expertise, and descriptions of workplace communities of practice. Hull argues for stronger distinctions between school-based concepts of literacy and workplace literacies, suggesting that worker education programs consider substituting on-the-job apprenticeships for classroom learning so that workers can observe the expertise of fellow workers in authentic work situations. Too often school-based literacy tests are used to assess the workplace competencies of employees. Instead, Hull explains, workers should be evaluated on the basis of the actual forms of expertise required in their specific jobs. In fact, highly complex skills and knowledge are required in the work lives of many employees, and more fine-grained studies of workers' on-the-job practices would reveal the complex forms of expertise that many workers possess. — BJG

252   Kalman, Judy, and Kay M. Losey. "Pedagogical Innovation in a Workplace Literacy Program: Theory and Practice." *Changing Work, Changing Workers: Critical Perspectives on Language, Literacy, and Skills*. Ed. Glynda Hull. Albany: State U of New York P, 1997. 84–116. Print.

As evaluators of a grant-funded workplace literacy project, Kalman and Losey observed a teacher using a student-centered pedagogical approach in which students were expected "to raise issues, direct the class, and organize the classwork," (89) instead of the more traditional teacher-centered approach, which favors the instructors doing most of the talking, determining classroom activities, and assessing learning. The grant writers argued that the newer student-centered approach was more appropriate for teaching adults in entry-level occupations such as ambulance drivers, vocational nurses, and maintenance workers. Despite the pedagogical goal of the grant, the teacher being observed, Deborah, made only minimal changes to her (mainly) traditional approach to teaching. For the most part, she continued to maintain control over student activities and classroom discourse. For example, she was observed denying students opportunities to articulate their experiences as writers in one class session and instead provided her own stock answers to questions about the writing process. The authors suggest that for teachers to change their curricular approaches and pedagogical strategies, teachers must receive adequate support for their development as teachers—they need sufficient time to develop and reflect on their curricula, institutional support, and mentoring strategies. — BJG

253   Merrifield, Juliet. "If Job Training Is the Answer, What Is the Question?" *Changing Work, Changing Workers: Critical Perspectives on*

Language, Literacy, and Skills. Ed. Glynda Hull. Albany: State U of New York P, 1997. 273–94. Print.

When an apparel construction plant was closed in 1988 to find cheaper labor abroad, workers were provided a relatively generous compensation package and three months' notification. Job training was also provided by the apparel company in conjunction with a government agency called the Job Training Partnership Act (JTPA). This essay explores the experiences of one group of displaced women workers and the challenges that they encountered while going back to school and seeking new employment. The author followed the progress of displaced women workers for two years after the company plant had closed and documents the outcomes for women who enrolled in a job training program. The story of one woman, Tracy, illustrates the larger narrative of women workers displaced by the plant closing. Tracy had been offered opportunities to earn a GED at the company workplace but had declined to take advantage of the opportunity because enrollment procedures occurred in public spaces. Tracy was fortunate in that she was young (age 30), healthy, and highly motivated to work; she quickly attained a new job at another sewing plant after the plant closing. Tracy took advantage of free job training classes for ten weeks after the plant closed; she studied four nights each week while working at her new job during daytime hours. After completing courses in typing, word processing, microcomputer use, and pharmacy technician job skills, Tracy was earning the same wages she had earned as a company textile worker but was no longer eligible for more job training classes. This example represents a larger finding of the study reported here: Job retraining opportunities can be helpful but are generally insufficient for the needs of displaced US workers. Another finding is that how job training and basic skills educational programs are structured matters, and "some [related] legislative changes are needed" (274). Recommendations for improving existing job retraining programs are offered together with the strong reminder that job retraining alone cannot meet the needs of displaced workers. — BJG

254   Meyer, Paul R., and Patricia Teel Bates. "Literacy Practices in the Healthcare Industry: The Challenge for Teachers." *Expanding Literacies: English Teaching and the New Workplace*. Ed. Mary Sue Garay and Stephen A. Bernhardt. Albany: State U of New York P, 1998. 133–54. Print.

A changing US economy has affected the health care industry by reducing jobs for unskilled workers and increasing a need for employees with strong literacy skills and technical expertise. However, according to a 1993 survey of adult literacy, about one-half of adults living in the United States possess weak reading, math, and information processing skills. Conducted by the National Center for Education Statistics (NCES) and the Educational Testing Service (ETS), the survey reveals that one-half of US adults are weak in everyday activities such as writing short notes, reading a bar graph, and using a calculator for simple arithmetic. Workplace skills needed today include (1) the ability to learn reading, writing, math, and computer skills, (2) interpersonal skills, (3) problem-solving skills, and (4) specialized technical expertise. Although the widespread existence of low-literate adults residing in the United States is commonly accepted, the notion that they cause harm to the US economy is controversial. In *Changing Work, Changing Workers: Critical Perspectives on Language, Literacy, and Skills* (SUNY Press, 1997), Glynda Hull argues that unskilled employees use complex competencies to fulfill their job functions. Meyer and Bates agree with Hull's analysis of unskilled workers' job responsibilities but disagree with Hull's interpretation of business leaders' views on unskilled workers. Business leaders don't cast blame on workers, the authors contend, but on a US educational system that produces less competent workers than their international counterparts. US schools need to produce far more highly skilled workers in order to meet current demands in US workplaces. Implications for teachers include educating students in reading, writing, computation, and computer processing and conducting student-centered classes that are activity-based rather than dependent on lecture. — BJG

See: Mike Rose, *The Mind at Work: Valuing the Intelligence of the American Worker* [98].

255 Tingle, Nick. "Literacy Development and the Working-Class Student." *The Writing Instructor* 7.1 (1987): 21–27. Print.

In describing an experimental literacy education project designed for young adult members of the California Conservation Corps (CCC) in the 1980s, Tingle contrasts mainstream middle-class values associated with work, education, and literacy with working-class students' views of work, education, and literacy. While writing and reading are regarded as worthy investments of time and labor in middle-class communities, these literacy practices are often far less well-regarded by working-class communities. Likewise, being willing to sacrifice individual free time for many years of education is a middle-class value that is not always taken for granted as a worthy investment in working-class ideologies. By contrasting these class-based ideologies, Tingle explains why some working-class students choose to withdraw from formal education and to spend less time reading and writing voluntarily than their middle-class literacy instructors expect them to. In experimental literacy classes that Tingle and his colleagues taught for California Conservation Corps members, it became clear that the mostly male adult students were resistant to writing more than a page in one day and did not view mental work as a priority in the ways expected of students enrolled in formal educational programs. Reacting to their students' resistance, teachers became bosses requiring completion of work rather than learning facilitators and instructors. Teachers began blaming their students for their own unproductive lessons, sometimes finding fault with the characters or mental capacities of their students. To overcome the unproductive roles that both teachers and students had fallen into, Tingle and his colleagues experimented with group learning activities focusing primarily on producing a video. The key lesson learned was that student resistance or even failure to engage with learning and literacy activities is not always best explained by finding fault with individual students. Rather, Tingle encourages learning about class-based ideologies and developing appropriate pedagogical strategies for working-class students. — BJG

Literacy in Family and Community

256   Addams, Jane. *Twenty Years at Hull-House*. Ed. Victoria Bissell Brown. Boston: Bedford, 1999. Print.

An editor's introduction provides details of Jane Addams's life (sometimes varying from Addams's own account) and a history of the Chicago settlement house that Addams helped establish. Born into a financially secure home with a politically liberal father, Jane Addams was encouraged to attend college and make a contribution to society, possibly in the medical profession. After graduating from college, Addams spent two years in Europe, returned home, and completed one year of medical school. An illness caused Addams to discontinue her medical studies. She spent a second tour in Europe with a friend, Ellen Gates Starr; they imagined creating a settlement house similar to the Toynbee Hall in London. With an inheritance received upon her father's death, Addams moved to Chicago in 1889 with Gates Starr. Together they established Hull-House, where Addams lived for much of her adult life. Hull-House provided basic needs, arts enrichment, and educational opportunities for poor Americans and immigrants. Children and adults alike attended classes and special events at Hull-House. Instructors provided English language instruction and civics lessons for immigrants. Addams grew to understand that the rich could learn from the poor while the poor learn from the rich, and that authentic relationships could be formed between people of different classes. She also challenged the view that people are born into pre-ordained circumstances that they cannot influence or overcome. — BJG

See: Yvonne Honeycutt Baldwin, *Cora Wilson Stewart and Kentucky's Moonlight Schools: Fighting for Literacy in America* [110].

257   Elias, John. "Adult Religious Education." *Expanding the Boundaries of Adult Religious Education: Strategies, Techniques, and Partnerships for the New Millennium*. Ed. E. Paulette Isaac. Hoboken, NJ: Wiley, 2012. 5–12. Print. New Directions for Adult and Continuing Education 133.

Elias argues that while religious education starts in childhood, it continues throughout the lifespan and has different meanings in different phases of life. In fact, religious maturity requires continuous learning during adulthood. In contemporary religious education, informal education and experiential learning are more common than formal education and direct instruction. Contexts for informal religious education can include homes, camps, and retreats as well as official sites for worship. Formal religious education takes place in forums such as "courses, sermons, lectures, directed study, discussion groups, seminars, forums and symposia" (10). Adults also learn about religion by means of self-directed study and in learning groups. Current modes of communication allow for learning via online social communications. — BJG

258   Hogg, Charlotte. "Beyond Agrarianism: Toward a Critical Pedagogy of Place." *Rural Literacies*. Ed. Kim Donehower, Charlotte Hogg, and Eileen E. Schell. Carbondale: Southern Illinois UP, 2007. 120–54. Print.

Framing her study in David Gruenewald's critical pedagogy of place, Hogg reports on the everyday literacy practices of older rural women (ages 77 to 100), their children, and close women associates. Moving beyond *agrarianism* (a view of rural farm life as more uplifting and morally sound than urban industrial life), *critical pedagogy of place* blends *place-based education* (emphasizing locality in education) with *critical pedagogy* "to address critically and comprehensively ecological, social, economic, and cultural issues that face rural areas" (121). A traditionally masculine concept, agrarianism fails to account for women's roles and the complexities of modern living in rural communities. Hogg describes the multifaceted literacies of a group of rural Nebraska women, who are sometimes college-educated and always deeply invested in their community. One former nurse and teacher, Fae Chistensen, helps organize records for a local cemetery, writes town histories, and contributes to her church by writing newsletters. Mona invites school children to learn about local grasses at her ranch and produces books for relatives about her geographic region and family history. Cathy, another former nurse and garden club president, gives talks at club meetings about wild flowers that she has photographed and mounted on slides. The older adult women described in this study contribute to their male-dominated community as botanists, historians, teachers, writers, editors, and librarians. In addition to their individual literacy practices, cooperative centers and public forums, like the online forum Rural Womyn Zone (RWZ), provide opportunities for rural women to communicate and post their own written texts, thereby empowering themselves and other women. — BJG

259   Isaac, E. Paulette, Guy Talmadge, and Tom Valentine. "Understanding African American Learners' Motivations to Learn in Church-Based Adult Education." *Adult Education Quarterly* 52.1 (Nov. 2001): 23–28. Print.

The history of African American churches reveals the church as a social place as well as a place for learning, with African Americans attending church more often than whites. This study focused on "identify[ing] and describ[ing] African American adults' motivations for participating in church-based education" (24). The authors developed their own instrument for their study since other instruments were based on white middle-class participants. The instrument was validated through its development with focus groups and interviews. For this study, the authors used three large Baptist African American churches. Most of the participants were over 25 years old and involved in both religious and secular education at the churches. Isaac, Talmadge, and Valentine discuss the seven motivational factors in their findings and observe that four factors—Spiritual and Religious Development, Love of Learning, Service to Others, and Social Interaction—were prevalent, which agrees with previous research. However, three new factors—Familiar Cultural Setting, Family Togetherness, and Facing Personal Challenges—emerged as important in the learning of these adults. The authors argue that adult educators overlook the importance of church-based adult education for African Americans and generally do not research the topic.—KKN

See: Jacqueline Lynch, "Print Literacy Engagement of Parents from Low-Income Backgrounds: Implications for Adult and Family Literacy Programs" [120].

See: Ronald J. Manheimer and Diane Moskow-McKenzie, "Transforming Older Adult Education: An Emerging Paradigm from a Nationwide Study" [63].

260 Mott, Vivian W. "Rural Education for Older Adults." *Adult Education in the Rural Context: People, Place and Change.* Ed. Jeffrey A. Ritchey. Hoboken, NJ: Wiley, 2008. 47–57. Print. New Directions for Adult and Continuing Education 117.

Rural adults are getting increasingly older as the US population ages nationwide. In 2000, 56 million of over 300 million US residents were age 55 or older. Of the 56 million adults age 55 or older, 12 million live in rural areas—defined officially by the US Department of Agriculture as "any unincorporated place . . . with fewer than 2,500 inhabitants" (49). These older rural adults are more likely to learn informally than formally, and they exhibit all of the learning orientations described by C. O. Houle in *The Inquiring Mind* (Oklahoma Research Center for Continuing and Professional Education, 1988); that is, they can be goal-oriented, learning-oriented, or activity-oriented. Rural-context learning opportunities are abundant and diverse; schools, farm organizations, libraries, health care providers, and social service clubs are all examples of agencies that provide learning opportunities in rural areas. Older adult learners in rural areas respond particularly well to dialogic, activity-based events focusing on content relevant to their lives and interests. Three case studies of older adult learner communities illustrate three approaches to learning: one community of older adults engaged in self-directed learning to satisfy community needs and increase self-sufficiency of individuals. A second community engaged in social action activities to learn about absentee landlords and preserve their community. A third group of older adult learners participated in learning events for enjoyment in leisure time. The overall finding is that older adults living in rural areas are participating in learning activities that are mostly informal, activity-based, self-sponsored, and embedded in communities of practice. — BJG

261   Mündel, Karsten, and Daniel Schugurensky. "Community Based Learning and Civic Engagement: Informal Learning among Adult Volunteers in Community Organizations." *Linking Adults with Community: Promoting Civic Engagement through Community Based Learning.* Ed. Susan C. Reed and Catherine Marienau. Hoboken, NJ: Wiley, 2008. 49–60. Print. New Directions in Adult and Continuing Education 118.

Mündel and Schugurensky review informal learning that occurs with volunteers in community organizations. Their work involves interviews with eighty-two people and discussion of two case studies. After discussing informal learning and volunteer work, the authors categorize their findings into three areas: instrumental learning, interpersonal learning, and "learning through formal and informal reflection" (52). Instrumental learning is needed for completing specific tasks and results in understood knowledge. In this case, learners were involved in learning by doing with little recognition of the learning achieved. Acquiring people skills was the largest area for learners, and this learning occurred not only on the job but also through training. The education also involved learning about the particulars of specific groups. Learning about engaging in a community and how volunteering fits within the political economy was not how most volunteers engaged in learning. While volunteers understood and could discuss changes that took place within the organizations, they could not discuss the policy changes made at higher levels. Mündel and Schugurensky conclude that most volunteers' learning was implicit and the extent of their learning was unknown to the volunteers. The authors make three recommendations: community organizations need to make learning more explicit so that mistakes would not be repeated; organizations need to foster learning by forming places and actions that nurture skills, attitudes, and knowledge; and organizations need to develop mentoring relationships so that new volunteers can learn from experienced volunteers or paid staff. — KKN

See: Victoria Purcell-Gates, *Other People's Worlds: The Cycle of Low Literacy* [96].

262   Ritchey, Jeffrey A. "Rural Adult Education: Current Status." *Adult Education in the Rural Context: People, Place and Change.* Ed. Jeffrey A. Ritchie. Hoboken, NJ: Wiley, 2008. 5–12. Print. New Directions for Adult and Continuing Education 117.

Adult education is historically a strong presence in rural regions, in part because rural residents live far away from schools and colleges and thus depend on extension services and correspondence courses. About 95 percent of US land is rural, and about 59.1 million people (21 percent of the US population) were living in rural areas, according to the 2000 US Census. Even though they share common issues and concerns, rural US communities are highly diverse and often have highly specific geographic identities. Therefore, rural educators need to connect with the needs and interests of people living in particular rural communities. The meanings of *rural* and *urban* are often defined by means of statistics. Communities with fewer than 2,500 residents are classified as rural. This statistical definition fails to account for cultural, social, historical, political, and economic factors often associated with rural communities. In addition to low population density, key features of rurality are cultural uniformity; sparsely available stores, medical care, and other public services; and economic reliance on agriculture, mining, or timbering (current or historical). Common concerns of people living in rural communities include the invasion of mass merchandise stores such as Walmart, which lead to losses of local retail businesses, less access to Internet services than in urban areas, an increasingly older population, loss of farm land and family farms, increased residential land development, and air and water pollution. —BJG

263   Rivera, Klaudia M. "Adult Biliteracy in Community-Based Organizations: Venues of Participation, Agents of Transformation." *Adult Biliteracy: Sociocultural and Programmatic Responses.* Ed. Klaudia M. Rivera and Ana Huerta-Macías. New York: Erlbaum, 2008. 75–95. Print.

This essay focuses on the role that community-based organizations (CBOs) can play in promoting biliteracy in adult education. An important feature of CBOs is their location: they are usually situated in communities where their clients live. Given CBOs' close proximity to their community members' homes, schools, and workplaces, CBO teachers and program administrators can observe, learn about, and come to value their adult learners' linguistic and cultural practices in everyday situations. Whether they are unincorporated grass roots community projects or formally incorporated nonprofit organizations, CBOs tend to focus closely on the communities that they serve and align their agendas with community members' needs and interests. Case studies of three educational programs (located in Los Angeles, Seattle, and New York City) are offered to illustrate various ways that Spanish and English can be taught together in one curriculum. Common characteristics of successful adult biliteracy education programs include developing a participatory bilingual curriculum, hiring staff from the adult learners' same community, offering learners opportunities for developing leadership skills and roles, and making contributions to learners' communities. A challenge common to many CBOs is the ability to meet their bilingual clients' needs while simultaneously addressing the values and goals of funders who require monolingual, English-only instruction and standardized curricula. A second challenge is the lack of stability that accompanies CBO grant-funded programs; classes and services are often impermanent while staffing relies heavily on volunteers and poorly paid part-time employees. Despite these challenges, CBO-based adult education programs are uniquely situated to provide innovative educational programs that can transform the lives of underserved immigrant populations — adults who often seek the most basic levels of basic skills education and English language instruction. — BJG

264   Winterowd, W. Ross. *Senior Citizens Writing: A Workshop and Anthology, with an Introduction and Guide for Workshop Leaders.* West Lafayette, IN: Parlor, 2007. Print.

Winterowd describes workshops he has led for senior citizens since 1997. Through the workshops, the seniors write stories, both fiction and nonfiction, and share their thoughts on what they see happening in the United States and the world. Winterowd begins by explaining his philosophy about this type of writing versus the writing he taught in college courses. He explains that he does not agree with "the Romantic philosophy of composition" (3) in college writing, but he does use the idea of voice, part of the "Romantic philosophy," in the senior writing workshops. Then Winterowd explains his approach to leading the seniors through the writing process as they express themselves, and he includes ideas to help others who might want to lead workshops for seniors. After this discussion, Winterowd offers writings by various seniors who participated in his workshops. A brief autobiography is provided for each author. The stories demonstrate the effectiveness of the workshops. — KKN

Adult Literacy Education Programs

See: Alisa Belzer, "'It's Not Like Normal School': The Role of Prior Learning Contexts in Adult Learning" [69].

See: Caroline Beverstock, Shanti Bhaskaran, Jacquie Brinkley, Donna Jones, and Valerie Reinke, "Transforming Adult Students into Authors: The Writer to Writer Challenge" [111].

See: Lauren Marshall Bowen, "Resisting Age Bias in Digital Literacy Research" [74].

See: M. Carolyn Clark and Marsha Rossiter, "Narrative Learning in Adulthood" [49].

265   Freire, Paulo. *Pedagogy of the Oppressed, 30th Anniversary Edition.* Trans. Myra Bergman Ramos. New York: The Continuum International Publishing Group, 2003. Print.

Arguing that oppressors dehumanize the oppressed, Freire also contends that the oppressed must free themselves as well as their oppressors. However, the oppressed tend to fear freedom, so they must analyze what caused the oppression and take transformative action to change the situation. Freire then presents the case for dialogue with people about what they need to do to change their situation. It is through the pedagogy of the oppressed that changes are made. Freire distinguishes between systematic education and educational projects, and he defines two stages of this pedagogy of the oppressed. According to Freire, it is when the oppressed realize that they have knowledge that changes occur in the education of the oppressed. The oppressors must realize that the oppressed have the ability to reason and to trust that reasoning. Freire then discusses the narrative character of the teacher-student relationship (71). This type of teaching changes students "into 'containers,' into 'receptacles' to be 'filled' by the teacher" (72). Freire calls this type of teaching "the banking concept of education" (72). Students (the oppressed) are not to know, but are to memorize what the oppressor (the teacher) wants them to know. Instead, educators must liberate students with "problem-posing education [that] affirms men and women as beings in the process of *becoming*" (84). Freire argues that people become significant as they dialogue with one another and name their world. Dialogue exists when love, humility, faith in mankind, truth, and critical thinking are present. Freire then discusses how this dialogue works and doesn't work in education and claims that people in this libertarian education must become masters of their own thinking. Freire continues to discuss the differences between the theory of revolutionary action and the theory of oppressive action, calling for more revolutionary action, particularly in education. —KKN

266   Hiser, Krista. "A Paragraph Ain't Nothin' But a Sandwich: The Effects of the GED on Four Urban Writers and Their Writing." *City Comp: Identities, Spaces, Practices*. Ed. Bruce McComiskey and Cynthia Ryan. Albany: State U of New York P, 2003. 57–70. Print.

Having tutored and taught adult literacy in San Francisco for nine years, Hiser designed a study to learn about the writing lives of four adult students seeking a GED. Two of these four participants informed Hiser that they enjoyed writing as a means of self-expression; however, all four adults reported feeling negatively about their writing as a result of studying for the GED exam. Although examining the effects of GED instruction on students' self-perceptions as writers was not her initial aim, Hiser soon discovered that the exam played such an important role in the experiences of these four students that she would have to factor it into her research. Hiser concludes that the pedagogical framework of GED writing and test-taking did little to support the literacy lives of these individuals, and—if used as the primary benchmark of their educational experiences—would not provide the information needed to understand these students' literacy learning experiences, self-images, and attainments. —BJG

267   Ntiri, Daphne W. "Older College Students as Tutors for Adult Learners in an Urban Literacy Program." *Journal of Adolescent & Adult Literacy* 43.1 (1999): 48–57. Print.

The issue of low literacy among older adults was addressed by an initiative in Detroit, Michigan, where there is a staggering 25 percent of low-literacy readers. The initiative took place inside a course titled "Adult Learning Methods," which was offered at Wayne State University's Interdisciplinary Studies Program (ISP). Adult college students enrolled in "Adult Learning Methods" were assigned the role of "tutors" who would work one-on-one with low-literacy adults—referred to as "adult learners." These adult learners ranged from 29 to 54 years old, were mostly African American, and were part of a ninety-day residency program. The tutors, as part of the larger demographic of Wayne State's Interdisciplinary Studies Program, were mostly African American, female, and averaged 41 years of age. The first five class meetings focused on instructional methods. The following ten class meetings comprised thirty hours of one-on-one reading tutorials. These tutors used learner-centered lesson plans that they developed themselves. An initial assessment of the adult learners involved use of the revised Woodcock Reading Mastery Test, which revealed a general lack of reading competencies. Portfolios used by the tutors were evaluated for the second semester. This portfolio evaluation revealed information about tutoring sessions, served as a reference for time spent and the number of sessions that took place, and indicated the organization and progress of both tutors and learners. The retention rate for the program was high. Out of all three groups of adult learners, about 74 percent stayed to complete the weekly program. Tutors reported feeling uplifted and inspired by the experience. They also reported being able to apply what they learned in their college class to their tutoring experiences. The learners reported a gain in confidence as readers and learned how to use reading strategies independently. The program is reported as having the "potential . . . to provide . . . benefits to tutors, learners and society" (57). Accounting for learners' needs and designing appropriate literacy instruction methods are both reported as important for the success of this program. —NVT

268   Rose, Mike. *Back to School: Why Everyone Deserves a Second Chance at Education.* New York: New Press, 2012. Print.

Rose presents a comprehensive analysis of nontraditional adult students and the institutions designed to serve their educational needs. While acknowledging the impact of proprietary schools, Rose focuses almost exclusively on publicly funded adult education programs and community colleges, explaining that second chance educational opportunities have "public, as well as personal, meaning" and that his own research interests lie in the "public domain" (31). The analysis of nontraditional students is supported by descriptions of educational programs and classrooms Rose has visited and by anecdotes of students Rose has met in a variety of educational institutions and programs (community colleges, English language classes, vocational classes, and GED preparatory programs). Rose's analysis supports his argument that educational institutions reflect and very often reinforce economic and social inequities, making adult education opportunities especially, though not exclusively, important for people who come from low-income families and neighborhoods. Rose also explores issues related to postsecondary institutions: who should attend college? why don't more undergraduates remain in college and earn degrees? how can high academic standards be maintained while we admit underprepared applicants to undergraduate degree programs? how can a vocational education be combined with academic learning? Rose connects these issues to the concerns of nontraditional students and their teachers. Professional education for adult educators and college faculty is a concern: not enough teachers have sufficient preparation or expertise to work with nontraditional adult students. Despite these challenges, entire colleges have been designed to encourage student success: one example Rose discusses is Valencia College in Orlando, Florida. And, as Rose notes, faculty can better serve their students by "learning about and responding to their students' needs" (166). Despite the fact that there are larger problems related to our economy and changing workforce needs, and the related fact that educational institutions cannot easily address these larger issues, Rose believes that issues related to developing educational opportunities for nontraditional adult students merit significantly increased public attention and support. — BJG

269   Silver-Pacuilla, Heidi. "Access and Benefits: Assistive Technology in Adult Literacy." *Journal of Adult & Adolescent Literacy* 50.2 (2006): 114–25. Print.

Silver-Pacuilla, with a grant from the National Institute on Disability and Rehabilitation Research, explores the gap in research on learners with learning disabilities in secondary and postsecondary institutions and notes that adult education students with learning disabilities have been omitted from the studies. She reviews several studies on adult education learners before presenting her study on eighteen adult education students with learning disabilities. The students used various electronic programs to develop their skills and participated in classes while working with a literacy coach. Silver-Pacuilla presents her methods and gives snapshots of the students' experiences with the technology and in-class sessions. In her findings, Silver-Pacuilla argues, "Small-group tutoring with assistive technology for students with learning disabilities can be enabling and empowering and can begin to bridge the multiple gaps in instructional practice and service" (123). She then calls for leaders of adult education programs to work with community agencies to bridge gaps that adult students with learning disabilities experience. — KKN

See: Jeff Zacharakis, Marie Steichen, Gabriela Diaz de Sabates, and Dianne Glass, "Understanding the Experiences of Adult Learners: Content Analysis of Focus Group Data" [31].

College Environments and Programs

See: Carol Berkenkotter and Thomas N. Huckin, with John Ackerman, "Conventions, Conversations, and the Writer: An Apprenticeship Tale of a Doctoral Student" [72].

270   Blanchard, Rosemary Ann, Felicia Casados, and Harry Sheski. "All Things to All People: Challenges and Innovations in a Rural Community College." *Journal of Continuing Higher Education* 57.1 (2009): 22–28. Print.

The authors describe a program at New Mexico State University–Grants, a community college established by NMSU to meet the needs of the rural adults who wanted to attend college. The adults are from a variety of ethnic groups and often have remediation needs for academic success. Thus, NMSU–Grants combined vocational programs with college programs. The institution received grants to assist working adult students who did not qualify for traditional financial aid, and it adjusted programs to meet the needs of the current economy. After providing two examples of the programs offered by NMSU–Grants, Blanchard, Casados, and Sheski review their findings from studying this type of institution and its programs for rural adult learners. — KKN

271   Brodkey, Linda. "On the Subjects of Class and Gender in 'The Literacy Letters.'" *College English* 51.2 (1989): 125–41. Print.

Contending that poststructuralist theories of discourse can illuminate basic writers' textual performances, Linda Brodkey reports on a letter writing project involving six graduate students who were white English teachers and six white women enrolled in an adult basic education (ABE) class. The project paired one graduate student with one adult education student and required them to write letters to each other. Brodkey then analyzed the rhetorical strategies used by both graduate students and adult education students as they wrote their letters to each other. Surprisingly, an analysis of the graduate students' letters revealed that they often made rhetorical missteps and sometimes misread their ABE pen pals' letters. One graduate student, for example, responded to an ABE student's story about a friend's murder by commenting on how one should respond politely to news of a friend's death. This is one example of the graduate students' repeated failures to respond to real-life events with empathy. The graduate students too often failed to recognize and respond appropriately to ABE students' preferred topics, which often related to "external threats to the well-being of themselves and their families or their neighbors" (130). Holding fast to the premise that class, culture, and gender inequalities can be left at the door of a college classroom and that academic discourse is a neutral, nonideological language, these graduate students sometimes failed to recognize and respond to their correspondents' socioeconomic and cultural realities. The ABE students reacted to their pen pals' communication failures by shutting down the conversations and by producing written language marred by increasing grammatical and word form errors. Brodkey argues that the basic writing errors frequently explained by cognitive or linguistic deficits can better be understood by discourse theories that present language as constructed by external realities such as social roles and power differences among readers and writers. She concludes by calling for teachers to become more aware of their own powerful roles in determining discourse topics and deciding what counts as appropriate responses to their students' oral and written communications. — BJG

272   Bruno, Frank J. *Going Back to School: College Survival Strategies for Adult Students.* 3rd ed. Lawrenceville, NJ: Arco, 2001. Print.

Bruno argues that adult college applicants can succeed in entering college and become successful students, even if their prior academic experiences have been far less than satisfactory. After presenting an initial explanation of different kinds of colleges and varying standards for college admissions, Bruno describes common admissions procedures and offers useful recommendations for applicants. He goes on to discuss several myths about college students (e.g., that they are exceptionally intelligent or especially talented) and provides an introductory, jargon-free discussion of learning theory. Common fears and questions experienced by returning adults are described, including anxieties about learning math, public speaking, test-taking, and writing. Among many useful strategies suggested are the SQ3R (survey, question, read, recite, review) method of reading textbooks (chapter 4) and information about how people learn (chapter 5). Affective dimensions of learning are addressed in chapter 6 and chapter 17, with related discussions of motivation, self-understanding, the underachievement syndrome, and self-actualization. A classification of five instructional styles is accompanied by strategies for coping with different types of instructors in chapter 15. — BJG

See: Lauren E. Clarke and Trent E. Gabert, "Faculty Issues Related to Adult Degree Programs" [164].

See: Nicholas Coles and Susan V. Wall, "Conflict and Power in the Reader-Responses of Adult Basic Writers" [131].

See: Jonathan I. Compton, Elizabeth Cox, and Frankie Santos Laanan, "Adult Learners in Transition" [2].

273   Ferretti, Eileen. "Between the Dirty Dishes and Polished Discourse: How Working-Class Moms Construct Student Identities." *Teaching Working Class*. Ed. Sherry Lee Linkon. Amherst: U of Massachusetts P, 1999. 69–84. Print.

Ferretti describes the learning experiences and writing and educational histories of working-class mothers who attend community college classes to earn credits needed for their jobs as education paraprofessionals. Fundamental to these students' educational experiences is the fact that they must juggle home, work, and school responsibilities to a greater degree than do other nontraditional students. Aware of this central fact about the students, Ferretti employs a Freirian pedagogical perspective in her college composition class. She encourages her reentry women students to examine their own lives and to articulate their experiences in autobiographical literacy narratives. The women's multiple roles and identities become more evident when portrayed in their autobiographical writing. And their learning is different as well: They must read and write in short spurts of time sandwiched in between childcare, house cleaning, and work. The women's responses to various readings reveal their attitudes towards their own circumstances as re-entry women students. Their writing also records a dissonance between their home and school cultures. Ultimately, Ferretti constructs a writing curriculum that encourages reentry women students to explore their multiple roles and potential conflicts between their original cultural communities and the academic community they hope to enter.—BJG

274   Fredericksen, Elaine. "Silence and the Nontraditional Writer." *Teaching English in the Two-Year College* 25.2 (1998): 115–21. Print.

Fredericksen argues that instructors need to be sensitive to nontraditional students, whom she describes as older, veterans, ethnic minorities, or foreign students, so that instructors can help these students have a voice in their courses. She states that nontraditional students, who may come to class with work and/or prior college experience, often are silent in the classroom because they fear ridicule or failure, or because they fear they will not be heard because they see themselves as underprepared compared to other students. Fredericksen then offers suggestions to help nontraditional students feel comfortable in the classroom and to let their voices be heard.—KKN

275   Holladay, Sylvia A. "Gladly Teach and Gladly Learn." *Teaching English in the Two-Year College* 36.4 (2009): 368–78. Print.

Reporting on her experience as a community college instructor during wartime, Sylvia Holladay calls attention to the educational needs of military veterans returning to the classroom as undergraduates. By recalling how her own worldview was shaped by the Cold War, the Korean War, and the Vietnam War, Holladay has been able to find common ground with students returning from combat in US wars and also with her younger, less experienced students who live during wartime without engaging in military service. Central to this essay are questions about a college instructor's responsibilities toward veterans enrolled in college courses: In particular, how should English instructors of writing and literature change or refine their pedagogical practices in order to address the needs of veterans? To explore this and related pedagogical questions, Holladay asked students who were military veterans to respond to a list of twelve questions regarding their reasons for entering the military and their subsequent experiences, both during their military service and after they returned home. She also asked about their reasons for entering college and their educational goals. Two male students' written responses are quoted extensively to provide the viewpoints of veterans who have enrolled in college classes. One issue their writing prompts is how a writing instructor should respond to personal narrative writing that records horrific, violent memories of wartime experience. Holladay resolves this issue by responding to veterans' writing in the same ways that she responds to other students' writing: helping the student to communicate effectively using linguistic forms and rhetoric patterns appropriate to genre, audience, and the writer's purpose. The author's major aim, however, is to call attention more broadly to the increasing presence of combat veterans in college writing and literature classes, to the corollary responsibilities of their instructors, and to their educational aims and needs.—BJG

276   Kiely, Richard, Lorilee R. Sandman, and Janet Truluck. "Adult Learning Theory and the Pursuit of Adult Degrees." *Developing and Delivering Adult Degree Programs.* Ed. James P. Pappas and Jerry Jerman. Hoboken, NJ: Wiley, 2004. 17–30. Print. New Directions for Adult and Continuing Education 103.

A comprehensive guide to adult learning theory looks at three areas: the nature of the adult learner, the context in which adults learn, and the processes that adult learners engage in. A four-lens model builds on the three-part typology and incorporates the perspective of educators as a significant fourth lens. The authors contend that when considered together as one model, these four lenses form a broader, more holistic view of adult learning than the three-lens model. The most prominent theorist focusing exclusively on the individual adult learner is Malcolm Knowles, whose central principle is that adults are a unique type of learner and require different instructional strategies from the teacher-centered, subject-focused pedagogies commonly used to teach children. The process lens focuses on how adults learn. The most prominent process learning theory is Mezirow's transformational learning model, defined as "the process of becoming critically aware of how and why our presuppositions have come to constrain the way we perceive, understand, and feel about our world; of reformulating these assumptions to permit a more inclusive, discriminating, permeable, and integrative perspective; and of making decisions or otherwise acting on these new understandings" (22). Adult educators and administrators informed by Mezirow's theory will encourage adult learners to reflect critically, engage in discourse with others, and derive tentative judgments through consensus. Adult learning viewed through the context lens describes learning as fundamentally a social process and views individual adults as primarily living in communities. The fourth lens focuses on the educator's perspective. Educators base their assumptions about effective teaching and practice on accumulated experience, intuitive insight, and practical knowledge gained over time. While some educators prefer the expert role that has primary control over the content and process of learning, others are more comfortable as a facilitator who shares responsibility for the content, process, and evaluation of learning with adult learners. The four-lens model of learner, process, context, and educator offers a holistic understanding of learning in adulthood and proves useful in planning instruction or analyzing and diagnosing problems. If carefully considered when designing and administering adult degree programs, the four-lens model could provide successful experiences as adults pursue and complete their degree programs. —NMM

277   Maehl, William H. "Adult Degrees and the Learning Society." *Developing and Delivering Adult Degree Programs.* Ed. James P. Pappas and Jerry Jerman. Hoboken, NJ: Wiley, 2004. 5–16. Print. New Directions for Adult and Continuing Education 103.

Maehl reports that the US educational system has undergone significant changes following World War II, and that education has become more accessible, especially for adult learners. General Education Diploma (GED) testing has provided a new opportunity for adults to complete secondary school and enter college; the Serviceman's Readjustment Act (the "GI Bill") has allowed veterans to pursue higher education; and the American Council of Education (ACE) has implemented credit awards for specific types of military training. The initial development of adult degree programs during the 1960s gradually contributed to educational reforms in the 1970s, leading to the evolution of innovative models of education such as Adult Degree Completion (ADC) programs. Newly established institutions emerged (e.g., Nova Southern University, Union Institute, California Institute of Integral Studies, Saybrook Institute, Walden University, and Fielding Graduate Institute) to address the needs of students interested in graduate education and professional studies (e.g., education, health, administration, management, clinical psychology, and human services). By the late 1980s, these programs had gained credibility via successful accreditation. More recently, globalization and technology have significantly impacted the development of adult degree programs. The author reports three trends in adult engagement in degree programs during the 1990s: increases in human capital development, distance learning by means of advanced technology, and the number of for-profit degree-granting institutions. —NM

278 Pappas, James P., and Jerry Jerman. "Accreditation Issues Related to Adult Degree Programs." *Developing and Delivering Adult Degree Programs.* Ed. James P. Pappas and Jerry Jerman. Hoboken, NJ: Wiley, 2004. 81–89. Print. New Directions for Adult and Continuing Education 103.

According to the Council for Higher Education Accreditation (CHEA), in order for degree-granting colleges and universities to become accredited, there must be a review of the quality of education they provide. There are three types of accreditors: (1) regional, (2) national, and (3) specialized. One benefit of obtaining accreditation is that it allows institutions and students to receive federally funded grants and loans. The US Department of Education (USDE) requires accreditation from higher education institutions that seek federal dollars. Accreditation also makes credit transfers among universities possible and assures employers that the credentials provided by their employees have come from expert-approved programs and institutions. However, Simpson notes that an increase in adult degree programs has introduced terms like *online*, *nontraditional*, and *distance education*, which has forced accreditors to adjust their approaches and standards for evaluating these technology-based learning opportunities. Proprietary institutions that offer adult degree programs often make use of these learning options and rely on accreditation as a central component in their marketing strategies. Many educational agencies both in and out of the accrediting system share principles when it comes to serving adult learners. Overall, the author claims that using the same guidelines and principles established by accreditors can lead to a well-designed adult degree or certificate program that can pass the toughest program review. —MCV

279   Pappas, James P., and Jerry Jerman. "Future Considerations." *Developing and Delivering Adult Degree Programs*. Ed. James P. Pappas and Jerry Jerman. Hoboken, NJ: Wiley, 2004. 91–96. Print. New Directions for Adult and Continuing Education 103.

Pappas and Jerman argue that higher education institutions should increase the availability and the quality of adult degree programs because the US workforce requires more college-educated people and also because tangible benefits tend to accrue to individuals with earned degrees. Education can become more available for adults via innovations such as accelerated short courses offered on the weekends or evenings, online courses, and blended programs that combine in-person and online learning. One approach to improving the quality of adult education is to focus on relevance; for example, a relevant program might involve "a practicum or service-learning component as part of its curriculum" (93). In addition to meeting the educational needs of adult learners, adult degree programs ought to use successful market strategies and address financial considerations. When faced with budgetary issues, some adult degree programs have moved toward becoming government-sponsored while others have allied themselves with corporations. In addition, adult degree programs should prepare for accreditation. In order to ensure that students receive a quality education, accrediting groups and state licensure boards evaluate programs based on outcome measures. Institutions can prepare for these evaluations by making sure their students receive an education that is congruous with their programs' objectives. Finally, the authors suggest that faculty should also undergo technical training and acquire knowledge of adult learning. To better serve adult students, faculty must be aware of the demands, skills, and preferences of adults, which can differ enormously from those of traditional students. — BB

280   Ritt, Elizabeth. "Redefining Tradition: Adult Learners and Higher Education." *Adult Learning* 19.1–2 (2008): 12–16. Print.

Ritt argues that in order to remain a leader in innovation and economic success, the United States should change state and federal policies to make higher education more accessible, especially for nontraditional students, a significant portion of the postsecondary landscape. The vast majority of the fastest growing jobs require at least some postsecondary education. While other countries are increasing their college graduation rates, the United States is failing to lift barriers to higher education. Despite common perceptions of college students, only 16 percent of US undergraduates are aged 18 to 22 years old and attending college full-time while living on campus (13). According to P. J. Stokes (*Hidden in Plain Sight: Adult Learners Forge a New Tradition in Higher Education* [2006, Web]), 37 percent of undergraduates are older than 25 (13). Furthermore, many younger students are considered "nontraditional" by National Center for Education Statistics criteria. Because of a rapidly changing economy, many adults are finding it necessary to return to school. In addition to long-term earning potential, which comes with a college degree, other benefits of a college degree include improved health, social mobility, and professional growth. The author argues that getting more adults into college is an urgent need and is essential to maintaining the United States' economic position in the global marketplace. However, even though more and more colleges and universities are offering programs geared specifically towards adult learners, there still remain many personal, professional, and institutional barriers. According to Ritt, greater collaboration among policymakers, state representatives, employers, and workforce development workers can lead to action that will address these barriers. — AA

See: Mike Rose, *Back to School: Why Everyone Deserves a Second Chance at Education* [268].

281   Tinberg, Howard, and Jean-Paul Nadeau. *The Community College Writer: Exceeding Expectations.* Carbondale: Southern Illinois UP, 2010. Print.

In a multipronged study of community college student writing, Tinberg and Nadeau evaluate both faculty and student perspectives through survey questionnaires and interviews in four community colleges. The research reveals that most writing produced by first-semester students occurs in English courses and that faculty favor essay writing assignments. Since essays are not typically produced in work environments, the authors question the notion that writing skills developed in English classes easily transfer to other courses and workplaces. Among the contrasts between student and faculty perception is the view of 48 percent of students that writing won't be important in their selected careers while 95 percent of faculty consider writing as highly important in those same careers. And while 80 percent of faculty view writing as critical to student success in college, 89 percent of faculty view their students as underprepared for college writing. Students surveyed range in age from 28 to 35. The authors profile sixteen students, fourteen women younger than 25 and two older than 25. The survey questionnaire asks further questions about students' attitudes toward writing, their own writing processes, and their high school preparation. While 90 percent of these students expected to write in college, only one-third viewed themselves as strong writers. Fifty-eight percent viewed their high school preparation in writing as sufficient for success in college. Implications for teaching and research, discussed in chapter 6, include the authors' conclusion that "we would all do well to ascertain the pressures faced by students who are no longer for the most part full-time students but rather students who work and attend school" (131). This conclusion has implications for the types of writing projects assigned in college classes, as well as for instructional approaches and faculty responses to student writing. Faculty responses suggest a need for improved instructional approaches. Students report disappointment with faculty feedback on their writing. But both students and faculty report being optimistic that community college students possess the ability to acquire improved writing skills. — BJG

See: Karen S. Uehling, *Starting Out or Starting Over: A Guide for Writing* [154].

Focus on Adult Learners

Adult Learners' Perspectives and Experiences

See: John M. Ackerman, "Postscript: The Assimilation and Tactics of Nate" [128].

See: Sharon M. Ballard and Michael Lane Morris, "Factors Influencing Midlife and Older Adults' Attendance in Family Life Education Programs" [42].

See: Carol Berkenkotter, Thomas N. Huckin, and John Ackerman, "Conventions, Conversations, and the Writer: Case Study of a Student in a Rhetoric PhD Program" [71].

282 Connors, Patricia. "Some Attitudes of Returning or Older Students of Composition." *College Composition and Communication* 33.3 (1982): 263–66. Print.

Noting the increasing presence of nontraditional students in higher education, Connors questions the use of traditional teaching methods for teaching nontraditional students. Connors argues that nontraditional students are serious about their studies in a way that traditional students usually are not, and that though they bring a wealth of experience into the classroom, older students are more hesitant about their insights than are traditional-age students. To measure her impressions more precisely, Connors developed a brief survey for composition students. She designed the survey to learn about whether there were measurable differences between these two student groups and, if so, to understand the pedagogical impact. The survey questionnaire was distributed to 182 students; 137 students were between 18 and 24, and the remaining 45 were between 25 and 50. For the most part, the groups' responses were very similar. Surprisingly, however, the question "I believe my own life experiences and interests give me plenty of material to write about" revealed that older students are less confident than younger students in this regard (264). This result suggests that nontraditional students should be encouraged to think more highly of their own experiences. The author also found that nontraditional students are much more likely to put time and effort into their courses and that nontraditional students are much more likely to want specific direction. The author concludes with a list of suggestions for classroom practice that respond to these findings. — TBP

See: Stephen Doheney-Farina, "A Case Study of One Adult Writing in Academic and Nonacademic Discourse Communities" [84].

283 Gillespie, Marilyn. "Profiles of Adult Learners: Revealing the Multiple Faces of Literacy." *TESOL Quarterly* 27.3 (1993): 529–33. Print.

Explaining that stereotypical portraits of adult illiterates have been substantially replaced by adult learner profiles derived from qualitative research, Gillespie summarizes the findings of several qualitative research studies and argues for increased effort to understand and describe adult literacy learners. Gillespie goes on to say that qualitative research on adult learners had come into its own during the ten years prior to this 1993 publication. Among the qualitative approaches used to study people's literacy practices are ethnographies, longitudinal case studies, and life histories. Citing Shirley Brice Heath's ten-year study of people living in three communities (*Ways with Words*), Gillespie notes that much of what we know about adult learners comes from ethnographic studies of people's everyday uses of language and literacy in their own communities. Despite all the gains reported by qualitative researchers, Gillespie argues that much more of this research is called for and that adult learners must become collaborators in these research projects so that their perspectives can better inform these studies. — BJG

See: Carol E. Kasworm, "From the Adult Student's Perspective: Accelerated Degree Programs" [237].

See: Francis E. Kazemek, "They Have Yarns. Writing with the Active Elderly" [118].

284 Keeton, Morris T., Barry G. Sheckley, and Joan Krejci Griggs. *Effectiveness and Efficiency in Higher Education for Adults: A Guide for Fostering Learning.* Dubuque, IA: Kendall Hunt, 2002. Print.

This book offers a research-based framework for increased learning effectiveness and efficiency in higher education. The authors argue that a set of key learning principles and related strategies, together with creative uses of technologies, can help colleges enhance accountability and reduce costs. This twin focus on demonstrating successful learning and increasing efficiency has come more sharply into focus as college student populations have trended toward older learners and working adults. Eight learning principles are presented along with strategies for their implementation and illustrative anecdotes. Principles one and two are "early and ongoing clarification of goals" and "deliberate practice" (6). Principle three advocates support for individual learners, while principle four emphasizes the value of experiential learning. Reflecting on learning achieved and pursuing solutions to actual problems form the bases for principles five and six. Principles seven and eight call attention to monitoring individual learners' experiences and creating college-wide cultures of learning. Concrete suggestions for teachers are provided in eight of the ten chapters. What makes this book distinctive, according to the authors, are (1) an emphasis on skills development rather than a sole focus on theory and fact-based knowledge, and (2) attention to recent observations about learning and problem-solving. — BJG

See: Vivian W. Mott, "Rural Education for Older Adults" [260].

See: Iswari P. Pandey, "Literate Lives across the Digital Divide" [231].

See: Elizabeth Ritt, "Redefining Tradition: Adult Learners and Higher Education" [280].

See: Mike Rose, *Back to School: Why Everyone Deserves a Second Chance at Education* [268].

285   Tinberg, Howard. "'Under History's Wheel': The Uses of Literacy." *Teaching English in the Two-Year College* 38.4 (2011): 338–46. Print.

Arguing that literacy learning continues in adulthood, Tinberg cites the cases of two community college students, Wendy (age 40) and Kim (age 35), who both learn academic writing after having acquired writing skills at their workplaces. In the same manner, faculty learn literacy after they are hired as college instructors. Tinberg illustrates this idea by recalling an experience in which he read a written commentary that he had produced twenty years earlier as a young college instructor. Though appreciative of the writing, the mature man recognizes that his written "words were not bought and paid for by experience" (346). Similarly, adults continue to learn about the uses of literacy as they grow older. — BJG

Multilingual Adults and English Language Learners

See: Linda Lonon Blanton, "Student Interrupted: A Tale of Two Would-Be Writers" [73].

See: Yongyan Li, "Apprentice Scholarly Writing in a Community of Practice: An Intraview of an NNES Graduate Student Writing a Research Article" [90].

See: Natasha Llovich, *The Multilingual Self: An Inquiry into Language Learning* [218].

See: Julie Mathews-Aydinli, "Overlooked and Understudied? A Survey of Current Trends in Research on Adult English Language Learners" [64].

286   McKay, Sandra Lee, and Gail Weinstein-Shr. "English Literacy in the US: National Policies, Personal Consequences." *TESOL Quarterly* 27.3 (1993): 399–419. Print.

The essay examines relationships between US immigration and naturalization policies, attitudes toward competency in English language and literacy in the United States, available English language and literacy programs for adults, and the needs of individual immigrants. Although knowledge of English was not historically a requirement for US immigration, English literacy competency is currently viewed as a valid prerequisite for US immigration and naturalization. To achieve legal immigration status, potential US citizens must now pass tests on English literacy, US government, and US history. For this reason, a strong need exists for courses that teach adult learners English language and literacy. However, available courses do not meet current demand. Furthermore these courses often emphasize utilitarian goals, such as finding employment, whereas adult immigrants' learning goals frequently include incentives such as being able to support children at home and at school and communicating with grandchildren about their native cultures and traditions. The authors argue that while teaching English is important for US immigrants, helping these immigrants to maintain their first-language literacies is also a valid goal. Moreover, since many immigrants live as multilingual individuals in multilingual communities, multilingualism merits closer attention from language and literacy educators and support from US immigration policy makers. — BJG

See: N. Eleni Pappamihiel, Takayuki Nishimata, and Florin Mihai, "Timed Writing and Adult English-Language Learners: An Investigation of First Language Use in Invention Strategies" [161].

See: Klaudia M. Rivera, "Adult Biliteracy in Community-Based Organizations: Venues of Participation, Agents of Transformation" [263].

See: Klaudia M. Rivera and Ana Huerta-Macías, "Adult Bilingualism and Biliteracy in the United States: Theoretical Perspectives" [194].

See: Gail Weinstein-Shr, "Overview Discussion: Directions in Adult ESL Literacy: An Invitation to Dialogue" [219].

Learning Differences and Styles

See: Royce Ann Collins, "The Role of Learning Styles and Technology" [221].

See: Tammy J. Freiler, "Learning through the Body" [207].

See: Nancy F. Gadbow, "Teaching All Learners As If They Are Special" [208].

See: Marianne Mazzei Hanlon and R. Jeffrey Cantrell, "Teaching a Learning Disabled Adult to Spell: Is It Ever Too Late?" [86].

See: Lynnette Pannucci and Sean A. Walmsley, "Supporting Learning-Disabled Adults in Literacy" [124].

287 Rocco, Tonette S., and Antonio Delgado. "Shifting Lenses: A Critical Examination of Disability in Adult Education." *Challenging Ableism, Understanding Disability, Including Adults with Disabilities in Workplaces and Learning Spaces.* Ed. Tonette S. Rocco. Hoboken, NJ: Wiley, 2011. 3–12. Print. New Directions for Adult and Continuing Education 132.

Increasing numbers of adults with disabilities are entering adult education programs. This is one of several reasons that research on disability should become a greater priority in adult education research. Research on issues of access to learning opportunities should be connected to research on power and privilege. Very often, when adult educators study issues concerning disability, they conceptualize disability as a medical condition or a functional impairment. However, Rocco and Delgado argue that disability is more than a medical condition: It is an identity marker or social construction that has the power to limit adults' access to "education, meaningful work and participation in civic and social life of the community" (8). Just as educators who are nonspecialists in race, gender, and social class conduct research in these areas, educators who are not specialists in disability studies can and should apply this orientation to research on adult learning and teaching.—BJG

See: Heidi Silver-Pacuilla, "Access and Benefits: Assistive Technology in Adult Literacy" [269].

Gender and Learning

See: Mary Field Belenky, Blythe McVicker Clinchy, Nancy Rule Goldberger, and Jill Mattuck Tarule, *Women's Ways of Knowing: The Development of Self, Voice, and Mind* [68].

288   Culley, Margo. "Adult Women in the College Classroom." *Equity and Excellence in Education* 24.3 (Fall 1988): 67–68. Print.

Culley uses her experiences with adult learners in her mixed-age classes as the basis for this narrative essay. She describes some of her female adult students and some of their issues as college students. Then Culley focuses on the point of her work: "pedagogy and classroom dynamics—in particular, interaction between teachers and older students" (67). She states that older students position themselves differently with the professor because of their experiences. Some adult students believe that professors box them in and feel intimidated by the adult students. Adult students also test what they are learning in class against what they have experienced and know as real. Culley states that adult students see education as changed since they were in school, and these students sometimes don't see the relationship between what they have experienced and the classroom. Finally, Culley argues that instructors need to put themselves in the place of the adult learners. —KKN

289   Gilligan, Carol. *In a Different Voice: Psychological Theory and Women's Development*. Cambridge, MA: Harvard UP, 1982. Print.

When this book was published, developmental psychology theories were based primarily on studies of boys and men. Piaget's theory of child development focused principally on boys, and Lawrence Kohlberg based his theory of moral development on a study of boys. When theories that explain male development are used as yardsticks for judgments of females, women appear less competent and less likely to mature as fully as men. Moreover, the absence of girls and women from research on psychological, moral, intellectual, and social development creates faulty theories and misleading contrasts between men and women. Three ongoing studies are referred to throughout the book: a study of twenty-five male and female college students enrolled in a course on moral and political choice, a study of twenty-nine women who were considering obtaining an abortion, and a study of males and females at nine points across an age spectrum ranging from age 11 to age 60. Using these studies to make observations on men's and women's preferences and choices, Gilligan points out that women typically share an orientation based on attachment and caring while men strive to separate from others and accomplish individual goals. This idea was not new. In 1926, for example, Virginia Woolf observed that women's values differ from men's values and that men's values carry the day. Gilligan explains that by "changing the lens of developmental observation from individual achievement to relationships of care, women depict ongoing attachment as the path that leads to maturity" (170). She goes on to observe that women's development in childhood and adulthood must take into account the realities of women's experiences and perspectives.—BJG

290   Gilligan, Carol. "Hearing the Difference: Theorizing Connection." *Hypatia* 10.2 (1995): 120–27. Print.

Having called attention to disparate treatment of women and men in developmental psychology (*In a Different Voice*, 1982), Gilligan describes a subsequent paradigm shift in development theory. It involves moving beyond a patriarchal frame in which women must choose between being selfless or selfish because they are "bound internally and externally by obligations to care without complaint" (122) and progressing toward a philosophy based fundamentally on connection with others. Rather than requiring women to view themselves as individuals separated from people, this philosophy prioritizes relationships with people and connections between private and public worlds. This new philosophy Gilligan terms "a feminist ethic of care" (123) and describes the view as an opportunity to resist oppressive, patriarchal frameworks. Applying the feminist ethic of care to research on women's development significantly impacts views of psychological maturity in adulthood.—BJG

291   Greenwood, Claudia M. "'It's Scary at First': Reentry Women in College Composition Classes." *Teaching English in the Two-Year College* 17.2 (1990): 133–42. Print.

The writer notes that the profile of a traditional college student is changing and that more of these returning students are women who interrupted their education to have children. These women have been "designated reentry women" (133). The author found little information about these students in the literature, so she designed a study that would help her understand her students' needs, especially with regard to the composition classroom. This extensive study includes data gathered from a "preinstruction questionnaire exploring reasons for their decision to return to school . . . a preinstruction writing attitude survey;

a writing history; an interview at the conclusion of the first three weeks of instruction; a video-taped writing session and retrospective protocol," three postinstruction surveys, and the analysis of student portfolios (134). Study participants included twelve students and four instructors. The researcher found that reentry women in this sample had a very high level of anxiety about their ability to be successful college students. They also felt guilty about making additional demands of their significant others so that they could return to college. The students believed that without family support they would not be able to complete their studies. Personal resolve to succeed, enhanced by positive classroom experiences, also helped students to complete their studies, as did the discovery that other students and faculty would become part of their support group. As writers, these students valued writing as a form of "self-expression and for maintaining personal relationships," but they found writing for purposes other than these threatening (136). Students did not think themselves capable of other forms of writing. There were a variety of forms of instruction in the four courses included in this study, and instructors tended to have very high expectations of reentry women since they were older and had more life experience. The students' self-perceptions changed over the course of the semester, but they were unable to reflect on changes in their writing abilities. At the end of the semester, they still did not perceive themselves as writers but rather as imitators of writers. Students who had been pushed intellectually, however, had a much stronger impression of themselves as thinkers at the end of the semester. Though they did not think their writing had much improved, they were pleased with their increased ability to think through complex rhetorical problems. All students agreed that successful writing required revision. All students continued to regard professorial authority as extremely powerful and did not question the professors' goals and methods. This power makes each instructor's mode of instruction and orientation toward reentry women very important. Instructors should create a welcoming, constructive classroom environment, recognize that these students have intense time constraints, and plan their course work accordingly. —TBP

292   Hayes, Elisabeth. "Social Contexts." *Women as Learners: The Significance of Gender in Adult Learning.* Ed. Elisabeth Hayes, Daniele D. Flannery, with Ann K. Brooks, Elizabeth J. Tisdell, and Jane M. Hugo. San Francisco: Jossey-Bass, 2000. 23–52. Print.

Women learn in a variety of settings, yet most scholarship on women's learning focuses on formal educational contexts. Among the scenes for women's learning are formal education, the workplace, home and family, and community-based social organizations. In her analysis of formal education, Elisabeth Hayes notes the increased presence of women in undergraduate and graduate programs during recent decades. When this book went to press (2000), more women than men were earning bachelor's degrees and master's degrees. Yet, despite their wider participation in higher education, women still face gender bias in higher education and in their workplaces. A hidden curriculum presents indirectly conveyed lessons on the roles of women and on their limited worth in school and at work. Furthermore, although women are earning more bachelor's and master's degrees than ever before, their opportunities for employment, financial rewards for work, and advancement remain less favorable than for men. Hayes argues that the learning women can experience at home and among family members can often be substantial, yet this learning is not sufficiently valued because of the social context in which it occurs. As for community-based social organizations, women often learn experientially by participating in group activities and sometimes learn by participating in formal educational meetings. Hayes describes higher education and workplaces as "greedy institutions" (47) requiring total commitment from women. This exemplifies a situation when different social contexts for learning can create conflict for women. Commenting on the need for adult educators to understand various contexts in which women learn, Hayes explains that adult education can offer opportunities to reduce inequities for women learners and help transform social environments in which women learn. — BJG

See: Elisabeth R. Hayes, "A New Look at Women's Learning" [56].

See: Charlotte Hogg, "Beyond Agrarianism: Toward a Critical Pedagogy of Place" [258].

See: Karyn L. Hollis, "Liberating Voices: Autobiographical Writing at the Bryn Mawr Summer School for Women Workers, 1921–1938" [141].

See: Karyn L. Hollis, *Liberating Voices: Writing at the Bryn Mawr Summer School for Women Workers* [142].

293   Hugo, Jane M. "Perspectives on Practice." *Women as Learners: The Significance of Gender in Adult Learning.* Ed. Elisabeth Hayes and Daniele D. Flannery, with Ann K. Brooks, Elizabeth J. Tisdell, and Jane M. Hugo. San Francisco: Jossey-Bass, 2000. 185–215. Print.

Jane Hugo comments on key issues in women's learning that can inform adult educators' practices and argues for greater emphasis on women's learning in all sites of adult education. Hugo's discussion is framed by a series of commitments outlined by Daniel Pratt and Associates in *Five Perspectives on Teaching in Adult and Higher Education* (1998). These commitments include an increased emphasis on meeting women's learning needs, an effort to deliver content effectively for women learners, a commitment to relying more heavily on apprenticeships and mentoring, increased attention to ways of thinking and constructing meaning (e.g., encouraging women to rely on their own beliefs and expertise and to become independent learners), a commitment to women's development of self-efficacy, and ultimately to building a better society. Recommendations for future work include offering staff development workshops on topics related to women as learners, making women's learning more visible in scholarship, and educators' putting into practice what they know about women's learning styles, preferences, interests, and goals. — BJG

See: Mary Kay Jackman, "Where the Personal Becomes Professional: Stories from Reentry Adult Women Learners about Family, Work, and School" [88].

See: Christine A. Jarvis, "Desirable Reading: The Relationship between Women Students' Lives and Their Reading Practices" [116].

See: Daphne Key, *Literacy Shutdown: Stories of Six American Women* [89].

294 Martin, Theodora Penny. *The Sound of Our Own Voices: Women's Study Clubs, 1860–1910*. Boston: Beacon, 1987. Print.

Early US women's organizations focused on religion, and during the Civil War, Northern women met to support the war effort. A well-heeled women's group based in New York initiated the women's study club movement; however, the movement existed primarily for ordinary women who wanted to learn together by reading common texts, discussing issues, listening to lectures, and participating in debates. Martin documents the study club movement, which offered a socially acceptable alternative to attending college. A few women did enter college in the nineteenth century and early twentieth century, but postsecondary education was widely viewed as unnatural for women, who were thought best equipped to remain at home and develop their talents as wives and mothers. Domestic themes dominated some study groups (who often explored the meaning of "true womanhood") while other groups focused on learning about art, literature, or history. The informal learning experienced by women participants in nineteenth-century study clubs helped contribute to the rise of women opting for formal learning in college classrooms during the early decades of the twentieth century. — BJG

295 Sealey-Ruiz, Yolanda. "Wrapping the Curriculum around Their Lives: Using a Culturally Relevant Curriculum with African American Adult Women." *Adult Education Quarterly* 58.1 (2007): 44–60. Print.

In a study of adult African American female students engaged in a culturally relevant course, Sealey-Ruiz reports that these students valued their life experiences and wished to share them as part of their learning process. Black female students especially wished to display their knowledge of what it means to be an African American female in our society. They sought ways to apply that knowledge to their course work. Sealey-Ruiz argues that personal experience can bridge the gap between lack of knowledge and what these students seek to learn from their college experience. Three different themes evolved during the research study: "language validation, the fostering of positive self and group identity, and self-affirmation or affirmation of goals" (59). In addition, the study promotes the idea of including experiential learning as a core part of the curriculum so that students are encouraged to maximize their learning potential. — LDB

296 Vaccaro, Annemarie, and Cheryl D. Lovell. "Inspiration from Home: Understanding Family as Key to Adult Women's Self-Investment." *Adult Education Quarterly* 60.2 (2010): 161–76. Print.

After providing a review of literature on women students in education, Vaccaro and Lovell describe their study of women in a small women's college. The authors found that women experience ebbs and flows in their education, which they accept as normal. Despite the challenges they faced, the women found the strength to continue their pursuit of a college education; they had learned to balance several factors in their lives. Additionally, family members were inspirational to these women, even when family responsibilities interfered with the women's schooling. The students also were invested in themselves, which encouraged them to keep working toward their degrees. Vaccaro and Lovell discuss their findings as compared to previous studies on nontraditional students and state that educators need to focus on the investment women are making in themselves instead of their earning capital. —KKN

Social Class, Culture, Race, and Learning

See: Anne Aronson, "Reversals of Fortune: Downward Mobility and the Writing of Nontraditional Students" [129].

297 Branch, Kirk. "In the Hallways of the Literacy Narrative: Violence and the Power of Literacy." *Multiple Literacies for the 21st Century.* Ed. Brian Huot, Beth Stroble, and Charles Bazerman. Creskill, NJ: Hampton, 2004. 15–38. Print.

The traditional adult literacy narrative portrays learning as rewarding and transformational. An adult voluntarily seeks educational opportunities in a romanticized classroom where successful literacy practices are facilitated by caring, inspirational teachers. However, some adults do not recall literacy learning so positively; in fact, for some people literacy education is remembered as punitive and alienating. Memories of teachers sending unsuccessful students out of their classrooms are common, and literacy learning memories are sometimes painful reminders of teachers' exclusionary practices and students' sense of themselves as failures. To explore this flip side of the literacy narrative, the author reports on his interviews with seven African American community college students. One student recalls being denied the opportunity to attend school by her mother. Several students report having been humiliated and physically beaten for educational failures. Less obviously oppressive are classroom assessment practices that divide students by publicly rewarding some and shaming others. The seven interviewees' recollections illustrate a power dynamic that allows literate adults to oppress children, adolescents, and low-literate adults. The author uses these examples to argue against naive or uncritical readings of adult education students' literacy narratives. —BJG

See: Linda Brodkey, "On the Subjects of Class and Gender in 'The Literacy Letters'" [271].

See: Tom Buckmiller, "Contradictions and Conflicts: Understanding the Lived Experiences of Native American Adult Learners in a Predominantly White American University" [77].

See: Nicholas Coles and Susan V. Wall, "Conflict and Power in the Reader-Responses of Adult Basic Writers" [131].

See: Eileen Ferretti, "Between the Dirty Dishes and Polished Discourse: How Working-Class Moms Construct Student Identities" [273].

See: E. Paulette Isaac, Guy Talmadge, and Tom Valentine, "Understanding African American Learners' Motivations to Learn in Church-Based Adult Education" [259].

See: Juanita Johnson-Bailey, "Race Matters: The Unspoken Variable in the Teaching-Learning Transaction" [58].

298   Kates, Susan. "Literacy, Voting Rights, and the Citizenship Schools in the South, 1957–70." *College Composition and Communication* 57.3 (2006): 479–502. Print.

This essay presents an analysis of the Citizenship School movement, a response to literacy tests used to prevent African Americans from voting between 1945 and 1965. The Citizenship Schools' principal founders were Esau Jenkins, Septima Clark, and Bernice Robinson, who garnered significant support from private funders and from Martin Luther King Jr. and the Southern Christian Leadership Conference (SCLC). Structured as night classes for adults, Citizenship School classes focused on civil rights and African American culture, topics that appear in a thirty-eight-page workbook promoting the view of literacy as empowering for individuals and a potential force for social transformation. Citizenship School scholarship is important to composition and rhetoric because this movement underscores the political realities and social structures that have denied many African Americans access to literacy. The movement also promotes the understanding that African Americans have played significant roles as educators and civil rights activists, a needed counterbalance to the current scholarly emphasis on African Americans as deficient linguistically and in need of remediation. Furthermore, the Citizenship Schools' curriculum models an early form of service learning: The curriculum encouraged students to collect information about registered voters in their communities and to become literacy tutors and teachers themselves. After extending into all eleven of the southern states and reaching a high point of 195 schools, the movement lost momentum when literacy tests were banned by the 1965 Voting Rights Act. Loss of needed funding, the death of Martin Luther King Jr. in 1968, and a struggle for SCLC leadership led to the end of Citizenship Schools in 1970. — BJG

See: Raymond A. Mazurek, "Running Shoes, Auto Workers, & Labor: Business Writing Pedagogy in the Working-Class College" [189].

See: Lauren Rosenberg, "Retelling Culture through the Construction of Alternative Literacy Narratives: A Study of Adults Acquiring New Literacies" [99].

See: Yolanda Sealey-Ruiz, "Wrapping the Curriculum around Their Lives: Using a Culturally Relevant Curriculum with African American Adult Women" [295].

See: Cynthia L. Selfe and Gail E. Hawisher, *Literate Lives in the Information Age: Narratives of Literacy from the United States* [100].

See: Nick Tingle, "Literacy Development and the Working-Class Student" [255].

See: Victor Villanueva, Jr., *Bootstraps: From an American Academic of Color* [176].

See: Audrey P. Watkins, *Sisters of Hope, Looking Back, Stepping Forward: The Educational Experiences of African-American Women* [102].

299   Wiley, Terrence G. *Literacy and Language Diversity in the United States.* 2nd ed. Washington, DC: Center for Applied Linguistics, 2005. Print.

Arguing that language diversity is a "rich national resource to be fully developed" (208), Wiley surveys US language education policies, national studies of literacy attainment, and the educational achievements of US children and adults in a book divided into ten chapters. Popular assumptions about literacy, major literacy studies, and education practices are analyzed in order to cast light on ways that multilingual individuals are sometimes misunderstood and shortchanged in educational settings. A key concept that is continuously challenged in all ten chapters of the book is *monocultural bias*, the belief of mainstream English language speaking individuals that their practices and standards are an appropriate benchmark for evaluating the literacy performance of multilingual people who come from non-US cultures or from non-English speaking ethnic enclaves within the United States. Instead, Wiley argues, US educators, language and literacy researchers, and policy makers should acknowledge the value of multilingualism and of people who possess multiliterate capabilities. In addition, educators, researchers, and policy makers should recognize the challenges faced by English language learners whose teachers are mainstream English speakers and know little of their students' home languages and communities. Of particular importance to teachers and researchers of adult learners is Wiley's critique of the 1992 National Adult Literacy Survey (NALS) in chapter 4, "Defining and Measuring Literacy: Uses and Abuses." While that survey does pay more attention to language diversity than did previous studies (by providing questionnaires in both Spanish and English), the NALS assesses only English literacy and fails to report on literacies attained in other languages. It is informed by the view that only English literacy counts enough to be assessed in a national study of adult literacy in the United States, a country where nearly 20 percent of US children and adults speak a native language other than English. — BJG

Soldiers and Veterans

300   Burdick, Melanie. "Grading the War Story." *Teaching English in the Two-Year College* 36.4 (2009): 353–54. Print.

Burdick reflects on the powerful presence of combat veterans' war stories and her obligation to respond to these narratives in the context of a college writing course. She argues that, while difficult for both her and her students, including former combat soldiers' stories in her writing curriculum is vitally important, for it allows veterans' voices and stories to be heard. A key challenge Burdick faces is critiquing these stories without allowing herself to become depressed by anger and sorrow expressed by veterans. — BJG

301   Cornell-d'Echert, Jr., Blaise. "Beyond Training: New Ideas for Military Forces Operating Beyond War." *Beyond Training: The Rise of Adult Education in the Military*. Ed. Jeffrey Zacharakis and Cheryl Polson. Hoboken, NJ: Wiley, 2013. 17–27. Print. New Directions for Adult and Continuing Education 136.

Adult learning principles have recently been integrated into the *Army Learning Concept for 2015* (Department of the Army, 2011). Whereas in the past, compliance with orders and an unquestioning stance were very highly valued within the military, today's military personnel are required to think independently, solve problems, rely on their prior knowledge — not just what they are told by military instructors — and adapt to new situations. These practices are no longer viewed as valid only for officers, but are instead considered valid for lower-ranking personnel as well. In many modern military conflicts, the soldiers are "unschooled, undisciplined, and largely unorganized insurgent forces" (18). Fighting these adversaries requires ingenuity and the ability to think on one's feet, not just the ability to follow a leader's commands. — BJG

See: Kristy Liles Crawley, "Renewing Our Commitment to Connecting to Student Veterans" [204].

See: Noreen M. Glover-Graf, Eva Miller, and Samuel Freeman, "Accommodating Veterans with Posttraumatic Stress Disorder Symptoms in the Academic Setting" [85].

See: Sylvia A. Holladay, "Gladly Teach and Gladly Learn" [275].

See: Denis O. Kiely and Lisa Swift, "Casualties of War: Combat Trauma and the Return of the Combat Veteran" [144].

See: Galen Leonhardy, "Transformations: Working with Veterans in the Composition Classrooms" [145].

302   Rumann, Corey B., and Florence A. Hamrick. "Supporting Student Veterans in Transition." *Creating a Veteran-Friendly Campus: Strategies for Transition and Success.* Ed. Robert Ackerman and David DiRamio. Hoboken, NJ: Wiley, 2009. 25–34. Print. New Directions for Student Services, Number 126.

Rumann and Hamrick call for colleges to partner with veterans organizations to offer programs that "build awareness of soldiers' experiences and assist campus administrators in being proactive in serving student veterans" (25). The authors review the relationship colleges and the military have had since colonial times and then note how college attendance delayed conscription with the military. The increase of the all-volunteer army through the National Guard and Reserve units also is discussed. Because Guard and Reserve units are being deployed regularly for the Iraq and Afghanistan wars, the college experiences of the members of these groups frequently are being interrupted. However, no standard guidelines are in place for colleges to follow regarding the deployment of students. Because most college administrators today have no military experience, they do not always know how to help veterans of these recent wars. The authors note that some inappropriate comments are made in the classroom, and these comments demonstrate bias against veterans, which marginalizes student veterans. When colleges partner with veterans organizations, they provide veterans with the help they need as they return to college. Rumann and Hamrick argue that colleges need to offer programs and other opportunities for staff, faculty, and students to learn about military experiences to provide a better understanding of the veterans' experiences. At the same time, institutions must also make sure that veterans have and are aware of effective support services. — KKN

See: Thomas G. Sticht, "Swords and Pens: What the Military Can Show Us about Teaching Basic Skills to Young Adults" [197].

303   Wallace, Robert M. "Twenty-Two Anti-Tank Mines Linked Together: The Effect of Student Stories on Classroom Dynamics." *Teaching English in the Two-Year College* 36.4 (2009): 365–67. Print.

Wallace discusses an American soldier who served in the Iraq war and the effect his presence had on Wallace's class. The other students sometimes were writing antiwar poetry, to which the student, D-Mon, responded only vaguely. When D-Mon writes about his experiences as a soldier in Iraq, excerpts of which Wallace shares, the class experiences what it was like in the war situation where D-Mon was. This soldier's presence caused both Wallace and the class to find the reality of the war. Wallace's discussion helps the reader to understand the importance of allowing war veterans to express their experiences through their writing and to share their writing with their classmates. — KKN

304   Zinger, Lana, and Andrea Cohen. "Veterans Returning from War into the Classroom: How Can Colleges Be Better Prepared to Meet Their Needs." *Contemporary Issues in Education Research* 3.1 (Jan. 2010): 39–51. Print.

Because most research on veterans in college focuses on post–World War II and Vietnam, Zinger and Cohen found that research on veterans of the Iraq and Afghanistan wars was needed as these veterans flood colleges. Veterans of these two wars experience multiple deployments and fight in an arena that has no recognizable front line, which has created their vulnerability to combat stress. When these veterans enter colleges, they are entering a world that is less absolute and less structured. Additionally, Zinger and Cohen note that because the wars are not over, the full impact of the situations on the mental health of soldiers is unknown, which also means that how their mental health affects their college experiences is unknown. The research that these authors did was completed to inform colleges on "policy making, program development and restructuring efforts" (40) as they relate to veterans of these two wars. The students who participated in the study ranged in age from 21 to 32 years and had served in various branches of the military in one or both of the wars. The volunteers in the study were interviewed on reasons why they enlisted in the military, the mental preparation they went through for the wars, how they had changed after serving in the military, emotional issues they were experiencing, how their personal and social relationships were affected, their reflections on their postdeployment sense of worth and personal goals, and their experiences at Queens Community College (QCC). The students noted that they wanted more assistance going through the various administrative processes of the school. One particular area in which schools need to help veterans is in their understanding and accessing of GI Bill benefits. Mental health counseling related to the transition from military life to college life and/or dealing with PTSD is another area that colleges need to develop to help veterans. Aiding veterans with understanding the unstructured world of college is yet another area that colleges need to improve. The veterans often felt alone as they could not identify with their peers in classes. QCC has a veterans club, which some veterans found helpful. College counselors who are trained in helping veterans are needed in colleges, too. Additionally, students and faculty need sensitivity training. Zinger and Cohen end the article with symptoms veterans may experience and therapies that veterans may need. —KKN

Index of Authors Cited

Numbers refer to entries within the bibliography.

Ackerman, John M., 71, 72, 128
Addams, Jane, 256
Adkins, Natalie Ross, 25
Adult Learning in Focus: National and State-by-State Data, 39
Agnew, Eleanor, 247
Alamprese, Judy, 248
Aldrich, Pearl G., 40
Aronson, Anne, 129, 162
Askov, Eunice N., 200
Auerbach, Elsa, 155

Baer, Justin, 41
Baitinger, Katrina, 156
Baldwin, Yvonne Honeycutt, 110
Ballard, Sharon M., 43
Bardine, Bryan A., 122
Bartlett, Carol, 107
Bates, Patricia Teel, 254
Baumgartner, Lisa, 1, 22
Bay, Libby, 43
Beaman, Ronda, 201
Belanger, Kelly, 104, 130
Belenky, Mary Field, 68
Belzer, Alisa, 69, 70
Bennett, Shelly, 44
Berkenkotter, Carol, 71, 72
Beverstock, Caroline, 111, 112
Bhaskaran, Shanti, 111
Bishop-Clark, Cathy, 62
Bjorklund, Barbara R., 34
Blair, Kristine, 220
Blanchard, Rosemary Ann, 270
Blanton, Linda Lonon, 73
Bowen, Lauren Marshall, 74
Boyle, Bridget, 61
Brady, E. Michael, 202
Branch, Kirk, 297
Brandt, Deborah, 75, 76
Brewer, Susan A., 179

Brinkley, Jacquie, 111
Brodkey, Linda, 271
Brookbank, Bridgett, 117
Brookfield, Stephen, D., 163, 180
Brown, Betsy A., 45
Brown, Judith O., 181
Brumagim, Alan L., 182
Bruno, Frank J., 272
Buckmiller, Tom, 77
Burdick, Melanie, 300
Butler, Marilyn, 10

Caffarella, Rosemary S., 22
Calvin, Jennifer, 46
Cantrell, R. Jeffrey, 86
Carman, Priscilla S., 200
Casados, Felicia, 270
Castaldi, Theresa M., 78
Castles, Jane, 79
Cercone, Kathleen, 203
Chao, Ruth, 47
Chen, Li-Kuang, 48
Choi, Hee Jun, 232
Clark, Gregory, 80
Clark, M. Carolyn, 27, 49
Clarke, Lauren E., 164
Clinchy, Blythe McVicker, 68
Cohen, Andrea, 304
Coles, Nicholas, 131
Collins, Royce Ann, 221
Colvin, Janet, 236
Compton, Jonathan I., 2
Connors, Patricia, 282
Cornelius, Sarah, 222
Cornell-d'Echert Jr., Blaise, 301
Corrigan, Dagmar Stuehrk, 228
Courage, Richard, 81
Cox, Elizabeth, 2
Crawley, Kristy Liles, 204
Cray, Ellen, 157

Cross, K. Patricia, 3, 20
Crow, Angela, 223
Culley, Margo, 288
Currie, Pat, 157

D'Amico, Debby, 105
Dallmer, Denise, 183
Darkenwald, Gordon G., 82
Delgado, Antonio, 287
DelliCarpini, Margo, 158
DePew, Kevin Eric, 224
Diaz de Sabates, Gabriela, 31
Diehl, William A., 106
Dill, Patricia L., 4
Dillon-Black, Liz, 83
Doheny-Farina, Stephen, 80, 84
Dominicé, Pierre, 184
Donohue, Tambra L., 50
Dougherty, B. Christopher, 5
Dunleavy, Eric, 61
Dzindolet, Mary T., 51

Elias, John, 257
Ellis, Carol, 132
Elsasser, Nan, 133
Evans, Tracy, 44

Fallon, Dianne, 113
Fenwick, Tara, 249
Ferretti, Eileen, 273
Fiddler, Morris, 205, 206
Fiore, Kyle, 133
Fishman, T. A., 224
Fleming, Cheryl Torok, 165
Flint, Thomas & Associates, 6
Fredericksen, Elaine, 274
Freeburg, Beth Winfrey, 46
Freeman, Samuel, 85
Freiler, Tammy J., 207
Freire, Paulo, 7, 265
Frey, Ruth, 52

Gabert, Trent E., 164
Gadbow, Nancy F., 208
Gaillet, Lynee Lewis, 134
Garner, J. Bradley, 165
Genisio, Margaret Humadi, 242
Gere, Anne Ruggles, 53
Giancola, Jennifer Kohler, 54
Gillam, Alice M., 55
Gillespie, Marilyn, 283
Gilligan, Carol, 289, 290

Glasgow, Jacqueline N., 114
Glass, Dianne, 31
Gleason, Barbara, 135, 136, 137, 138
Glover-Graf, Noreen M., 85
Goldberger, Nancy Rule, 68
Good, Glenn E., 47
Gordon, Carole, 222
Gowen, Cheryl Greenwood, 107
Grabill, Jeffrey T., 225
Grabowsky, Adelia, 215
Greenberg, Elizabeth, 61
Greenwood, Claudia M., 291
Griggs, Joan Krejci, 15, 284
Guth, Gloria J. A., 216

Hagedorn, Linda Serra, 59
Hale, Andrea D., 127
Halio, Marcia Peoples, 226
Hamrick, Florence A., 302
Hanlon, Marianne Mazzei, 86
Hansen, Craig, 162
Hansman, Catherine A., 8, 139
Hashimoto, Irvin Y., 166
Hawisher, Gail E., 100
Hayes, Elizabeth R., 56, 292
Haynes-Burton, Cynthia, 140
Heimlich, Joe E., 167
Henley, Tracy B., 4
Herman, Lee, 168
Hill, Robert J., 9
Hillard, Van E., 217
Himley, Margaret, 115
Hinkson, Christina, 10
Hiser, Krista, 266
Hoffman, Al, 115
Hogg, Charlotte, 258
Holladay, Sylvia A., 275
Hollis, Karyn L., 141, 142
Holton, Elwood F., 18
Holyoke, Laura, 185
Holzman, Michael, 209, 250
Hoover, Polly, 147
Horinek, Jon B., 187
Houser, Marian L., 57, 87
Hoy, Cheryl, 220
Hsu, Yung-chen, 61
Huang, Hsiu-Mei, 227
Huckin, Thomas N., 71, 72
Huerta-Macías, Ana, 194
Hugo, Jane, M., 293
Hull, Glynda, 251
Hunt, Jen, 214

Inman, James A., 228
Isaac, E. Paulette, 259

Jackman, Mary Kay, 88
Jacobi, Tobi, 243
Jarvis, Christine, A., 116
Jenkins, Lynn, 60
Jerman, Jerry, 278, 279
Jin, Ying, 61
Johnson, Helen, 143
Johnson-Bailey, Juanita, 58
Jones, Donna, 111
Jones, Jill, 117
Jungeblut, Ann, 60
Jungkang, Kim, 159

Kalman, Judy, 252
Karpiak, Irene, 210
Kasworm, Carol E., 11, 12, 13, 211, 237
Kates, Susan, 298
Kazemek, Francis E., 118
Kazis, Richard, 14
Keeton, Morris T., 15, 284
Kenner, Cari, 186
Kerns, Lorna, 16
Key, Daphne, 89
Kiely, Denis O., 144
Kiely, Richard, 276
Kilgore, Deborah W., 17
Kim, Karen A., 59
Kim, Kyong-Jee, 229
Kim, Young Sek, 48, 66
King, Estelle, 26
Kirsch, Irwin S., 60
Klein, James D., 179
Knightley, Wendy M., 230
Knowles, Malcolm S., 18
Kolstad, Andrew, 60
Kutner, Mark, 41, 61

Laanan, Frankie Santos, 2
Lamoreaux, Annalee, 29
Largent, Liz, 187
Larrotta, Clarena, 160
Larson, Erick, 185
Laughlin, Thomas, 119
Leaker, Cathy, 238
Lee, Jenny J., 59
Lees, Elaine O., 212
Leonhardy, Galen, 145
Li, Yongyan, 90

Losey, Kay M., 252
Lovell, Cheryl D., 296
Lvovich, Natasha, 218
Lynch, Jacqueline, 120
Lynch, Jean M., 62
Lytle, Susan L., 35

MacKinnon, Jamie, 108
Madden, Chris, 115
Maehl, William H., 277
Maher, Jane, 244, 245
Mandell, Alan, 168, 239
Manheimer, Ronald J., 63
Mann, Kenneth E., 179
Mansfield, Margaret, A., 213
Marienau, Catherine A., 211, 205, 206
Marshall, Brigitte, 169
Marsick, Victoria J., 19
Martin, Theodora Penny, 294
Massengill, Donita, 121
Materna, Laurie, 188
Mathews-Aydinli, Julie, 64
Mazurek, Raymond A., 189
McAlexander, Patricia J., 20
McDonough, Jennifer, 117
McIntyre, Sue, 112
McKay, Heather, 170
McKay, Sandra Lee, 286
McShane, Susan, 190
Melichar, Barbara E., 65
Merriam, Sharan B., 21, 22, 48, 66
Merrifield, Juliet, 253
Meyer, Paul R., 254
Mezirow, Jack, 23, 24
Michaud, Michael J., 91
Michelson, Elana, 239
Mihai, Florin, 161
Mikulecky, Larry, 106
Miller, Eva, 85
Miritello, Mary, 92
Mohammed, Methal R., 191
Moon, Paul, 48
Morris, Michael Lane, 42
Moskow-McKenzie, Diane, 63
Mott, Vivian W., 260
Mueller, Julie, 214
Mündel, Karsten, 261
Munz, David C., 54
Murray, Donald M., 109

Nadeau, Jean-Paul, 281
Nash, Susan Smith, 233

Navarre Cleary, Michelle, 93, 146, 147, 171
Nerney, Brian, 162
Nishimata, Takayuki, 161
Nixon-Ponder, Sarah, 192
Norland, Emmalou, 167
Novak, Richard J., 82
Ntiri, Daphne W., 267

O'Connor, Patricia E., 243
Oliver, Renee, 127
Orem, Richard A., 172
Ostman, Heather, 238
Ozanne, Julie L., 25

Padak, Gary, 123
Padak, Nancy D., 122, 123
Palmer, Barbara C., 126
Pandey, Iswari P., 231
Pannucci, Lynnette, 124
Pappamihiel, N. Eleni, 161
Pappas, James P., 278, 279
Park, Ji-Hye, 232
Parrish, Betsy, 173
Penrod, Diane, 115
Pfahl, Nancy Lloyd, 125
Pies, Timothy, 148
Pompa, Lori, 246
Popken, Randall, 94, 95
Pourchot, Thomas L., 36
Pratt, Daniel D., 193
Prior, Paul, 149
Purcell-Gates, Victoria, 96

Quinn, Edward, 150

Ray, Ruth E., 97
Reinke, Valerie, 111
Richardson, John T. E., 26
Riedle, Joan, 44
Ritchey, Jeffrey A., 262
Ritt, Elizabeth, 280
Rivera, Klaudia M., 194, 263
Rocco, Tonette S., 287
Rodriquez, Frank G., 233
Romberger, Julia E., 224
Rose, Mike, 98, 174, 268
Rosenberg, Lauren, 99
Rossiter, Marsha, 27, 49
Ruetenik, Bridget Fahey, 224
Ruey, Shieh, 234
Rumann, Corey B., 302
Russo, John, 130

Sabitini, John, 41
Sanders-Betzold, Suzanne, 147
Sandlin, Jennifer A., 25
Sandman, Lorilee R., 276
Sax, Linda J., 59
Schnee, Emily, 105
Schugurensky, Daniel, 261
Schwarzer, David, 175
Sealey-Ruiz, Yolanda, 295
Selfe, Cynthia L., 100
Shaughnessy, Mina, 20, 195
Sheckley, Barry G., 15, 284
Sheski, Harry, 270
Silver-Pacuilla, Heidi, 269
Simpson Jr., Edward G., 280
Skinner, Christopher H., 127
Smith, Beatrice Quarshie, 151
Smith, M. Cecil, 36, 37
Sommer, Robert F., 196
Sommers, Nancy, 152
Sork, Thomas J., 101
Southers, Tracy, 103
Spitzer, Tam M., 38
St. John, Peggy, 147
Steichen, Marie, 31
Sticht, Thomas G., 197
Stine, Linda, 235
Stino, Zandra H., 126
Strom, Linda, 104, 130
Swanson, Richard A., 18
Swift, Lisa, 144

Talmadge, Guy, 259
Tarule, Jill Mattuck, 68
Taylor, Edward W., 28
Taylor, Kathleen, 29
Thompson, Merle O'Rourke, 67
Tinberg, Howard, 281, 285
Tingle, Nick, 255
Tisdell, Elizabeth J., 30
Tom, Abigail, 170
Trares, Shawn, 54
Truluck, Janet, 276

Uehling, Karen S., 153, 154

Vaccaro, Annemarie, 296
Valentine, Tom, 259
Van Horn, Barbara L., 200
Villanueva, Jr., Victor, 176

Wall, Susan V., 131
Wallace, Robert M., 303

Walmsley, Sean A., 124
Walvoord, Barbara E., 240
Watkins, Audrey P., 102
Watkins, Karen E., 19
Weinerman, Jason, 186
Weinstein-Shr, Gail, 219, 286
Weinstein, Lawrence, 51
Whitaker, Urban, 206
White, Sheila, 41, 61
Wiessner, Colleen Aalsburg, 125
Wiley, Terrence G., 299
Williams, Mitchell R., 103
Wilson, Arthur L., 139
Winn, Beth, 127

Winterowd, W. Ross, 264
Wlodkowski, Raymond J., 177, 241
Wong, Eugene H., 50
Wood, Eileen, 214
Worthman, Christopher, 178
Wright, Melissa, 215

Zacharakis, Jeff, 31, 198
Zachary, Lois J., 199
Zaffit, Cynthia K., 32
Zemke, Ron, 33
Zemke, Susan, 33
Ziegler, Mary, 127
Zinger, Lana, 304